Dread

King of S

raught

ropunk

D. H. Peligro

A Barnacle Book   Rare Bird Books

THIS IS A GENUINE BARNACLE BOOK

A Barnacle Book | Rare Bird Books
453 South Spring Street, Suite 531
Los Angeles, CA 90013
abarnaclebook.com
rarebirdbooks.com

FIRST TRADE PAPERBACK ORIGINAL EDITION

Printed in Canada
Set in Goudy Old Style
Distributed in the U.S. by Publishers Group West

10 9 8 7 6 5 4 3 2 1

Publisher's Cataloging-in-Publication data

Peligro, D. H.

 Dreadnaught : king of Afropunk / D. H. Peligro.
 p. cm.
 ISBN 978-0-9854902-7-0

1. Peligro, D.H. 2. Dead Kennedys (Musical group). 3. Red Hot Chili
Peppers (Musical group). 4. Punk rock musicians. 5. African American
musicians —Biography. 6. Punk rock music. 7. Rock musicians —Drug
use. I. Title.

ML3534 .P448 2013
781.66 —dc23

This Book Is Dedicated To My Loving Family

INTRODUCTION

by William Knoedelseder

You hear a lot of stories in twelve-step meetings—shocking narratives of brutal childhoods, shattered families, hard falls from grace, harrowing descents into degradation, desperate time spent in detox, emergency rooms, psychiatric units, and jail cells. After awhile, you begin to think you've heard it all, that nothing will ever surprise you again about human behavior under the influence of drugs and alcohol, or about the human spirit's ability to recover.

I thought I knew D. H. Peligro's story. Sitting across the room from him most Monday nights for eight years, I'd learned that he was a successful rock musician, the drummer for Dead Kennedys and the Red Hot Chili Peppers, whose life and career had been derailed by the disease of addiction. I'd heard how he'd struggled for years to stay clean and sober, relapsing a number of times, undergoing multiple stints in rehab. I'd seen him come back from the depths on at least two occasions, chastened by the experience, upset with himself, but always upbeat, never despairing, determined to really get it right this time.

That was the thing that most impressed me about D. H.—however dark the places he'd been, he still radiated joy, hope, and humor. You couldn't help but be drawn to the guy. I recently watched him captivate my thirteen-year-old daughter with a funny comment and a fist bump. It took all of five seconds. I saw the light in his eyes leap into hers. She had never heard his music, knew nothing about him, but she was instantly enchanted. "Who is that guy?" she asked me later. "I didn't know you had any friends that cool."

I don't think I want her to read this book, at least not for a few years, or maybe ten. Because it turns out that I didn't know the half of D. H.'s story. *Dreadnaught* contains such guts-out honesty and unflinchingly graphic description of the physical ravages of heroin addiction that, at times, it literally took my breath away, causing me to stop reading and walk around the room to shake it off. D. H. (for his birth name Darren Henley) was born and raised in St. Louis, which is also my hometown. But it was definitely a case of same city-different planets. His description of growing up in urban housing projects with a drunken stepfather who would wake him up in the middle of the night with a double-barreled shotgun pressed into his cheek and then force it into his mouth while screaming, "Are you a man, now, Motherfucker?" defies the comprehension of a white kid from the suburbs. How could that little boy NOT become a heroin addict?

Music saved him, giving him a ticket out of the craziness, but only temporarily. As he moved through the fascinating and disturbing world of West Coast punk music in the 1980s, running with the Peppers and the DKs as well as lesser known punk practitioners with names like The Dicks, the Dirty Rotten Imbeciles and the Slug Lords, D. H. constantly coupled career highs with personal lows, finding deeper and deeper "bottoms" to hit on his toboggan ride down into addiction, reaching a point where his body began sloughing off fist-sized chunks of flesh where he had repeatedly injected himself. He remembers laying in a hospital bed in a haze of drugs as a doctor on his morning rounds matter-of-factly told an entourage of medical students: "This is Mr. Henley, thirty-four-year-old African American who has what's known as a 'shooter's abscess.' We extracted approximately a *liter* of puss from his left thigh." Next to *Dreadnaught*, a typical episode of *Behind the Music* seems like *My Little Pony*.

At the same time, however, the *Dreadnaught* narrative is infused with wry humor of a man who appreciates the ironic ridiculousness of shooting heroin into abscesses in his butt while complaining about the food served in rehab: "I can't eat this! I'm a vegetarian!"

It's the D. H. I know who relates the story of the scary ex-con in yet another rehab (his twenty-eighth or twenty-ninth) who asks rhetorically, "You know how you rape a guy in prison?" and then proceeds to list the steps, employing the prison expression "grippins" to describe the sphincter muscle. D. H. instinctively processes the man's story emotionally by writing an old time-y blues song titled "Grippins to the Grave," thereby transforming a truly horrific mental image into something genuinely funny. I would not have thought it possible if I hadn't read it. Writers this good rarely play drums so well

As the author of nonfiction books, I confess there were times when I was reading *Dreadnaught* that I envied D. H. for having such a rich, colorful true story to tell. But I am grateful I didn't have to live that story, because I'm fairly certain I would not have survived it. From now on, whenever I see D. H., I will always marvel that he is alive and that his sense humor and sweet nature have somehow survived as well.

If you don't believe in miracles, this book may change your mind.

Dreadnaught
King of Afropunk

PROLOGUE

L.A. County Hospital I'm in L.A. County Hospital, and it's a nightmare. I've spent four days shivering and sweating in the emergency room before being taken into the examining room. I was obviously a strung out mess, but guys with knife and gunshot wounds were rushed in ahead of me. I clutched a bottle of Valium that I had stashed away. A nurse came out once to check on me and tried to take it, but I yelled and we had a tug of war. I hollered and wouldn't let go. I was too much trouble so she got fed up and left. She didn't come back.

I was constantly shifted around various hallways and corridors for four days. Sweaty, dirty, and bloody, I sat in the rancid air of that emergency room feeling the cloud of death around me. A suffocating death was inside of me, too.

I felt deep shame and humiliation. I couldn't stand anyone seeing me like this.

When the orderlies finally brought me into the examination room the doctor was actually shocked, surprising considering what he must see every day.

"What have you done to yourself?" he asked as he looked at me.

I had red and blue tracks up and down my arms, and an abscess had taken over my entire left thigh. I had no veins left. I had been shooting Dilaudid straight into my leg. The pills had a thick plastic coating that stayed where I injected them and made a spongy lump similar to silicone. The doctor had an entourage of medical students following him as they wheeled me into the operating room, all poking at me, "oohing" and "ahhing" in disbelief. They would have to cut the abscess open, find out just exactly what was in there, then cut away all the necrotic tissue.

They tried to knock me out with anesthetic, but with my high tolerance it didn't work. I went out for a moment, but soon came to and stayed awake. My body was paralyzed but my eyes were wide open, my brain fully functioning. I could not speak or move through the rest of the operation.

The doctor took liberties in regions that he found needed attention but were not signed off on the release form. He ushered the students over for a look and discussed what they all saw. The scalpel was handed around so each one of them could practice, and I could see the horror in their eyes above their surgery masks. For four hours I lay there watching them, feeling every probe. It was like a horror film, until I finally passed out.

I came to, screeching and screaming, not sure where I was. Smoldering coals of pain ran through my entire body. My leg was packed with gauze. I writhed in pain as a nurse filled my IV with morphine. She moved me to

D. H. PELIGRO

the special ward reserved for junkies with abscesses. The familiar taste of bacteria was gone, so at least I knew they had removed it all. The room was airless, only flickering fluorescent lights and slimy, puss green walls. I didn't need to die to go to hell. I was already there.

That day there were six of us in the ward: three in the men's room and three in an adjacent room for women. Victor Vasquez was an old school tweaker with skin like a string of volcanoes. He insisted that he got his abscess from a nail at work. The other guy, Kevin, was a bad prison junkie out on parole. I recognized him from the main recovery room at County Hospital where I had been on a previous visit. One of the women used to drift into our room when the nurses weren't around. She'd wobble in, dressed in her sea green hospital gown and dirty, stained, burgundy, satin hooker boots, flashing her two teeth at me.

"Oooh, you look like my son," she'd say, sitting down on my bed, crossing her emaciated, track-scarred legs. "I like your dreadlocks," she said, trying to caress them.

I snapped my head to the left and gave her a sideways snarl. "Never touch a Rasta's dreads," I said.

"Rasta? You 'bout a junkie...junkie rass. You 'bout a ragamuffin—

"Ooooo," she crooned, "Let me rub your shoulders."

Ugh, nasty.

I was there about three weeks, but it seemed like an eternity. I would wake up sweating and check the sheets for blood and the nurse would come in with that smirky little nurse expression.

"Oh! Bob Marley's awake," she'd say as she refilled my IV of Demerol.

The vato down the hall in the big room, where they kept the worst offenders—ya know, like cats from county jail—sported a Doobie Brothers/Cheech and Chong brush. They called him Chuy. Some of the cats were handcuffed to their beds, some were chained to the beds, and the other motherfuckers just looked like criminals wandering free.

So this cat named Chuy, a patient/hustler, would come around to collect money for dope. Everybody would put their money in—but I had overheard from one of the male nurses (because I'm an eavesdroppin' fucker) that Chuy had *full blown AIDS*. So ain't no way I was fuckin' with that motherfucker, hell naw!

I wanted to go to rehab anyway. This way of living was fucked and change was welcome. We were in the biggest dope house in the world, and we had a young doctor who was "cool." If I made enough noise he wouldn't hesitate to increase the volume of Demerol, then Morphine, then Dilaudid, and then the grandaddy of 'em all—Fentanyl—which is 100 times more potent than Morphine. Every once in a while in the middle of the all-consuming cravings and self-pity, I would objectively look at myself and wonder why I was still alive. I was supposed to die the year before when I was in Cedars-Sinai with renal kidney failure and massive sciatic nerve damage in my right leg. But I rolled out of there in a wheelchair with a bottle of Vicodin in my lap. My friends, family, and supporters were not happy with me, but some were still willing to help.

Three weeks later I was back on the streets, hobbling on my crutches to cop down at 6th and Union, or 5th and Broadway—better known as "the nickel." The dealers would shamelessly hustle their wears, screaming, "cheeba, outfits, works"—and a veritable smorgasbord of illegal drugs like Vicodin, Oxycontin, crack, Klonopin, Valium, and Xanax. After that, even those who had stuck around to help me were starting to lose hope and evaporate, leaving me to my demons.

I did try to clean up on my own, but I couldn't do it. So I called Buddy Arnold from Musician's Assistance Program (MAP).

"You're in Dead who?" he asked me on the phone. "Dead Milkmen? What are you, another guitar player?"

"A drummer...*man*," I told him and filled him in on some of my drug history.

"Goddamn it! You kids gotta stop wasting our money and wasting our time! Do you see a revolving door around here anywhere?!" he shouted.

When I went in for the intake he was a lot cooler. "Oh, come in, young man, have a seat," he said a little more kindly when he saw I was black.

Buddy was a jazz musician and one of the most notorious junkies still alive. He sounded mean, but he had a big heart. He had a poster on the wall of himself, when he was strung like a Stradivarius, to remind him of what he used to be like. He was pencil thin, his hair looked like long Amadeus locks surrounded by an encroaching bald spot. The walls were covered with Charles Mingus posters and Jazz paraphernalia. A little Yorkshire Terrier named Mingus scampered around the office.

I handed him my paperwork and discography. "Dead Kennedys? Plastic Surgery Disasters? What the hell is that?" he said. "I haven't heard of that band." He sighed, "I'll be honest. Most of y'all don't stand a chance. I don't think you are gonna make it but we'll give it a try. We did help that guy from that Chili Pepper group a couple years ago."

The mention of Anthony made my blood boil. At that time I still had a seething resentment against the Chili Peppers for kicking me out of the band in 1990. I hated them for the longest time. I couldn't listen to them at all. "Higher Ground" was in heavy radio rotation, and I had worked on preproduction. I knew it would be a hit. I knew when they kicked me out it was hard for them, but it was also hard for me. I was suicidal afterwards. I thought brothers should be there for each other, but I felt they weren't there for me at all. For that, I hated their fucking guts. We all supported Anthony as he went through his detoxes and addictions. However, when it was my turn, I was ostracized after a few chances.

I didn't stay clean after my time in Tarzana Detox, either. Had I proved Buddy's case?

For the second time in my life I was lying in the abscess room at County Hospital. Memories flooded my mind as I lay there, some hopeful but most despairing. On a good day I was glad I did not stay in St. Louis where I grew up. What would I be doing there now? Working in some dead end factory job? Driving a UPS truck? Having kids and drinking myself to death? FUCK that! I had left and taken a chance, which is more than most can say. Not to mention, I had done more than most would actually do in a lifetime. On a bad day, lying there jonesin' like a motherfucker for a hit and looking down at the ruined state of my body, I felt like a real failure. Defeated. *Jesus*...this was not the dream or the plan I had when I left St. Louis many years ago.

Now, as I lay with tubes attached to me, flat on my back in a cot surrounded by those puke green walls, I started remembering things—moments in my life, trying to weigh it all out and make sense of it. I remembered that first time I left St. Louis, hung over, jumping on the Greyhound bus at seventeen with only my drum kit packed full of clothes. I remembered how excited I was before the first big gig I ever played with Dead Kennedys in 1980. I thought of my girlfriend, Sherry, who I met in Los Angeles...the first time I shot cocaine—the rush, the ritual, the red register, the slow push...the weightless fade shifter sound and feel before the paranoia sets in— the creepy crawly sounds of *What's that? Who's that? Did you hear that?*...the first time I nodded out on China White, the warmth, the euphoria, the six hours of noooo problems. Then two weeks later waking up in a pool of sweat trying to figure out how to get enough dough to cop.

Halloween—Chicago 1982—fully pumped on coke, excited that my cousins came to The Metro Club all the way from the projects at Westlake in Damen to see me perform. I thought it was the worst gig ever. I knew I didn't need the coke, but I did it anyway. What a bad idea to mix the natural high of performing with some ten-times-stepped-on-smuggled-through-six-countries-in-a-mules-ass-cocaine. I was so irritable, sweating bullets behind my drum kit, impatient for the gig to be over so I could do more coke. I remembered how devastated and demolished I felt, lying naked on a cold floor in the fetal position, shaking from cotton fever. Hell felt real. And that was it.

Even with those memories in my head and with the throbbing in my leg I still wanted to get high more than anything on earth or in heaven.

1

Growing Up In St. Louis

*M*y life began in 1959 on a hot summer afternoon at City Hospital #1 in St. Louis, Missouri. I was the second born of premature twins to a tired and irritable Blanche Godfrey.

City Hospital was the poor man's hospital, across the railroad tracks in a city famous for high-end health facilities. The patients were mostly black, as St. Louis's proximity to the South meant that it was, in practice, racially segregated. In spite of our premature arrival, my twin sister and I both had a strong will to live, which we would need growing up black in America. Our mother brought us home to 2704 Hickory Street, where we lived for the first three years of our lives with Aunt Doris, Uncle Sam, and our older brother, Bruce.

Our neighborhood was downtown, southwest of the Mississippi River, in East St. Louis, near a series of factories. There were only a few white people living there, and they were poor and considered black, like us.

Our mother worked long, underpaid hours as a nurse on the night shift and later as a security guard at a psychiatric ward. For our first six months our biological father lived with us. I don't remember him at all.

Our family worked hard and played just as hard, if not harder. Blanche was an everyday woman, but she could fly into a rage if provoked. She beat my ass a lot because I was known as Satan's child according to a lot of different folks. But when Blanche let loose she sure knew how to get down and party.

My sister Dianne and I are products of her relationship with the guitarist from my Uncle Sam's band, James Yokely. We never knew James. My mother didn't even tell us about him until my stepfather Russell's death. Or maybe it was after I got sober the first time, I can't fully remember.

Sam Carr was my uncle and my very first musical inspiration. Uncle Sam is from the Mississippi Delta. He is the son of Blues guitarist Robert Nighthawk, a truly amazing musician who could play any instrument he came across. I don't know whether it's an old legend or not, but it has been said that he was the first man to ever play slide guitar.

My twin sister Dianne and I were very different from each other as babies. We didn't look alike, and our temperaments were night and day: Dianne was a calm, quiet baby, while I was a wiggling, squirming, buzzing pain in the ass. I was destructive. I threw tantrums, and I was what my mother called "vigorously infuriating."

My mama tells me that when she would put me in our convertible playpen with the wooden gates I would shake the sides until the whole thing collapsed. Each time she put it back together I'd shake it down again.

When Dianne and I were about three years old Aunt Doris and Uncle Sam moved back to the Delta— to Sam's hometown of Lula, Mississippi—to take care of his mother. They still live in the Delta today. They have a nicer house now, but back then they lived in an old ramshackle wood porch house. We visited them every summer.

I don't remember who took care of us while my mother was at work, but I do remember her coming home in the morning, the sound of her key in the latch, and the ghostly white of her nurse's cap, dress, and shoes in the grey dawn light. I remember her shouting at us. Short, hot words hitting us as hard as her hand slapped our faces. We were always scared of her when she came home from work. She was pissed off most of the time. I think she both loved and resented us. I don't know how or why, but she sure could whoop some ass—mostly mine.

She started going to church on Sundays, and I remember her getting ready, the sound of the aerosol can and the horrible smell of her hair spray as it cast a misty halo around her head. I remember the feel of her starched, elbow-high gloves on my arm as she got us out the door. When Dianne and I were three years old, my mother met a man at church named Russell Henley. He soon moved in with us, and we all moved from Hickory Street to 3609 North Newstead Avenue. We quickly adopted him as our father, but it wasn't until 1995 that my mother told me he had legally adopted all of us as his own.

We were very poor—dirt-eating poor, as they used to say. But my mama always did her best to provide for us all, no matter what. I didn't realize we were poor until I reached Junior High, but the empty fridge, the empty kitchen shelves, and the memory of near constant hunger still stick out in my mind.

There was always fury and frustration in the air around us like a relentless, suffocating cloud. This toxic air was what we breathed with every breath and it poisoned us all. My stepfather drank to escape the pressure. He always had a beer or a bottle in his hand. When he wasn't drinking he was just about to. On the weekends he just didn't stop. He was a cruel drunk and took it out on those closest to him. The most vulnerable, namely, me. His other kids, Russell, Renee, and Cheryl, didn't get it half as bad as me because they were his biological kids. Of all of us, though, I got the worst of his rage.

The minute I heard him stumble in the house I would quickly make myself scarce, especially if I had done something wrong. I knew what to expect: a long thrashing that wouldn't end until his arm was tired. Sometimes I was guilty of some small infraction, but often I had done nothing at all.

Sometimes, when he was really drunk, he would wake me up out of a dead sleep, and I would be staring into both barrels of his twelve-gauge shotgun pointed directly in my face.

"What's yo' sweat? Are you a man?" he would ask me. I can still feel his hot alcohol breath on my face and hear his hoarse, sloppy whisper in my ear.

"Wake up! Are you a man?"

No, I'm a kid, I would think to myself.

I remember once he had the gun pressed into my chest, then moved it to my temple, and then to my face. He then forced my mouth open with the barrel and whispered, "Are you a man now, motherfucker?"

I stayed absolutely still waiting for him to either blow my head off or leave me alone. I was numb until he stumbled out of the room. Often I would wet the bed out of fear, but I never, ever, cried. None of us did. We had all made a pact that no matter how bad it got, we would never cry. But when no one was around I did end up crying—I couldn't help it, it hurt.

From Hickory Street we moved to the Peabody housing projects on 14th Street and Chouteau Ave, blocks from the Mississippi riverfront. The Peabody was in a complex of low-income housing units, better known as the projects. We lived in one of three apartment buildings. Between them were concrete courtyards, and the complex was surrounded on all sides by high metal fences. These were and still are dangerous projects. Our address was 1441 Moorson Lane. It sounded as if we lived in some country village but we were completely surrounded by concrete and steel. In front of the apartments were tiny plots of grass, some kept alive by the old ladies who lived near them. They would shoo us kids away from their little patches of green for fear we would damage them.

"Ya'll kids, get off that grass now! Ya'll lil' bad ass devilish chilrren!" they would shout. Beyond that and all around us were steep hills and tall fences topped with barbed wire. This bleak existence formed the outer perimeter of our lives.

Russell and Renee were born while we lived there, making our small apartment overly full. Bruce, Dianne, and I shared one bed until we got a three-tiered bunk bed that Bruce, Russell, and I would sleep on for years afterwards. We survived on federal assistance, which provided food and food stamps. The so-called food the government gave us was horrible: canned peanut butter, huge blocks of orange cheese, and loaves of sliced white bread. We also got food stamps that we were allowed to spend at the food store in the neighborhood on overpriced sugar cereals and lunch meats pumped full of additives. All that food we grew up on in the ghetto was poison, drained of any nutritional value. Being forced to eat that food was one of the reasons that later in life, even when I was strung out on heroin, I remained a fanatic vegan.

There were lots of children living in those projects, and I can remember playing hide and seek with what seemed like about a hundred kids. We would play all afternoon and into the night, hiding and running and roughhousing. As long as some grown ups were around we could stay on the courts, so the parents would come downstairs, sit on the steps, talk shit, and drink beer. Later at night they would have parties in some of the apartments. I remember the walls would rock with the beat of Boogaloo and everyone would get drunk and dance the funky four-corners and the James Brown.

The projects were full of pimps, pushers, and hustlers of all kinds. Us children could train in any number of these trades but in the midst of it all, I chose not to. I guess there was a certain level of ethics that I was acquiring along the way, an inner sense of right and wrong. My childhood was more like a twisted version of *Huckleberry Finn* than *Last Exit to Brooklyn*.

Southwest of our buildings, six or seven blocks away, was Lafayette Park. There was a pond where we used to go fishing. It was dirty and polluted with industrial waste. We would walk there barefoot, the hot concrete burning our feet. With no fishing rods or poles, no trees dropping branches for us to use, we invented our own system of catching fish. The fish were really sick and small, basically the size of minnows, so we scooped them up in Dixie cups. What we really wanted was to catch the puny crawfish. For this we used bacon that we stole out of the fridge, tied it to a string and lowered it into the water. When the crawdads pinched on it we could pull them right out. We ate a few of them. Later we found that if we peed on the bacon first we attracted more of them. Considering all the toxic waste these fish were swimming in, they were probably very poisonous, so it's probably a good thing we didn't eat many of them, just kept most of them as pets until they eventually died.

The kids from the projects were all tough—we could endure a lot of beating. We could hop a train, fall off and skin our knees, and never cry. I was the filthy little kid that couldn't be kept still long enough to bathe. I had a couple sets of school clothes, some hand me downs, and some funky, fucked up shoes. My clothes were always torn and raggedy from falling down and skidding and getting skinned up on the asphalt, from frequent fights, scrapes, and from being pulled over the barbed wire fences around the apartments.

It was a bad idea to be too close to the barbed wire running along the tops of the fences that surrounded the perimeter of the apartments, because you couldn't see it when the lights came on at night. Packs of wild dogs came out at night and paced outside the fences. Crazy as I am, I used to run along the side of the fences for the thrill of it, daring those dogs. Once I got truly freaked: a huge snarling black dog, eyes glaring, teeth glinting, reared up at a section in the fence which looked like it could be easily broken through. I ran away as fast as I could, ripping the shit out of the sleeve of my shirt and my arm. It was so dark and I was running so fast I got clotheslined neck first and nearly hung myself on that barbed wire fence.

Around the apartments the streets that we played in were full of garbage: dumpsters, boxes, newspapers, rusted oil barrels, old cars, tires, lots of broken bottles, and beer cans. A few blocks northeast of us were train tracks, industrial yards, and a huge Wonder Bread factory. We were constantly taunted by the smell of bread baking. I can still vividly remember that smell as it mixed with the smell of factory smoke and dog pee from the concrete.

We did not have many toys to play with so we made our own; the little girls didn't have Easy-Bake Ovens so they would make mud pies, mud meatballs, and rock sandwiches. One game we played was called Mumbly Peg. We would try to get a knife to stick in the ground by flicking it off the wrist, and whoever couldn't do it would have to literally eat dirt. We would take the knife, stomp it into the dirt, and the loser had to get it out with their teeth.

One of our favorite pastimes was to set fire to all the shit on the street. We would set a dumpster on fire just to see the firemen come in, and to watch all the pretty lights and to hear the sirens. Everyone would come outside to watch them put it out. The smell of smoke would hang around until it rained, sometimes for weeks.

My favorite act of arson was to line the inside of a car tire with newspaper and other bits of trash, set it on fire, and then send it rolling down the street. I would chase it, running alongside to keep it rolling, the smell of burnt rubber permeating my clothing. Finally, I'd give it a kick and send it down the street until it would topple and burn—usually coming very close to setting the parked cars on fire. The best time to do this was at night when the effect was beautiful and exciting. The flames swirled out like a ghetto asteroid.

The other side of the wasteland we lived in held more of the spectacular grandness of the city. The St. Louis Arch was being built very close by when Dianne and I were about five years old. We could see the cranes from our house, and we couldn't figure out what they were building.

What is that? we thought. It was mysterious, like some kind of space station. The cranes reached so high into the sky as they built this thing, I was fascinated how they could make such a huge structure that stood on its own. *What's gonna hold it together? What is it gonna be?* we wondered.

They were also constructing the first Busch Stadium on the other side of the arch but even as kids we knew that none of this was for us. As young black kids, all of that construction, that newness, seemed so unattainable, just like the Anheuser-Busch Brewery. We just watched *The Three Stooges* and *Batman* on the black and white television, and danced to *Soul Train* on Saturdays.

As a kid I had an overwhelming energy, and was constantly feeling like I had to keep moving so I wouldn't explode. Part of this energy was just my nature and part of it was anger—deep-seated anger. I now know it came from my fury at the world I lived in, but back then I had no words to put to the feelings. I was never cruel or violent like some kids, at least not to other people. I just became self-destructive.

I used to jump off of this one two-story roof into a dumpster just to see what would happen. Every summer I had some kind of traumatic injury that needed stitches. Once playing hide and seek I launched myself into the bushes, just stage dove right into them thinking a kid was under them. I landed straight on a bottle and cut my lower leg open below the knee so deeply that you could see my shin bone. For that one I needed stitches and crutches, and I had to hobble around for the rest of the summer.

One time, when I was seven or eight, I was thrashing around and I landed square on a huge, jagged piece of glass. It went straight through the bottom of my foot and came out the other side. Dianne heard my screams and ran to me out on the courtyard.

"Ooh, Momma gon' be maaaad!" were her first words. "You gonna have to go the hospital!"

This was a bad moment for several reasons, the biggest being that we never had any insurance. Every time I got seriously injured it cost a lot of money, and that was hard on my family. I was also scared that I would get beaten for causing problems. My parents' frustration was often taken out on whatever part of me was still exposed. Even unwounded I would get beaten, sometimes until I passed out. It's a wonder I lived through much of that, but, like I said, I have always healed quickly and as soon as I was okay I would be back at it again.

Much to my surprise, with the glass still sticking through my foot, my mother was very gentle and caring. She filled a bowl with cold water and told my sister to get as much ice as she could find to stop the bleeding. She cleaned and bandaged the wound then took me to the hospital. They operated on my foot in the ER. My father, Russell, grew tired of waiting—he needed a drink—and split. My mom stayed until the operation was complete, then took me home. I healed up pretty quickly, but being a rambunctious kid it was hard to get used to walking on my heel so I didn't rip the stitches.

That wasn't the first time our dad bailed out for a drink. My sister Cheryl was born on December 21, 1965. That night Russell was so drunk he didn't even show up to the hospital. Two days later, when my mom was discharged, my dad was still drunk, and she had to walk home in the wicked St. Louis winter with my newborn sister in her arms. Not only did she have a new baby, but when she got home she made Christmas dinner for the rest of her kids.

2

Big Hats, Holy Heifers, and Jumpin' Jesus

*E*very Sunday, my mom brought all of us kids to Second Corinthian's Baptist Church, which was based out of a small storefront on the corner of Hickory and Jefferson Streets. Second Corinthians was a truly old school, inner city black church. Now it's a beauty shop. Most of the time Dad was too drunk or hungover to go, so Mom would take us. The church was only about ten blocks away so sometimes we would walk, but usually she would pile us into the Rambler. She didn't have a license and couldn't drive at all but she would grind those gears and throw us all around the backseat of the car until we were damn near dizzy with the spirit of Jesus.

The church was always full, and the ladies of the congregation reigned. They were always decked out in huge ornate and decorated hats, shiny, brightly-colored dresses, and matching handbags. There were gloves and hand fans everywhere. When they were all sitting in the pews it was as if a flock of bright birds had landed in the church, fluttering, twittering, and fluffing their wings. My mother would sometimes ask one of the women, Sister Hutchinson, to babysit us. Dianne said Sister Hutchinson was a drunk. While Reverend Nance rallied the congregation on its feet for a song, Sister Hutchinson would rear back and take a nip from her flask—and she'd be nipping all day long while she babysat us. Funny how my mom never figured that out, but she had enough things to worry about. When Dianne told her, she dismissed it, "What?? Naw...can't be."

After Russell, Renee, and Cheryl were born, we were such a big family that we took up an entire pew. Reverend Nance, who ran the church, would greet us as we came in.

"The Henley family is here, come up and sing us a song," he'd say.

I remember singing "Come and Go with Me to My Father's House." While we sang I didn't feel quite so antsy, as if the music calmed me down and served to keep me calm for the rest of the service.

At six years old, my sister and I were baptized by Reverend Nance. Water freaked me out at the time, so on this day when the entire floor in front of the stage opened up to reveal a huge pool I thought, *Well, they are going to drown me.* The music throbbed and voices were raised to "Praise Jesus!" Dianne and I were lowered backwards into the water. All the water stories from the Bible raced through my mind: Noah on the Ark, Moses as a tiny baby being sent down the Nile River in the reed basket, Moses parting the Red Sea. The Reverend pressed his hand on my chest and I froze as I was submerged, unable to breathe with water flooding my nose. Finally, he yanked me up, dripping and gasping.

"In the great name of Jesus!" the Reverend bellowed, "Great God ALMIGHT-AY!"

Sitting still and listening to the sermon on Sundays, especially the reading of the scriptures, was torment for me. It seemed to take forever. Most of the time us kids would be cutting up and making fun of the old ladies falling asleep. Mom would reach over and whack us, hard. But I really enjoyed watching people catch the Holy Ghost. As the pitch rose in the service people went wild, really letting themselves go: hats and shoes would fly, ladies fainted and fell out all over the church. People would shout, bellow, cry, and sing all at once. I loved all the action, the energy, the movement, and the fact that no matter what was going on, the group maintained the main song—somewhere in the room the melody or a phrase from the chorus could still be heard. I loved the way that all of the chaos could be so quickly brought right back into one harmony as everyone joined in with the band playing amidst the bedlam.

We went to Second Corinthians our entire childhood. The Reverend had two children, Christopher and Betty. Christopher was my age and a musician in the choir; he sang and played guitar. Many years later I would jam with him at their house when the Reverend was not at home. Chris got really into Jimi Hendrix, as did I, and we would come in the house, flop down, light a pin joint, and listen to *Electric Ladyland*. Then we'd start messing around with his music. I would bring my drums and we would play downstairs in the basement. My brother Bruce would be there, too. He was dating Betty, the preacher's daughter. So there we'd be at the Reverend's house, all smoking weed before Bruce and Betty had sex upstairs, and Chris and I played Hendrix jams in the basement.

Our favorite place to go after church, though, was to our Aunt Bea's. Aunt Bea was my stepfather's sister. She loved all of us, and we really loved her. She was a large, light skinned woman with long hair—"good hair," as we called it—and she spoke in a gentle southern drawl. We enjoyed our visits so much we would all rush to change out of our church clothes so we could go to her house. Like us, she lived in this hot concrete box of an apartment. Portraits of Martin Luther King, Jr. and John F. Kennedy hung on the wall, portraits that could be found in the living rooms of almost every black home at that time. Later, many black families, including ours, added Malcolm X to the wall. Aunt Bea would cook us greens, catfish, and cornbread as she moved through the kitchen with a gentle slowness. Her house was one of the few places we felt safe.

3

Uncle Sam

$\mathcal{S}$ome Sunday afternoons we would go down to Soulard Market to get fresh fruits and vegetables. This area was historically a center for blues musicians who would meet, play, and compose together in the 1930s. St. Louis Blues is a certain style, usually centered on the piano with a little jazz and ragtime influence and a jumpy, up-tempo beat. The blues men put St. Louis on the musical map and most good rock musicians listen to and get their riffs and styles from these guys, guys like Uncle Sam. This is why St. Louis is a regular touring stop for stadium and club rock. Many very famous musicians came out of St. Louis—the ragtime pianist, Scott Joplin, for one; Miles Davis from East St. Louis; Chuck Berry, the godfather of rock himself, was from there.

But out of all those guys, Uncle Sam was my earliest musical influence. Sam's father played in St. Louis and recorded for Victor Records, Bluebird Records, Decca Records, Aristocrat Records, Chess Records, United Records, and States Records. He introduced the use of the slide with the electric guitar and the harmonica. Muddy Waters heard Nighthawk sliding up and down that neck and loved it so much he took it up himself and became very famous for that sound, but it was Nighthawk who did it first.

My Uncle Sam is in his eighties now and still plays drums, bass, piano, and guitar, like his father. Playing with Frank Frost and Big Jack Johnson he backed up Sonny Boy Williamson. Forming the band Jelly Roll Kings, he recorded for Sam Phillips of Sun Records, who launched the careers of B.B. King, Howlin' Wolf, Carl Perkins, Jerry Lee Lewis, Johnny Cash, and Elvis Presley. Even though Jimmy Page, The Rolling Stones, and Eric Clapton made journeys to his house to learn at his feet, Uncle Sam never became fabulously wealthy or famous.

Lula, Mississippi, where Uncle Sam and my Aunt Doris have lived for over forty years, sits in the heart of the Delta. It's close to the crossroads of Highways 61 and 49 (where, the story goes, Robert Johnson met the devil on the road at midnight). There is a local joint in Lula where Uncle Sam plays regularly, but he also still tours. He used to tour in Europe and Asia, but he has slowed down as he's gotten older. He still plays gigs and Blues festivals all over the South. It's a way of life for him; wherever he finds himself he picks up and plays. In the summer, busloads of tourists come in on Blues tours. They pour in from Japan, Germany, Italy, Brazil, Switzerland, all over the world to hear the music of the Delta. Sam plays the King Biscuit Blues Festival in Helena, Arkansas, and in Chicago, St. Louis, and various states of the union. Every year he is voted Best

Blues Drummer. Our family in St. Louis would all go down for the King Biscuit Festival when I was younger. Aunt Doris especially loved this weekend and would stay through the duration. She didn't care whether it was burning hot or pouring rain or what time the last act went on, without fail she would be there until the last act finished their set. She was so set in her ways, sometimes the rest of the family had to leave her and let her find her own way home.

Uncle Sam and Aunt Doris live on a huge former plantation owned by a white family named Powell and have been there for over forty-five years. During slavery this was a working cotton plantation and the land was given back to the former slave owners, the Powell ancestors, in 1877. Mr. Powell sold a lot of the original land off, but he kept the plantation and still farms it. He tore down all the slave quarters at some point, which a part of me is sad about. Uncle Sam works the land for him, just like it's been forever in the South on all the big plantations.

Rows and rows of cotton fields and groves of pecan trees surround my Aunt and Uncle's shack. When I was a boy I looked across all of those cotton fields and had the strangest out of body experiences. Visions of slaves picking cotton flashed before me, and when I closed my eyes I saw women in the hot sun leaning over in big long dresses, some in hats, and men with their shirts off, pouring sweat as they worked in those back-breaking fields. In my mind's eye I could see them drinking water from a bucket with a ladle and then dumping it on their heads. I heard them singing together, religious songs and work songs. Maybe the ancestors were there speaking to me, maybe it was just my overactive imagination.

Every summer we would drive down to Lula to stay with Uncle Sam and Aunt Doris for a couple of weeks. We'd all pile into my father's 1974 Fury 3 for the drive across country. When my dad was working, drunk, or, for some other reason, couldn't come, Mom would herd us all onto the Greyhound Bus for the nine-hour ride. The bus would drop us off in front of the general store—I think it was called Powell's General Store—and Uncle Sam would come get us in his old pick-up truck.

Although Uncle Sam and Aunt Doris lived off of famous Highway 61, to us city kids it looked like nothing more than a street. The first time we visited I started walking down it like a sidewalk.

"*Get off the highway, boy!*" my uncle shouted. The fact that they called that tiny road a highway cracked me up.

To get to Uncle Sam's we'd pull off the highway and turn down a long dirt road overhung with pecan trees. On either side were fields, acres and acres of squash, rows and rows of corn, greens, lettuce, beans, and the largest tomatoes I had ever seen. Further off to the right, on the way to the house, was a long, corrugated steel building that turned out to be a chicken slaughterhouse. That was it for miles around.

Nothing but mangy old dogs covered with fleas and swollen with tick bites wandered on the side of the dirt

D. H. PELIGRO

road. Some had chain collars that had been on their neck so long that the skin had grown around them, so their necks were raw and rotten, producing maggots and flies around the collars. You could smell them from miles away. At night they would bark and howl into the dark, which always scared the shit out of us.

When the dogs weren't barking at night you could hear the symphony of cicadas chattering and screeching—while you shooed away blood-sucking mosquitoes. Fireflies provided meandering light late at night, glowing like beacons in the blackness of the country.

The house was a dilapidated old one-room wooden cabin with no electricity, heating, running water, or inside plumbing. They had sectioned off a part of it with a curtain for a bedroom. The kitchen had a huge potbelly stove in the middle of it for a heat source. Very primitive and pretty much unchanged since they moved in—similar to the outer decor of House of Blues in Hollywood—but this was no stage set, this was real life.

Their outhouse was one of the creepiest places I've ever been, especially at night. There were no streetlights, so the dark was the darkest dark I had ever experienced. I would wake up and have to face that walk in the pitch black, surrounded by raccoons and other wild animals. The stench and squishing sounds of the living organisms devouring the feces in the outhouse—maggots, snakes, whatever was crawling around—made me gag.

I remember the first time we saw the well, too. "Wow, look! What is that?" I ran over and started pumping on it.

"*Boy-ee*, stop pumpin' that water! Don't be wastin' it!" my uncle shouted. This was their sole water supply ,and I soon learned to respect that fact. We all took turns taking our baths, pumping water from the well and filling up this big corrugated steel tub. My Auntie would heat water in a big pan on the stove and pour it in our tub for warm water.

We gathered vegetables from the garden and fished from the creek. I would go fishing with my Uncle Sam, and as soon as we got in the door he would hand the fish to Aunt Doris. She would debone, gut, and clean them, roll them in a little cornmeal and throw them in the pan in a matter of seconds. I never saw anybody do that before. I was horrified watching my aunt tear the fish's head off, but that's country life; it's how they cooked and had done so for ages. Sometimes they would have pieces of meat for dinner—pig's feet or left over scraps from the chicken factory: giblets, livers, and neck bones. Ten cents worth of hogshead cheese from the dry goods store was considered a delicacy. They grew everything else themselves. They were self-sufficient, didn't need a lot and didn't want for anything. All of the fresh fruit and vegetables, lettuce, carrots, tomatoes, potatoes, squash, peaches, blackberries, cherries, watermelons, and pecans—"pee-cans" as they called them. This is what I loved the very most about being there: the vernacular of everyday life.

Uncle Sam was as country as they get, yet still managed to be dapper. He was a tobacco chewing, straw hat, bib-overalls wearing kind of cool cat. He and Doris would dress up and go out when they could afford it, and he would turn into a slick Stacy Adams, brim hat, fancy shoes type of dude. But that was rare and where they could go was limited. When he and Doris were young, black people weren't allowed to go into some of the bigger hotels and the concert halls. My uncle, as great a musician as he was, just wasn't allowed in these venues.

Back then black people didn't start anything. That shit had been ingrained in them since birth: "Don't start no fuckin' shit because white people will fucking lynch you in a heartbeat and hang you from the highest tree." That's just the way it was. The real hot spots where black people went and where the music was really happening were the juke joints and old backwoods taverns. That was where it jumped off, and where white musicians got their inspiration.

It was Uncle Sam who first planted the seed for me to become a musician. I got my first vibe on musical instruments there in his shack in Lula. He didn't have much in the way of living there in that cabin but he had piles of musical gear: a drum kit, a bass, some guitars, a piano. He never learned to read or write so when people ask for autographs he just scribbles.

My first memory of touching those instruments and really feeling them was when I was about six or seven. I touched the keys and the strings and notes and tones and sounds magically emerged, something inside me woke up and answered back. Uncle Sam was always curious about the music I was making as a kid. He was also interested later when I started playing drums with Dead Kennedys. "Let me hear some of that music you been playing," he asked at a family reunion in St. Louis—and he really listened. He nodded his head even as loud and noisy as it must have been to him.

In 1995, I finally got to jam with Uncle Sam a little bit in the basement of my mom's house with Russell. I was just out of a St. Louis rehab. I was a shaky mess, but it felt good to play again, especially with my family.

Years later I figured out why he was so curious about my musicianship. Sam had come to St. Louis and played around with a lot of musicians. At one point, Aunt Doris was lead vocalist for Uncle Sam's band, and my mother would go along to the shows. My mother met one of Uncle Sam's guitar players, James Yokely. She started seeing him, and a year later she was pregnant with Dianne and me.

Aunt Doris was the only one that would talk about James Yokely. She told me that my mother was seeing James Yokely pretty seriously. After we were born he lived with us. He hung around, smoking and drinking in the house during the day and staying out at the bars and clubs all night. He began leaving the house for longer periods of time, showing up again only to disappear as quickly. One day he left and never came back. Uncle Sam saw him once, years later, out of work and drifting, and talked to him briefly. That was it. I have never met him, though I hear from my Aunt Doris and Uncle Sam that I look, sound, and move exactly like him.

4

From One Ghetto to Another

When I was eight we moved to Wellston, a section of town west of the Peabody projects. For my family it was a step up; we had a bigger house, garage, and even a yard. It wasn't the projects, but it was still the ghetto. Now it is even more of a deprived area—rough, fucked up, and bombed out. It wasn't so great when we lived there, either, but we didn't know the difference. All we knew is we had more room to run and play.

Wellston, in its day, had been a major shopping district. It was a black neighborhood, but everybody shopped there in the three city blocks of stores along Easton Boulevard, which has since been renamed Martin Luther King Drive. It had everything from Thom McCann, Kinney's shoes, J.C. Penney, and Sears, to Woolworth's. There were also smaller businesses run by black folks like barbershops, pawnshops, a House of Wigs, television and shoe repair shops. There were still electric streetcars running up and down Easton, which turned around in a depot called The Loop.

The Woolworth's was near The Loop, but we didn't go there. Even then, in the late 1960s, black people still couldn't sit down at the food counter in St. Louis. You could order something to go but you took it with you, you did not sit down. Black people went to Steak 'n Shake or White Castle—both were further out in Wellston. We didn't really think about it, we just accepted it. Even as a kid I knew it was fucked up. Our stepdad, Russell, told us about the first sit-ins by the members of the Student Nonviolent Coordinating Committee that protested segregation at Woolworth's lunch counter in Greensboro, North Carolina. As he was from Mississippi, he directly experienced the hatred that fueled racism and segregation in the South. The violence and beatings he inflicted on me were due to alcohol, but that urge to drink, in many ways, came from the frustrations of racism, of not being seen as a man. There were guys who were ninety years old and were still called "Boy."

Russell was angry, militant, and followed the Black Panthers. He wore all black and was pretty much the only guy around rocking those Rampuri caps, which I always assumed were attached to the Nation of Islam. He hung Black Power posters around the house and listened to the speeches of Dick Gregory, Stokely Carmichael, and Malcolm X.

I remember going on marches with Russell before Martin Luther King, Jr. was assassinated. When I was very little he took Dianne, Bruce, and me to hear Malcolm X speak at the VFW Hall in St. Louis. I remember standing next to him as he was frisked by the

Nation of Islam security guards. Depending on their rank, some guards wore red fezzes with yellow tassels, some wore brown and black caps embossed with yellow moons and stars, others were just clean cut with no caps. After they frisked my father they shook his hand and said, "Welcome, my brother."

When we sat down I remember the feeling in the room—like a powerful field of electricity. Everyone stood or sat up tall, erect, and proud. Everyone was clean, dressed in suits, with their hair freshly clipped. This was 1965, before the afros and raised fists that became synonymous with the Black Panthers.

Our house in Wellston was an old one-bedroom house. It is hard to believe that all six of us kids lived in that one tiny house, but it seemed big enough at the time. When we moved in, Dad started converting the house—moving the kitchen, family room, and dining room downstairs into the basement and making the upstairs kitchen into a bedroom for us boys. Before that we had slept in the tiny pantry room on the same three-tiered bunk bed we had shared in the Peabody Projects. Bruce was on top, I was in the middle, and Russell Jr.—Rusty, as we called him—was on the bottom. Whenever I peed the bed it would drip down in Rusty's bed. We were forever hanging the mattress out to dry.

Daddy had left the house unfinished for years. There were half torn down walls, stacks of sheet rock in the corner, and fiberglass insulation hung from the ceilings.

That house also had a funky old wooden porch with dry rot. All the girls would jump double-dutch on it, which drove dad crazy. The porch was so tore up one day my middle sister Renee stepped back into a crack, the board broke, and she fell inside the porch floor. After that, Dad started to fix it. He bought cinder blocks and ready-mix concrete. He pulled up the wooden boards, and we helped pull out all the junk underneath. Because he was half-assed about his building and remodeling we lived with the porch like that for two years, sitting on the cinder block steps before mom and us kids finished it and finally poured the concrete top ourselves.

One of my most vivid memories from Wellston is sitting on those steps of the half-finished porch on hot summer nights watching *Playboy After Dark*. Neighbors would usually come by and sit for a while, and one of those nights was the first time I ever played electric guitar. My dad had bought this Silvertone with the amp built into the case, but he didn't know how to play it. I had a friend, Rocky, whose father was a musician, and he would come over and play sometimes, strum a few chords, play some James Brown songs.

One night I grabbed the Silvertone and started sliding up and down the neck, wrrreeenk wrroow, making noise, having fun with it. Running my fingers up and down the neck felt amazing; the mere idea that something so beautiful could come from my fingertips, from the depths of my un-nurtured soul, was mind-boggling.

D. H. Peligro

We had a record player in the basement, and my folks belonged to the Album of the Month Club. Next to the record player lived a stack of Motown 45s: Gladys Knight and the Pips, Marvin Gaye, The Temptations, The Spinners. Next to them sat LPs: Bill Cosby, Diana Ross, O.C. Smith, Wilson Pickett, and a few Beatles records. My dad's favorite was Lorne Green's spoken word version of "Ringo," a western tune about an outlaw in the Wild West. He played it over and over, always chuckling at the end. Most of the time there was some kind of music playing in the basement. Before Dad converted the house we would have Kool-Aid dance parties with our cousins. We would listen to those 45s and copy the dances we saw the groups doing Saturday mornings on *Soul Train*, *American Bandstand*, and a local St. Louis show, *Black Circle Hour*. Then we would kiss and dry hump our girl cousins. It was much more innocent than it seems.

My mother could be merciless. She would beat me for anything and everything until I was bleeding. Then she would beat me some more like I was someone she hated. When she was beating me she would be saying things like, "Goddammit ya little sonofabitch! I told you to watch what ya doin'...you little ungrateful bastard. You're always breaking something, tearing something up. I'm tired of your little ass breaking shit. C'mere. Shut up! Turn around. Don't you run from me." She wouldn't stop until she was tired or until the switch, belt, hanger, or other device broke. It was sometimes a ritual and there were special places in the house where she would drag me while the other kids would beg her to stop.

Looking back on it, it makes me wonder how close this was to the way slaves were beaten on the plantation. I wonder if this is in our cellular memory, if the violence inflicted on the slaves had been passed down through the generations. My mother is the daughter of Mississippi sharecroppers and grew up among all the ghosts of those plantations. All that had been done to them was done to her and became her legacy, a legacy that she handed down to us. It is a miracle that I have never been violent, at least not to others, but always somewhere in the back of my mind I still think of physical punishment as a logical and natural response to conflict.

When I went back to St. Louis for rehab, I sat down and had my first real talk with my mom. She told me about her childhood, growing up dirt poor in Mississippi and moving to Chicago as a little girl. When she arrived she didn't even know what a toothbrush was. Now that she's older she's really fearful, maybe because she knows that she's done some really awful things to me, and she has to live with those memories. I see it in her face when I'm back visiting, but I forgave her long ago.

5

The Tribal Solution

*G*rowing up, my mom was strangely tolerant of my drumming. As soon as I came home from school, I'd burst through the front door and head to the basement. As I passed them, I could see my sisters roll their eyes and turn the volume on the television all the way up, groaning, "Oh damn, Darren's home." As though the world would end if they missed a line from *Family Affair*, *The Patty Duke Show*, or *The Flying Nun*. But Mom ruled the house, and she let me play. I did have to stop when Mom was watching the evening news—heaven forbid you came between Moms and Walter Cronkite. She was a watcher. Even still, she's always watching the news or *Law & Order*, and only gets out of the house to go grocery shopping.

Decades after Cronkite announced the death of John F. Kennedy on the news, my mom remembered every detail. "It was devastating," she said. "We was all settin' around prayin' and hopin' that he wasn't gonna die. When Walter Cronkite came out he was talking about what happened. He was all choked up or something...he took his glasses off and wiped his eyes then said that the President was dead."

Later on, my boy Pat O'Brien told me he gave a copy of *Too Drunk to Fuck*, the first single I recorded with Dead Kennedys, to Walter Cronkite. "D. H.," Pat smirked, "You should have seen the look on his face." I didn't put the two together until I talked to my mom about the day Kennedy died.

The violence that spun around me as a child made playing drums an intense pressure release. It centered me, gave me focus and purpose. I just beat the hell out of my kit and, as angry as my mother was at everything I did, she would let me play. I don't know if it derived from her guilt, or from a soft spot she had for my father as a musician. Maybe she saw something in me, but if she did she never said anything. She never complimented me, or even commented on my playing. It was as if my drumming were just another part of the household cacophony—unless we were around my bandmates or relatives. Then she'd boast, "That's my boy" and "I'm so proud of him."

One winter, after a recent visit to Uncle Sam's, I became curious about musical instruments. I loved my Dad's Silvertone, and when I was ten I asked my mother to get me a guitar for Christmas, you know from Santa Claus, but she bought me a little child's play acoustic guitar.

I was like "No, Mom, I want an electric guitar like Jimi Hendrix. I can't play no acoustic guitar...be all like John Denver, all 'Rocky Mountain High' and shit!" This was very bratty for me. I usually didn't spit in the face of what my mother gave me or talk back. I usually thanked her and moved on. But this time I knew what I wanted. One thing I knew was that you had to have the right tools for the gig. But my mother couldn't afford to get me an electric one.

In the Sears and Roebuck catalogue, I saw this toy drum set, and I asked for that instead. She could just about afford to get me that on an installment plan. So I had this little twenty-nine dollar plastic drum kit—and that was it. I loved that little kit, and it was tore up in no time. I just beat it, beat it, beat it, to fucking death. From the beginning, I practiced all the time. "Here comes the racket!" my mother would say.

From my first set of drums made of plastic, paper, and metal, I developed a need to play music. It focused me, took me out of running around and causing trouble, and gave me an insane drive and purpose. It took away all of my inhibitions and gave me something to strive and live for. With music, and especially drumming, I had a direction and a focus for all that wild energy ripping and running through me. My need to play was more of a deep hunger than a simple need. Playing music stilled me. It was the only way to calm the savage beast within me. I learned drums, at first, by watching another boy in the neighborhood play. His name was Jeffrey, but we called him Yoke because when he walked or ran he looked like he was doing a dance popular in the 1970s that we called The Yoke. He was also on the track team and ran long distance. "Go, Yoke, go!" we'd shout and laugh as we watched him run. But as uncoordinated as he looked running, when he sat down to a set of drums, he played his ass off.

The first time I heard him play was at one of the many talent shows we had in our grade school. After I saw Yoke drumming I decided to organize a little band of my own.

When Dianne and I were ten years old we moved to Elmwood. I started my little band with the Roberts brothers who lived down the block. I played drums, Michael Roberts sang, and his younger brother Reggie played the guitar. My little kit was made by Polaris, which was written on the front of the bass drum so, I proudly painted a number six under the Polaris insignia. We named ourselves after my little drum kit, The Polaris Six. Reggie jangled out simple chord progressions while Michael sang in a high falsetto voice like Michael Jackson and shook a tambourine. We were like bad Cosby kids inspired by The Jackson 5. We wrote several little songs, one of which was called "Open Highway," after the title of a geography book we had at school. Another was "Are You Mad?" The lyrics went: "Are you mad / are you mad / are you out of your mind / are you mad / are you mad / are you out of your mind." That was the entire song— punk before it was punk.

Our first gig was at a typical black kids' talent show with lots of dance teams and solo singers. We were one of two bands to play. In the other band was a kid named Lamont Thompson. His father owned the local barbershop and also played drums so he had a real professional drum kit that he was letting Lamont use for the competition. All I had was that same tore up little plastic drum kit, which by then was way too small for me. Lamont promised that he was going to let me use his dad's kit, but just before we were supposed to go on he reneged on the deal and took it off the stage. I was mad and humiliated, but I was determined. I had left my crappy drum kit by the side door just in case so I quickly jumped off the stage, walked through the crowd, and grabbed it. The whole kit was so small I could practically carry it under my arm. I could barely sit at the drum kit; it was so small my legs and arms stuck out all over the place. When the curtains opened, everyone laughed at me. But the laughter quickly came to a hush once I started playing. I played really hard and didn't need to be wired for sound. I beat the shit out of those drums and everyone stood up and clapped for us when it was over. We blew the other group away even if Lamont did have his daddy's drums.

6

A Divided Loyalty

*E*lmwood was in the cuts. It was poor, but it was in the county so it wasn't as bad a ghetto as down in the city. There were houses and yards so there weren't as many shoot-outs and hold ups, but besides some newly built tract homes, it was still mostly projects and government funded housing. Elmwood was surrounded by white neighborhoods. Above us, separated from us by railroad tracks, was Olivette, a rich white section. Below us was an area called Overland, which was middle class white families. To the Southwest was the upper middle class St. Ann area. Black folks were literally across the tracks.

The residents of Olivette and Overland were the most racist. White kids drove down in packs to our neighborhood to hassle us. We would just be hanging out in our own street, and a car full of these white kids would drive by shooting at us with pellet guns.

"You fuckin' niggers!" they'd shout as they shot at us and threw shit out of their windows. "Hey you fucking tar baby! Spear chucker!" I remember hearing as a beer bottle hit my ass. "Hey, jungle bunny! Why don't you go back to Africa?" All we could do was run and try to keep from getting nailed.

It all changed once we started getting bussed out to white schools—then we fought back. Even though we were greatly outnumbered, nobody, not even the football players, could kick our asses.

I tried to stay out of the fights. It was a constant tug of war, though; by Junior High School I had found the band room and started to listen to and play rock music. I had made friends with a few white boys, and later when I was playing in bands I felt like I had divided loyalties. I loved music, and I loved rock music more than having to take sides or belong to any tribe, race, or creed. Other people didn't see it like that, and I had problems when I was back in the neighborhood. My neighbors didn't like that I was hanging with the white boys. Our street was the last street to go into the plot so there were no sidewalks or electric lights when we first moved in. The street had a couple of low-income apartment complexes and new cheaper developments. There were big apartments next door and later on the neighborhood turned into Section 8 housing that was zoned for people receiving housing subsidies from the federal government, and hundreds of kids moved into that apartment complex.

Then it was just like when we lived at the Peabody projects, playing all day and into the night with hundreds of other kids. We all played hard, and most everyone played sports. For the first year we lived there I was a wrestler on the varsity team at school, and my sister Dianne played softball. Quite a few professional athletes and musicians came out of that neighborhood. The soul singer Donny Hathaway grew up around there, and when he came into town off tour he stayed with his cousin Lavalle who lived just a few doors down the street from us.

At the time I didn't really appreciate who Donny Hathaway was. I knew he was a singer and keyboardist, but to us he was just Lavall's cousin who shuffled up and down the street every day in his house slippers and pajamas, talking to himself and smoking pin joints. You could tell something was really torturing his soul. He had episodes of madness, I guessed, and came home when he was having a breakdown. He wouldn't bathe or take care of himself so he was fat and filthy, hair matted and his skin ashy. We'd try to have conversations with him and most of the time he just would not make sense, but every once in a while he'd say something intelligent and beautiful.

In 1976 or 1977 he came and stayed for a while. Later we learned that this was when he was severely suffering. I think he had mental problems and anyone with mental problems we just thought was motherfucking crazy. At our young age we just didn't know any different, we'd say shit like "Ooh, he's touched! He's touched by Satan!"

I remember sitting with Donny on the porch next door to our house. No one was living there at the time so we used to chill there and watch the movies playing across the way at the drive-in. He'd talk with us kids in sometimes coherent, sometimes mumbling ways to a conversation that only he was following. After he left that time I guess he got better, at least enough to record "The Closer I Get to You" with Roberta Flack. Six years later we heard he had jumped out of the window of the Essex Hotel in New York City.

Our Aunt Mae Bell, Russell's sister, lived nearby us in Elmwood. She was pencil thin and wore a fire-red wig, always with a Pall Mall cigarette perched on her bottom lip and a large German Shepard by her side. One would die. She'd get another one and name all of them King. She always had a pot of greens on the stove at her house. She had a filthy mouth too. "How the fuck you doing, you little bastards?" she'd say to us.

Aunt Mae Bell worked for the Levitz family in Ladue who would donate clothes to us. That's the only way we had decent clothes to wear. She brought us boxes and boxes of these really expensive cast-offs. We were amazed at how rich people shopped, buying seven of the same shirt in all different colors. We had shit from Saks and Brooks Brothers. It never had our names on it, but we dressed sharp. We all wore each other's hand me downs. Because I was so hyperactive I still managed to be raggedy, and my clothes were always torn and full of holes. The kids on the street gave me a nickname: the bum.

"Hey you, Bummish Bum!" they'd shout. Or I was "Bummish Bum the Third," as if I was dubbed some sort of royal British Sir, Duke, or Earl, King of the Hobos, like it had been passed down to me from my forefathers as a legacy.

Beginning in Junior High we were bussed out to school in the white suburbs. We were part of that required 3-5% quota of blackness needed to integrate the schools. But integration went one direction: no white kids came to our tore up old school, and nothing was done to make that school a better place. We were in awe at the white school. Everything was so clean. The stall doors worked in the bathroom, there were seats on the toilets, toilet paper, mirrors above the sinks, and soap in the dispensers. The lights in the halls worked, the lockers were freshly painted without jagged edges or rust. And in the classroom there were supplies, whole pencils, fresh paper, clean books, desks with smooth tops and special places to put everything. Best of all there were free school breakfasts and lunches provided as a layover courtesy of the Black Panthers.

That was the main reason I went to school everyday and had perfect attendance. The laws of life were very different for these white kids. I remember being astounded the first time I heard a kid talk back to his mother. He was actually arguing with her: "Fuck you, Mom!" he shouted.

My mama would have killed me if I ever said anything close to that. Even if I looked like I was going to swear, Mom would raise her hand ready to hit me. One reason black parents were so harsh on their kids was fear for their lives. Black kids were not allowed that kind of leeway in life, not forgiven in the real world, not given that second chance. One "fuck you" to a cop or boss and who knew where we could end up—in jail or dead.

7

For Those About to Rock

*L*iving in black neighborhoods, we were not as exposed to Hard Rock, Metal, or Punk music. I had some knowledge of Prog Rock—my brother Bruce turned me on to bands like Yes, Frank Zappa, and George Duke—but mostly it was Blues, R&B, and Top 40. That changed once we started getting bussed out to white schools where the kids were listening to nothing but hard rock. Hard rock was the first new music I got into. The local radio station played different kinds of rock, and soon it broadened my horizons to include a range of what is now called Classic Rock: Foghat, Aerosmith, Black Sabbath, the Moody Blues, King Crimson, Van Halen, Led Zeppelin, Ted Nugent, KISS, and AC/DC, then more Psychedelic Rock like Wishbone Ash, Captain Beyond, Jimi Hendrix, Jefferson Airplane, Pink Floyd, and Ten Years After.

Since St. Louis was a Midwestern town touched by southern states there was also southern bluesy rock like ZZ Top, The Charlie Daniels Band, Lynyrd Skynyrd, Marshall Tucker Band, and Black Oak Arkansas. When I was at rock shows I didn't think about the crowds or the attitude and racism of the rednecks that came to see the show. I just loved being there.

"What is that, pubic hair on your head?" some of the rednecks would say. I'd just ignore them and keep on rocking and move away. I would sometimes get the feeling that I didn't fit in; to get rid of these feelings I would drink. All I knew was that it didn't matter when I was drunk.

I was not the only black kid into rock. There were other kids in the neighborhood that started digging it, too. There was my friend Darius. He was very cool in his little horn-rimmed spectacles, and his mom would always let us smoke joints in the house. We listened to Prog Rock bands like Genesis, Yes, Frank Zappa, and Queen. We would have long arguments about who was the better Yes keyboardist, Rick Wakeman or Patrick Moraz. Darius had cerebral palsy so his voice was high pitched and tight and you could never understand what he was saying. "Yo, check this out, listen to this part," he'd squeak, dropping ashes from the pin joint onto the record as he picked up the needle and dragged it across to the part he wanted me to hear again. He'd be drinking Ripple, and that was when he would start to slobber, but only after playing "The Prophet Song" and "Seaside Rendezvous" from *A Night at the Opera* over and over again, squealing out his explanations to me. It was nothing for us to listen to album sides for hours.

Bruce is the one that brought rock to our home and turned the rest of us onto it. We didn't really have a choice in the matter. He had control of the radio in our basement bedroom, which was part of a huge old busted up console stereo that Dad had given to my mom. The television didn't work but the radio did, somewhat. It would tune into the FM stations where the rock and classical stations were, but the AM stations, where the R&B stations could be found, came in a bit fuzzy.

At that time, radio was segregated: all the black music stations were programmed on AM, while rock and other white music stations were on FM—which offered much higher clarity and quality of sound. Bruce took possession of that console and moved it into the bedroom, and we started listening regularly to the local hard rock station, KSHE-95, partly because it was one of the only stations we could tune in. At night when we went to bed he would turn it on real low, and we would listen to KSHE all through the night.

Bruce, Dianne, and I actually grew closer through our love of rock. My sister loved Journey and Queen. Bruce loved Deep Purple and REO Speedwagon. We would crank that console up as high as it would go. I didn't know music could sound like that. We played "Brother Louie" to death, so much so that my mother even started to like it, and after a while she would join in singing. There we would be, listening to KISS or whatever, and the whole family would start singing along.

The first song that Bruce and I really appreciated together was Deep Purple's "Smoke on the Water," which played on every major white radio station. We had to have Deep Purple's album *Made in Japan*, but didn't know how we were going to get the money. I pooled my money together with a bass player from the neighborhood, and we bought the album. We listened to it over and over and over again, memorizing every lick and line. After that I started discovering music for myself: KISS, Alice Cooper, Blue Öyster Cult. For Christmas I asked for Rush's album, *2112*, and developed my own record collection: *Axis: Bold as Love*, Yesterday & Today's first album, Alice Cooper's *Billion Dollar Babies*, and Blue Öyster Cult's *Secret Treaties*. My neighbor even gave me Iggy and the Stooges' *Raw Power* for washing his 1972 Dodge Challenger.

I grew up with some real wild characters. Black Mike's real name was Robert McKee; he was skinny, muscular, and quick, and rode around all the time on black roller skates. He was always carrying this flute even though he didn't play. "What's up, Bummish Bum?!" he'd shout while waving his flute as he flew by on his skates.

One day we saw Mike hauling ass down the hill on his skates from the direction of the cab stand with three cops chasing him. Later we found out he had robbed the stand. There were rocks on that hill so we all gritted our teeth watching him shoot down the hill and then BAM! He hit the rocks hard and fell head first. Somehow he scrambled up and kept ahead of the cops as we cheered him on. They almost caught him, but he was too fast for the slow ass St. Louis County Sheriff.

Black Mike later went crazy from taking too much PCP, what white kids called "Tee." We called it "whack" or "dip." Mike would get lit on that PCP, hike himself up the telephone pole, and start hollering. We'd hear him from down the street.

"Mike's up the pole again," we'd say. Once I remember him hanging up there for an entire day and a night. "I'm not coming down until you get me some whack!" he was shouting. Someone finally got him to come down in the early morning.

All of us had nicknames; some made sense and described someone's character or habit, other names came straight out of a creative child's mind. As well as Bummish Bum the Third, kids called me Headly because of the way I moved my head when I played drums.

When I was a little older, I got a job washing dishes at the Hacienda Mexican restaurant and saved a little money pretty quickly that year. So the first thing I bought was an old beat up drum kit. I picked up things here and there for my kit, stole a snare drum and two cymbals from the band room, scrounged around and picked up a tom here and a cymbal there, but bought most of the drum parts from Rich Shapiro. Rich was my schoolmate and couldn't play drums as well as I could. I was in a band with his older brother Dave. Dave was really into acid rock and Grand Funk Railroad. And pot.

I kept my drums in the basement bedroom that my stepdad had walled off for me. Not really a room, but plywood and paneling nailed up to partition off the area. In the winter that bedroom was freezing cold, Antarctic cold. Just like with the rest of the house my father never really finished the room so there was no insulation, just pieces of sheet rock and paneling with the nails exposed. There was no heat at all except where my stepdad had cut a hole in the duct that ran upstairs and tried to squeeze a vent in. It was not very effective so the only way to deal with the cold was to play really hard. The icy wind whistled through the cracks in the wall and seeped through the sliding glass doors. I would play for hours and hours and hours in that basement room, and when it was really cold I would wrap myself up in a big wool blanket. I was practicing every available moment and when I couldn't I was listening to records through my headphones. My mother worked nights so we all had to be quiet when we got home while she was sleeping and tip toe around while she got ready. She was not to be messed with then, so I would start practicing as soon as she left until late at night when she got home, and then again when I came home from school.

In the early 1970s, I started going to live shows. Some of the shows I went to were outdoor rock concerts held at the drive-in right around the corner from my house. These drive-in shows often hosted local bands such as Bang, Sway, and a band from Canada called Bachman-Turner Overdrive. I think there was an admission price but we just snuck in under the fence.

Later on in 1974 we went to KSHE's Kite-Flying Contest sponsored by the radio station in Forest Park, and several top bands played. I distinctly remember KISS. I had never seen anything like it, a concert where the cops put their badges away. Very rare for St. Louis. Everyone was smoking pot and drinking beer but there was no violence or murders. (Bruce insists that this was the first concert I attended—I think he's wrong.) That year the audience was mostly white. There were a few dark spots, like us, but for some reason at that show, at least while the music was playing, no one bothered us. Racism didn't seem to exist at that moment.

The second time we saw KISS, Bruce and I were electrified by the makeup and tongue-lashing. KSHE didn't think KISS would do well so the entire arena sold for $2 a seat. They had pyrotechnics: huge plumes of fire and smoke exploded all around them, a very awesome spectacle for a young black ghetto child. After that, I saw KISS as many times as I could whenever they played. I knew right then and there that a band didn't have to be a bunch of veritable virtuosos to rock simple music.

When I was twelve or thirteen, Bruce lifted some tickets from Dave Shapiro, the same Dave Shapiro I bought my drums from, and we went to my first indoor big stadium rock concert: Emerson, Lake & Palmer. I guess Dave had gotten some more tickets because we saw him at the show. It felt very awkward at first, but peace was easily made in those days by smoking a joint. I was not a full time smoker yet, but I was thoroughly and absolutely intoxicated by the huge light show and even bigger sound. Everything was larger than life. Best of all, ELP did a ton of drum solos. In fact, it was the first time I got to see somebody play drums indoors, on the big stage, and as I watched I decided, "That is what I am going to do!"

After that I went to shows with Bruce all the time. He was working at Steak 'n Shake and would buy my tickets. I remember we once drove my mother's burgundy 1966 Pontiac LeMans, a leather wine flask strapped to my side with Mad Dog 20/20 inside, down to the Kiel Auditorium to see Lynyrd Skynyrd and REO Speedwagon play with a terrible opening band called Cockney Rebel.

From then on I fell in with the stoner crowd, and I continued to go to as many concerts as I could. St. Louis was a major stop for rock bands to come through so I saw everybody: Led Zeppelin, Ted Nugent, Aerosmith, Blue Öyster Cult, Alice Cooper, Marc Bolan & T-Rex, Foghat, Black Oak Arkansas, Rush, and Triumph. When I got to high school I moved on to seeing bands like Judas Priest, Eddie Money, Nantucket, Ram Jam, Jeff Beck, Black Sabbath, Queen, Steppenwolf, Tom Petty, UFO, Nazareth, Elf, Slade, Angel, and the Sensational Alex Harvey Band. These bands played huge stadiums, and after that I would daydream of playing high production shows. All that inspiration I would later translate into my own way of making music.

I punished Bruce by learning to play drums, but he and the rest of the family tolerated it because it was one of the most constructive things I had ever done. I was already a fairly good drummer by then through playing and practicing with a bunch of garage bands. Since I was always the class clown, people wouldn't take me seriously and didn't believe I could play until they heard me. My self-esteem was always a little fucked up so I would downplay the fact that I played drums like it didn't make me anything special. But I did, and still do, experience an incredible feeling when I play, as though I was giving away something that only I could give.

8

The Short Bus Serenade

After my seventh grade year at Hoech I was sent to Ritnour Vocational Prep for eighth and ninth grade in another white neighborhood called Overland. I was given a standardized test that was compared with the white kids I was going to school with, which resulted in the school proclaiming that I was a slow learner and that I had some learning disabilities, namely dyslexia, which often accompanies ADD and ADHD. As a result I was sent to another school. That is what happened to black kids all the time: "We're not saying you're stupid, but you're black and slow so we had you tested and survey says that you can go to tech school. Isn't that great?" Then two buses would come to the neighborhood to get us. They were the short busses that said Special School District on the side; it was so humiliating.

We had very few options, regular academic classes along with small engine repair, auto mechanics, woodwork, sheet metal, home economics, and all that kind of shit. The school was an old firehouse that had been converted so the classrooms were only areas sectioned off by partitions. This is where I met the real rocker kids, the stoner crowd. I remember thinking that I definitely did not want to get caught up with them, but just the same I would hang out with them to talk about music. They would always talk about smoking weed, muscle cars, rock bands, and beer.

After Vo Prep I went to North County Technical School for tenth, eleventh, and twelfth grades. We had academic classes in the morning: English, Math, Science, History, etc., and shop classes in the afternoon. We had to pick a vocation, and I chose welding. Every morning we'd have the standard academic classes, then we would go in for the academic portion of welding class where I learned how to use various welding equipment. Every afternoon we had shop. With my welding skills I built myself a bicycle chopper at school. My family thought I was going to be an automotive welder.

Even though I listened to rock and hung out with stoners, I still sat with everyone from my neighborhood in the back of the bus. By then I was a full-fledged stoner, but the fact that I hung out with white boys made some guys suspicious, and some tried to force me into situations where I would have to choose.

I remember one incident with Prentice Walker, a shit-stirrer from a truly rough part of town called Kinloch. We were in welding shop class, and he got right up in this white boy named Walter Maybe's grill and stood up to him. Some of Prentice's friends from Kinloch backed him up so then he looked at me. "Right, yo Bummish Bum? You got this? Come on, back me up," he ordered.

I said, "Naw." I refused. I was not about to take on a situation that wasn't mine just for the sake of it. He knew he was in the wrong.

But from then on all the guys from Kinloch would give me hell on the bus, giving me that attitude to try and intimidate me. I didn't give a shit; I was stoned every day by then. There was usually a huge cloud of smoke in the back of the bus. Some of the other bus drivers would call in and snitch on us, but our bus driver at this time was a little petite young white chick named Lynn. She was so innocent I bet she didn't know what weed was or what it smelled like.

That year I kept the same job I'd had since I was fourteen years old and gathered high school credits, a sort of OJT (on the job training) working as a dishwasher/bus boy/prep cook at The Hacienda, a Mexican restaurant in Overland. I worked at The Hacienda until I left for San Francisco many years later. At that time there were not very many Mexicans in St. Louis, but The Hacienda was authentic, not one of these jock-filled papas and beer places.

It was owned and run by Roberto Rodriguez, who had moved there from Mexico with his family. His daughter, Patty Rodriguez, used to hang out with my friends and me all the time, drinking beer, smoking weed, and listening to music in the park or in someone's carport. Another Mexican family worked there also: Carlos Macias, his two sons, Charles and Philip, and his daughter, Kim. Carlos would clean the restaurant by day, but at night he played mariachi music in the restaurant. He had a Les Paul guitar and a little tiki-tat-tiki-tat-tiki-tat drum machine, and he would jam and sing all night. Drum machines weren't popular then, so his was really primitive.

I had the biggest crush on Kim. She had huge, soft, pillowy breasts and a face full of pockmarks. I absolutely loved her. I was too socially awkward to ever ask her out.

Around then I started playing in local bands. One of my first was with a guitar player named Tom Schliemann who lived with his parents right down the way from Hoech Junior High. Tom and Bruce Wade were the guitar players. Bruce Wade was one of the few black rock guitarists that was into the same stuff as me. Tom Price played bass along with Randy, who filled in sometimes, and Charlie Bean was our singer. Everyone but Bruce sang backup vocals. Sometimes they would have me drumming or put in Mark Lee. We played a lot of southern rock and some Pat Travers, that sort of stuff.

Later I started playing with Fred Dickerson. Fred was a tall, dark-skinned, geeky brother with a medium afro, coke bottle glasses, and polyester collared shirts tucked into his high water bell bottoms who loved Jimi Hendrix. Once we became friends, we would sit around for hours smoking weed and listening to Jimi. Fred and Tom were much older than me, and I sowed my musical roots with them. Later Fred and I formed another band we called Fred, Broke and Darren because Larry, our bass player, was always broke. We would jam for hours and hours, endless blues and rock riffs. This is what we called doing originals. But basically it was an excuse for a lot of beer drinking and raising hell. We were a classic garage band, and we didn't play many venues. We played mostly in backyards, at keg parties, in a couple VFW halls, Lion's halls, and other lodges. It was when I came back to St. Louis with Dead Kennedys that I got to play at real places downtown, like Mississippi Nights. But Fred, Broke, and Darren played classic rock covers and whatever was hot on the radio at the time at keg parties, as those were the only places to play.

I was constantly changing bands because there were only two good drummers in the St. Ann-Webster Groves area, Mark Lee and me. We were drumming rivals, but of course we hung out and would go drinking in the park. With Mark, I learned the art of competing and working together. Our bands would sometimes have two drummers. He would take a solo and then I would take one; we complimented each other well. Mark was older and also really funny and outgoing. The girls loved him because he had cool, long, dirty blonde, feathered hair with a full beard. Socially, I felt inadequate next to him, but not when it came to the drums.

I was in the other band with Tom Schliemann and Bruce Wade. Bruce never had a car, never had any money, but he was the best guitar player hands down anywhere. It was always a hassle going to pick him up. He was like Jimi Hendrix in that way, never had any money but all the talent in the world. He lived way out in Normandy with his parents, of course, so you'd have to go out and get him, and then you'd have to bring his knucklehead brother, Marshall.

Marshall was great for parties, full of jokes, but he was a real pain in the ass. After rehearsal or a gig somebody would have to feed both of them and then take them home. Fortunately, most of the time Tom Schliemann's parents let us rehearse in their basement so we didn't have to pay for rehearsal space, and they had food and beer for Bruce and his brother. Tom's parents generally liked our music and would listen to us from the stairs.

In the summer, our regular venue, if you could call it that, was our carport in Elmwood at my mama's house. People gathered there to smoke weed, drink beer, and just hang out. That's where I met Fred. He was visiting his grandmother and saw us jamming and came over. I don't think he thought he'd seen anyone playing rock at that level in Elmwood. He asked me to come jam with him sometime. I said sure.

Bruce, Tom, Mark, Charley, Randy, and I started setting up out there and jamming, and pretty soon it was a regular gig. Other musicians, white and black, would also come there to set up and jam. We played all the rock tunes: Journey, Skynyrd, Queen, Kansas, and lots of blues. The guitarists—often there were two—would play solos for twenty minutes at a time. It was really hot so we'd play a couple songs, and then the cops would come, and everyone took a beer break, and after they'd leave we'd start playing again. It was a party but we took the licks very seriously. Anytime we had a chance to rehearse we would go play.

It always felt completely natural for us black guys and white guys to get together and play, as we were already drinking buddies and a lot of us played music. There would always be one guy around who played guitar, one who played bass, and the drummer, Mark Lee or me. Of course, St. Louis also had a bunch of rednecks, so we were usually playing to an all white crowd. Bruce, Marshall, and I were almost always the only black dudes in the place, and after people got drunk they would get belligerent. I remember one guy drunk as hell wobbling up to me: "You're pretty good for a nigger!"

I would hear racist shit a lot, even touring with Dead Kennedys. "Go home, yeh black bastard! If they're black, send 'em back," some skinhead dude said to me as we walked into a gig while we were touring in Australia. Very ironic, as he screamed that at me while he was standing in the long queue waiting to pay to get in to see Dead Kennedys. He had no clue what the band looked like since there were no pictures on the record.

Of course there was a lot of drinking and smoking going on in the Elmwood carport. Considering what a hardcore alcoholic and addict I turned into, I wasn't really that bad at this point. I was a late bloomer when it came to drinking, drugs, and sex. In fact I was kind of straight and prudish. I was a teetotaler because I saw my dad drunk so often and my brother stoned almost constantly. My brother, Bruce, was a big smoker and actually went to prison for a few years for dealing weed. I was so disapproving when he and my cousin Linda would smoke. "I'm never gonna smoke pot, man, that's illegal!" I declared.

The first time I got stoned was at a Foghat concert. I went with Matthew Williams, this black dude from my neighborhood, his brother Malcolm, and my white friend Dave Erwin. At first nothing happened, but then I started laughing and I couldn't stop. Everything was more intense—the music, the lights, the arena, my body sensations. I could feel the music more. One thing pot would do for me was to make me a part of whatever I was doing, as if I was completely absorbed in it. The guys sent me to go get some food, but I got lost getting back so I sat down on the floor of the concrete hallway and ate all the food that I had bought for everyone.

When I finally made my way back to the seats, the fellas asked, "Where's the food?" I thought about what I just did and laughed, that uncontrollable, belly-whopping, spit-up kind of laughter. After that I smoked occasionally, but it wasn't until a few years later that I started to get high every day.

My first love, and my first drug, was alcohol. I was fifteen when I had my first drink. It was one night when we were playing in the carport. I only drank a few beers but the feeling was electric to me. I instantly lost all of my inhibitions and as a result became a menace. I chased a girl down the street. I stole a mini-bike and rode after her yelling "Give me some pussy! *Give Me Some Pussy!*"

Those were my exact words. I had no sense. No social skills. And I was still a virgin.

The girl ran away from me and ducked into a house. "Get away from me, you crazy nigger!" She shouted at me looking as if I was disturbed.

I fought with Randy, the bass player, belligerently talking shit about his pockmarked, ugly, acne-covered face—just like the rednecks would call me names when they got drunk. Somehow they got me into the back of Randy's 1972 Plymouth Barracuda. I was obnoxious, shouting and yelling. The change in me was dramatic between the good kid, the wrestler who didn't smoke or drink at all, and the maniac I became.

I got home and my mama said something to me and I was like "zul zull zull im..." spouted some total drunken gibberish and then passed out.

9

San Francisco: Greyhound
Rocket to the Twilight Zone

After I graduated from high school I still lived in my mom's basement. I was sitting around smoking pot all day when I wasn't working at The Hacienda. Bruce was gone, as he had joined the Air Force a few years or so before. Dianne was busy going to Lincoln College and training to teach special education. Fred Dickerson had moved to San Francisco about a year before to live with his brother.

One day I was sitting at home smoking a joint watching *The Gong Show* when I got a call from Fred Dickerson, "Hey man, you gotta come to San Francisco, right now. It's a great scene out here, and you can stay at my brother's."

I said, "Huh?" all stoned and shit, "Can you call me back man...I'm watching *The Gong Show*...you know, Gene Gene the Dancin' Machine and The Unknown Comic Chucky Baby Chucky Baby..."

"You want to sit around watching *The Gong Show* on television for the rest of your sorry ass life or do you want to be on it?" Fred asked.

Fred and I never did do *The Gong Show*, but it was incentive enough to get me off the couch and on my way to San Francisco. I told Fred I had no money, but he insisted. "Come on, man, borrow some money and get out here!" So I borrowed enough money for a bus ticket and jumped on the Greyhound with my drums. I left a note on my mother's fridge written on a piece of paper bag, "Gone to San Francisco—Love, Darren."

I didn't have any suitcases, just my double bass drum kit. By this time I had bought a proper drum kit. It was a raggedy one; it had no bottom heads, and at the time I did not know how to tune them anyway. But it was a real kit, and that is what I played on for my first four or five years with Dead Kennedys. I played on that tore up kit for all of our gigs and used it on all of our early recordings. My drums were all I had so I stuck my clothes in the kit and handed the whole thing to the bus driver, like a little kid.

The bus driver sighed, "I'm sorry, but you're going to have to pay for that extra luggage."

"Sir, I don't have any more money and I have no suitcases, please, please, please!" I begged and begged for him to let me on the bus. He finally did.

I had no money at all, so for the next six days on the bus ride I ate next to nothing, a few crackers and apples I had in a bag from my mom's house and a bologna sandwich.

When I got to San Francisco, I was starving and I felt terrible. I was grubby and stinky and my mouth was cottony. In the Greyhound station I looked around, getting my bearings and figuring out where I was. I wanted to keep all my stuff in one spot so I put my drums near a payphone. The payphone rang. For some strange reason I answered it.

"Hey man," a voice that could only be Fred's said through the receiver. "We're in Daly City, be by to pick you up in about twenty minutes." Not twenty minutes later, Fred came walking through the door with his brother AJ who was dressed in a sky blue daishiki cut off at his midriff and matching blue parachute pants, complete with black sequined leg-warmers pulled over his calves and Birkenstocks on his feet. A black sequined scarf was tied around his neck, and in his arms he held a Pomeranian named Pal. Fred was rocking some bell-bottoms and a '70s augie shirt unbuttoned to his navel, and he had on those ever-present Woody Allen black framed coke-bottle glasses.

"Welcome to San Francisco," AJ said with a big grin. It was great to see them and excellent to get off that bus. We went straight to a party at his uncle's house. Coming from St. Louis and the Midwest, I looked around in amazement seeing for the first time palm trees, the streets, hills, and architecture that San Francisco is famous for; the sun shone brightly that day, which I soon learned was an anomaly in foggy San Francisco. Although San Francisco is one of the coldest cities in California, it felt warm and inviting to me.

D. H. PELIGRO

Sitting on the coffee table at the party was a huge, fancy, cobalt blue glass bowl. It was full of glorious, big, purple buds, and there were people smoking weed everywhere. Free weed in a dish? I knew then that I had arrived.

I was ecstatic and forgot about my hunger. San Francisco was lush, green, warm, and beautiful, and everyone was so friendly. No more freezing cold winters in St. Louis for me. From Fred's uncle's house we went to a club on Castro Street. Fred and AJ gave me a hit of acid and a tab of mescaline. This was my first acid trip, and the first time I had ever tried mescaline. On the way to the club I started feeling higher than I ever had. My body was tingling and vibrating all over. The entire world was bathed in soft light and gorgeous colors.

As we entered the club the music washed in warm waves over me. Dancing and grooving bodies made room for me and welcomed me in. Everyone was so friendly. After a minute it seemed strange that there were no women in the club.

"Fred, why are there no girls in here?" I asked. Then it slowly dawned on me.

"Fred...oh my god...is this a...ga...mmmmph–"

Fred slapped his hand over my mouth and hissed, "Sssh!" Then he grabbed my arm, "It's cool, man, be quiet!"

All I remember about the rest of the night is that once I knew where I was, it didn't ruin my buzz at all. I had never been anywhere like that—it was like entering a new sweaty man universe. The wave of acid hit like a thousand charging horses rushing me with the smell of leather and trails of chains whipping by my face glittering beneath the flashing disco lights amid visions of guys kissing, dancing cock to cock. It was like nothing I had ever seen.

This was my first exposure to a gay scene and to the wild land of drugs and sexual experimentation that San Francisco is legendary for. It was all about going to the limits and taking it to the limit. Everyone was doing or taking whatever, tea-bagging, felching, docking, wild bondage, fisting, tweaking, amyl nitrate. Whatever shit they were into, it was extreme.

My formative late teen years in San Francisco were a baptism by fire.

In a few months I had done and seen things my friends in St. Louis would never see, do, or believe.

Fred's brother AJ was a big old flamer. He sang backups for this queen named Pearl. Pearl was a white, nelly Jewish man with long curly brown hair who used to live with Janis Joplin. His act was a Janis Joplin impersonation in drag, and he had it down, the bracelets, long paisley dresses over bell-bottom jeans, peacock feathered hats, and, of course, the white girl blues voice. Since I had nowhere to live, Pearl offered me a room in his place. He had a huge three bedroom Victorian on Stanyan and Frederick, right across the street from Kezar Stadium—where Led Zeppelin played one of their last gigs—and right down the street from Golden Gate Park.

Back then, everybody lived in these huge flats, which were really cheap to rent. Also living in this house on Stanyan Street was a nurse named Linda, a gorgeous Native American woman, and her nine-year-old daughter, Rachel.

I got a job at Verdi's delivering pizza. But delivering pizzas, getting stoned, and not knowing the city turned into a mess. People were pissed about some black stoner kid showing up an hour late with cold pizza, so I got fired pretty quickly.

Pearl's house was gigantic, and I had it to myself most of the time. I got ahold of a little old futon and set my drums up in my bedroom. I felt so free. No one cared if I practiced in the house, so I would play my drums all day when I wasn't working. This was also the house where I was initiated into real drugs and real sex.

Pearl and Linda were both into lots of sex and cocaine. Linda may have been a nurse by day but all other waking hours she was a coke-sniffing, drunken maniac. She was a fag hag, going out to the gay clubs with Pearl all night. They would bring home hustlers all the time. They had one regular guy, a Colombian scam artist named Ernesto. He ended up stealing a bunch of money and coke from them and running off. Snorting and fucking, that's what went on in that house all night. I woke up every morning to Pearl singing at the top of his lungs, and Linda groaning, swearing, and trying to get ready for work.

I was still sexually naïve at the time. Sex was not my first thought; I was too hyperactive, and if I spent time on anything it was my music. Of course I masturbated, but it was always quick, and I was on to something else. My first time was in the seventh grade with a girl named Cheryl who lived across the street from us in Elmwood. She was about sixteen, a big dark-skinned girl with huge breasts. I didn't really like her like that, but Henry Head who lived next door and who also had a severe stutter dared me to come with him.

"I'm g-g-g-onna g-g-g-g-o over there and f-f-f-f-fuck her," he boasted like it was climbing a tree or something.

So I had to accept the challenge. "Here I come, too," I said as we ran across the street.

Her mom wasn't home so Cheryl opened the door and told us to come upstairs. She pulled off her clothes and laid on the bed. Henry Head pulled down his pants, climbed on top of her, and started fucking her. I went downstairs for a few minutes and then went up again to peer in the door to see what was going on. He was finishing up, and I went next.

My dick was hard, and I climbed on top of her not quite sure what to do. She took my dick and pushed it in. The rest was easy, and I came quick—I gave her the six-second rock. Then I tried to do it again.

"What are you doing?" she said, laughing, and pushed me off of her.

That was it, very cold and matter of fact.

D. H. PELIGRO

I did not have sex after that until I moved to San Francisco, where, in a very short period of time I would more than make up for my early chastity. In St. Louis it wasn't that I didn't think of sex or want it, especially when others were talking about it all the time, but I always felt inadequate. I had a crippling lack of self-confidence. I was the only black guy in the group of rockers I hung out with, and despite the fact that they were cool with me, there was always that racism in my face that made me feel like a second-class citizen. It was unspoken but understood, *It's okay if you hang out, but you cannot sleep with the white girls.* The history of lynching and segregation constantly lurked in the corners.

I was practically a virgin when I moved into Pearl's house, truly a temple in the city of sin. One night when I came home from my shift at McDonald's, where I started working after I got fired from delivering pizzas, and went into the kitchen to put my burgers in the fridge, I found Linda in the kitchen lit up on coke. She was sitting on the kitchen table facing the doorway and wearing her tight nurse's outfit. When she saw me walk in she stretched her legs wide open, pulled her knees up and pulled up her skirt, grinding her hips and moaning. She began to play with herself then lifted her fingers to her mouth, sucking on them.

"You want this pussy, don't you? You want it. Do you want it?" She wriggled out of her shirt, began twisting her nipples with one hand and sticking her fingers in her pussy faster and faster and moaning louder.

What was I going to say? I dropped my bag and went to her. She yanked off my pants, grabbed my dick, and started sucking it, hard.

"You wanna eat it?" she asked.

I had heard about this pussy-eating stuff. It sounded exciting, but I had never tried it. So I sloshed my tongue around like a wet serpent. She was so coked out and horny she just grabbed my little nappy head and ground it into her cunt.

I couldn't breathe, though I liked it when she clamped her thighs around my head. And then I just drilled her boney ass to China.

She said "Damn, baby, yer gonna fuck me raw!"

I had no idea about soreness, dryness, or wetness. This was my first real pussy and it felt so good and I could not stop.

The next day Pearl was disgusted when I told him.

"EEEUUW you ate her out? That stinky, rotten FISH! Ewwww!"

Then I felt bad, like I had broken a rule or something. Was I going to get a beating?

"What? I wasn't supposed to do that? Was that the wrong thing to do?" I asked him. I guess I was looking for guidance, and as a child I learned to respect elders and listen because you never know when you might have an opportunity to learn something. Pearl yelled so loud, so vigorously, that it seemed like my mama's hand was going to come through the San Francisco fog and slap me back to the second pew of the Second Corinthians

Church. I could just hear her screaming, *"Who told you to eat that white girl pussy?? Who told you to eat that Native American pussy?? You ungrateful little bastard!"* SMACK.

Of course Pearl knew that Linda was fucking everybody, but so was everybody else. It was 1977. That was pretty normal in San Francisco during that pre-AIDS era. Everyone was fucking everyone all the time. There was very little jealousy because you knew you would be getting it from someone else. It was pretty common to get STDs, too—but you'd just go to the free clinic and get penicillin. Plus, everyone was so high on coke and acid, there was no room for something as conventional as possessiveness.

The sexual hijinks in that house were phenomenal. Later on things got a bit tense, and there was some fighting, but it was nothing that serious. Linda and I fucked like animals for hours—on the table, the floor, the pantry, her bed, my bed, everywhere. I discovered things about myself I had not known. This was truly my introduction to manhood. After that, I started having sex with her all the time but never when she was sober. She would be so fucked up sometimes that she would pass out in the middle, and I would end up coming in her as she lay there limp and snoring and pissing the bed.

Linda had a boyfriend named Larry, not really a boyfriend, but he was one of those coke fiend player hustler brothers who lived off of women—San Francisco was full of them. So he lived off Linda, hanging around the house during the day, sleeping with her friends, and doing coke. But he was a great drummer and an amazing musician. He could play guitar, bass, and sing his ass off. He was one of those guys with loads of talent that could never get it together, but he taught me a lot.

We would do a bunch of coke and sit around the kitchen table or on the couch, smoking cigarettes. He explained jazz and fusion, and he turned me on to other drummers. He would give me these sweaty coke lectures about percussion, which turned out to be very useful. He was one of the first cats to show me how to read drum charts.

"Quarter note, quarter note, whole note, rest. This is the kick drum line," he'd explain.

I didn't like school much, but somehow I learned easily from him. Plus, his lifestyle inspired me. *See,* I thought, *he doesn't have a job and he does okay.*

He and Linda turned me on to coke. One afternoon they came home with a huge bag. I asked for some, so they gave me a little line. Then Larry went off into the other room and came out twitching, saliva exploding from the corners of his mouth, talking a mile a minute. He was on fire.

Pearl threw some twisted parties in that house. One night that I call the "Crazy Leather Acid Party" is etched in my mind forever. All of Pearl's friends from the Castro district were there, naked except for thick leather chaps, motorcycle vests, and spike-studded cock pieces. Some had handlebar mustaches, others had beards—bare asses and chests were hanging out everywhere. Some of them even had their nuts hanging out, tied up in string so that they bulged over the edge of the chaps like skin balloons.

It was an S&M scene so some of the guys dragged their subs behind them on chains and leashes. Some of these sex slaves had gags or masks covering their entire face. These weren't performances or demonstrations of love, this was sadism, domination, masochism, and submission. All I know is that I'd never seen it before.

One dom pushed his slave on the floor. "Lick my boots!" And the little Asian sub started licking.

"Suck my dick!" another said. His slave started sucking away.

Linda was the only girl there except the girl I had with me who I met in Golden Gate Park that day, a lazy-eyed rocker chick. Fred was there, too, wandering around, but he was so calm and seemed used to it, and there were plenty of drugs to distract him.

At the beginning of the party Pearl and this skinny half-naked young guy with acne came up to me and told me to hold my head back. "Are you ready for the trip of a lifetime?" they asked.

"Sure," I said, all naïve with trust. They then put two drops of liquid LSD into my eye. What a place to have an acid trip. I started getting really breathless and the leather all around me started to look very strange and to move like water. My peak was absolutely crazy, watching these two guys getting dominated by their masters. And just when I was peaking I nervously stuttered to my rocker chick, "Let's go to my room." We fucked for the rest of the party, tripping our brains out. I remember her toe kept hitting the edge of my drum kit. *Tap, tap, tap.*

What made this time so strange was that life in the house was sometimes the exact opposite of all the craziness that came through. Just like Beaver Cleaver and family, we would have sit down dinners where it was all about, "Pass the bread" and "Lovely meatloaf, Pearl—love this cheese!"

By this time I was getting tired of the hard rock scene. I was never going to fit into the arena rock/big hair mold, and I knew it. I would never have long, blonde hair. I was not going to be struck white, and I didn't really want to be. I was beginning to feel my own style, and I knew I couldn't be confined to a conventional hard rock kind of sound.

After a while I got really tired of all the disorganized drama in Pearl's house, too. Fred and I were supposed to start playing in Pearl's band—Fred on guitar, Pearl on lead vocals, and AJ on backup—but there was so much silly fighting going on between them that the whole thing just fell apart. Both Pearl and AJ had huge egos, so when we tried to have a band meeting these queens would just start screaming at each other—hissing, clawing, and a lot of finger waving.

I did start to meet some other people. I met Eddie at McDonald's where I was working. He was from

Florida and was into Judas Priest. We saw them at the old Waldorf, and later we witnessed the wrath of Motörhead. Eddie was a guitar player that couldn't play guitar to save his life.

We eventually quit working at McDonald's, and he got me a job at a fancy restaurant called the Sun Grove as a night porter from 11:00 P.M. to 7:00 A.M. We were later fired for drinking, sleeping, and being high on LSD. One thing about the Sun Grove is that we got to eat all this rich food and grog. I vomited sausage out of my nose high on LSD one night. It was so vivid, and the vile smell of the meat made me gag even more. That smell was forever imprinted in my mind. After I joined Dead Kennedys, I saw Eddie speaking with an English accent, and it became clear to me that everybody wanted to be somebody else. I was still trying to find out who I was. I guess that was the point of all that LSD.

10

Yes, I Digress

I eventually ran out of money, and the Pearl drama was getting to be too much, so I decided to move back to St. Louis. I was planning to move in with some old friends and keep playing music, but the minute I got back there I changed my mind. Everything was grey and dismal and nobody had any future other than secured factory jobs. I knew I had outgrown it there and had to get back to California, but this time I was going to do it right. I began saving up as much money as I could by working as a spot welder and Arc grinder back at Brash Heaters, Inc. They had me cutting huge sheets of 1/8 inch metal, but my math was so far off, and I fucked so many sheets of metal up, that they transferred me to the welding department. That's were all the fun was and where I wanted to be anyway. It was a typical factory job, and I worked hard by pulling ten-hour days. All I did from morning to evening was work, drink, smoke weed, and hang out with my sister Dianne, who took a cleaning job at the factory.

We became good friends with a white boy named Phil Black, who Dianne was soon involved with. The three of us hung out all the time. The first thing I did once I had some cash was to buy this beat up 1963 Ford Econoline van with a six-banger which I kept for years. During the lunch break we would ride up to the liquor store, get a thirty-two ounce of beer, smoke as much weed as we could before we went back to work. When we weren't in the factory we were in my van listening to music.

Finally, the time came when I thought I had enough money and was ready to head back to San Francisco. I was hanging out with good old Dave Irwin again, who still lived at his mom's in St. Ann. He still lives there today. But I had convinced him to come to San Francisco with me.

"Come on, Dave, let's take a road trip!" So we made a bunch of bologna sandwiches and packed up the Econoline. I said goodbye to my family and to grey, depressing St. Louis.

We drove as crazy as we could with a straight six and a three-speed tranny. By the time we got to the Colorado Rockies my little six-banger started to sputter, spit, and stop. It just wouldn't make it over the Great Divide or keep us going for the next hundred miles or so till we got to a service station to get the carburetor adjusted to the altitude, so we got a gallon of gas and poured it into the carburetor. It took us what seemed like four days, and the lion's share of my dough, to get over those mountains.

Dave wanted to stop at his cousin's place in Palmdale, which sounded like a resort town, like Monterey or Palm Springs—Palmdale is the exact opposite, in fact. His cousin lived in an old, dilapidated trailer plopped on the desert sand with no trees or shelter, just hotter than hell.

"Dave," I said, "Let's get out of here. I wanna go to San Francisco."

"Maaaan, I dunno..." he said.

The next morning I didn't even say goodbye, I just looked in my pockets at the forty or fifty bucks I had left and headed on to San Francisco.

As I approached the Bay Bridge, I remember having eight dollars in my pocket and a half tank of gas. "Damn," I thought. "Where did all my money go?"

My worries soon faded as I saw the view of San Francisco from the Bay Bridge.

I've always loved that view, its absolute magnificence. I felt invigorated to be back in my adopted home.

Once back in San Francisco, I quickly ran out of money again and was living in my van. Things weren't as easy this time. People were not as generous with their homes, money, or drugs. For a while I was parked outside of John Pintoff's. He was an excellent bass player and a so-so porn star. His father was a director, Ernest Pintoff, famous for his soft-core porn films. John had a very cool yet conservative style on the bass. Later he would play with me in our band, Reverend Jones and the Cool Aid Choir. He would let me park and hang out with him during the day but not come in to shower or sleep. I was put off by this. People had been so friendly the first time around, I figured that he would extend the same courtesy and let me stay there.

I had met John when I was living at Stanyan Street. I was hanging out at a club at the top of Haight Street near Golden Gate Park called the Omnibus, which later became the infamous Nightbreak. There was a whole music scene there; bands like Moby Grape, The Doobie Brothers, some members of Jefferson Airplane, and Skip Spence would frequent the Omnibus. It was very informal, and musicians would get on stage and just jam for hours. That shit does not happen anymore. People were playing a lot of blues and rock. I would go there and sit in, play around, which is how I met John.

I outgrew that scene because everyone was so apathetic and complacent. It was really easy in San Francisco to just hang around and not get anything done. Most of these guys were content to just jam their life away, playing shitty rock covers. I was living in my van hanging out in Golden Gate Park on Hippie Hill a short distance from the Omnibus and taking drugs, any drugs, all day, mainly smoking a lot of weed, drinking a lot, and taking LSD. I was wasting the days away. I knew I had to do something, and I felt in my bones that something was about to happen.

While I was living in my van, John introduced me to Paul McKinney, the front man for a punk rock band called SSI (which stands for Supplemental Security Income). SSI was government assistance for the mentally ill and otherwise incompetent. A lot of drug addicts, drag queens, tweakers, and Vietnam vets also relied on the supplements as their total source of income. At the time, peg leg pants were becoming very popular amongst punk rockers and new wavers in San Francisco. However, Paul would rock pleated slacks, a tight leather jacket, a button down shirt with a flipped-up collar, and the pointiest Italian shoes he could find. His suspenders had been cut by accident on the right side—with just the left attached—which he thought made him look more like a detective with his SSI badge adorning the attached left side suspender, three diagonal black and white stripes leaning left that were also on his three pickup Gibson SG.

He looked like a young Joe Strummer. It was said that Joe actually stole Paul's look. On 5th Street and Folsom at a breakfast place, Paul saw a poser who was dressed almost identical to him—turns out it was Joe Strummer himself. The Clash had a show that weekend, so he was in town. Paul's ego and judgment inhibited him from going up and talking to Joe. Joe was known to be a very down to earth, cool cat who was interested and curious to learn about the San Francisco scene. He would have talked to Paul for hours if Paul had just walked up and said, "Hi." But Paul was too busy calling him a poser and walked away.

Paul lived at 21 Falmouth Street, two doors down from a sex shop, around the corner from the warehouse at 227 Shipley Street, south of Market. Joy, the bass player of SSI, lived in that warehouse with Danny Vinik and Debby Parkins. The guitar player, Kevin Halloran, lived across town but was always at the warehouse. Kevin was very into the Yardbirds and Jeff Beck, and he incorporated it into his punk rock style. He would always pawn his guitar for beer money. He owned a two pickup SG, but somehow he'd always show up at gigs and rehearsals with Stratocasters. This was great for our sound because Paul had a low-chunking, humbucker sound, and Kevin had a high-pitched, Strat sound, which complemented Paul's sound. Joy played a Rickenbacker bass that was two sizes too big for her, but she also had a small scale Fender Mustang bass that was previously owned by Richard Hell.

They were kind enough to let me in to eat and take a bath. Since I had no place to live I was dirty and freezing cold. They told me I could stay there, which were magic words, and they gave me a key, told me I was free to come and go as I pleased. At one point Paul let me know that they needed a drummer. Up to that point I had been skeptical about punk rock. All I thought about when I heard it mentioned was the typical stuff most Americans thought—beer, puke, and safety pins, basically the Sex Pistols. I was into rock and metal, and I just didn't think punk was my style.

Joy grilled me, "Do you like the Sex Pistols? Dead Boys? Do you like the Ramones?"

"No way," I insisted in my own narrow mindedness.

"What do you think of Television? Radio Birdman? Iggy Pop?" she pressed.

"I told you, I'm into Judas Priest, Metal. You know. That is who I am."

"Well," she said, "have you ever actually listened to the Ramones?"

I had to admit that I hadn't. So she started playing the Ramones for me. This was a profound moment of self-realization. How could I have been so naïve? This was perfect music for me. The beat was in the band. We started playing around the city to pretty big crowds all around town: Mabuhay Gardens, The Def Club, and then The Hong Kong Café in L.A. We even opened for Dead Kennedys at the Mabuhay Gardens, which was when I first met East Bay Ray and Klaus Flouride. At one point we opened for the rock band called Yesterday & Today at Ruthie's in Oakland. After the gig Paul was carrying his amp to his taxi (he doubled as a taxi driver) and had a shotgun pulled on him by two black Oakland militants having a lovers' spat. He could have been the unfortunate and untimely recipient of some serious Oakland buckshot. The double barrels weren't meant for him, but he was in the line of fire. Since lovers are lovers, peace was made over a spliff. It took Paul a while to calm down, but it was just another day getting to and from a punk rock gig in and out of Oakland. Oakland wasn't so nice back then.

D. H. Peligro

Kevin was a real guitar player, not just a 1-2-3-4 go kind of guy, and that made our sound interesting. Paul wrote the songs, and we would all work out our parts and fit them in. Now, Paul was a 1-2-3-4 goer, four on the floor, full speed ahead. I loved this guy, He was a coffee-guzzling, Coca-Cola-drinking, over-caffeinated, well-dressed ball of fire who had part of his finger missing. I never asked why. He later told me on his own, but I never pried.

One day in 1973, before I met him, he was sneaking into a pool in San Jose. Kevin climbed over a fence and a ring on his right ring finger got caught. It tore the top half of his finger off to expose the bone. He screamed for help, but no one was around, so he had to put the finger in his mouth, climb back over the fence, and find help with blood squirting from his finger. He got to the hospital with his finger in a paper bag—but it was too late, they couldn't save it. He still wears a ring on that finger.

SSI and the San Francisco punk rock scene were really political. We didn't spout shit about elections, we were proactive, outspoken, we protested, demonstrated. When shit was fucked up we said and did something about it. Even if we just made noise, someone, somewhere would take notice. They were either for us or against us, but we always got a reaction. Sometimes our lyrics were just about how fucked up the world was and how empowering togetherness and the music could be— we would stand more of a chance together than apart.

SSI was my first real introduction to revolutionary music. I began having more political discussions and insight than I ever had before. It woke me up to all the injustice I had ignored for years. The band dialed me in on how the government was really a gang of corrupt, corporate, money-making elites, and they aimed to keep it that way by keeping their foot on the necks of people like us. Paul wrote a song called "Who Shot John?," about the CIA's involvement in JFK's assassination and the possible conspiracy surrounding his death.

Drumming became my expression for how alienated and pissed off I felt. My reasons were not exactly the same as the other guys', but I had a place for my rage and all my energy. I had so much anger I kept bottled up, I didn't quite know what to do with it, and I didn't want to act out on it. I started learning how to channel it through my music. It was really liberating to have a creative freeway for this anger and some way of understanding its source—it wasn't *all* my fault, the system was set up for me to fail.

When I was with the SSI we moved to Los Angeles for a brief time. This was my first introduction to all the L.A. pop punk bands. The Northern California attitude about L.A. was that they were all phony, plastic, Hollywood assholes. L.A. punk bands were posers who strummed a few chords by the pool and then ran to the record label, all style and no substance. San Francisco by contrast was truly an underground scene, and the bands there were part of it.

SSI and the bands we played with did all their own production and promotion, and people came to hear us based on these funky little flyers. Bands made stickers then, every band had one. Kids would be covered in them: on their skateboards, hand painted jackets, homemade bags, and even shoes. Bands made t-shirts really cheaply, so everyone wore those as well. The band kept all of the profit. It didn't go into the pockets of some fat record executives. Bands were proud to not be controlled by the record labels or any other entity in the music industry machine. That was the attitude.

SSI was doing okay. It wasn't like we were trying to be anything other than ourselves. Paul was offered a record contract and refused it because they wanted to keep the masters. So, he responded with a song called "Not to be Released":

We need the money
But not bad enough to sign the dotted line
'cause if we sold 'em
we'd be guilty of a serious crime

We don't have to sell if we don't wanna and you
know we ain't gonna
We don't want your money, your marijuana, cocaine,
free tickets to a rock show

These are—our tapes, these are not your tapes
These are—our tapes, these are not your tapes
These are—our tapes, these are not your tapes
These are—our tapes, these are not your tapes

People in Southern California liked us, and we were getting some gigs around L.A., so we thought what the hell. We opened up for X at Madame Wong's and did some other fairly big shows. While there I met some cool people and other musicians. We eventually disbanded right before we were going to record the debut SSI album, but we left on good terms. People wanted to go their own way and do their own things, so I moved back to San Francisco.

11

Hippies, Weed, and Veggie Burgers

When I got back, I started doing painting and construction up on Haight Street for a guy named Pat. I met him through Jim Boldman who had worked with me at Verdi's Pizza back when I first came to San Francisco. This is when I got introduced to vegetarianism.

We were on a job painting a couple of houses for these two potheads, Billy and Ezekiel. They were true hippies—long, dark, dry, frizzy hair, and smelling of patchouli. They had bought the buildings with money made dealing huge quantities of weed. They came into some tax trouble, so they had also bought a health food store on the corner of Cole and Haight. We were painting one of their Victorian buildings above the health food store, so we saw them everyday. Each day we were out there swooping around on swing stages, no health coverage and one safety rope. I would stop only to eat, usually some crap hamburger and fries, while on one of our many weed breaks.

So one day Billy says to me, "Hey, brother, why are you eating that McDonald's burger and drinking that Coca-Cola?"

I said, "I don't know. I'm hungry." That was what I had been taught to eat, bread and meat.

"Bro, there's a better way," Billy told me as he took a huge toke off a fat joint. "You gotta take care of your body, bro. It's your temple, man. Animal flesh is the worst thing for us," he said, exhaling through his Charles Manson beard, "and the way they raise and slaughter animals in this country is criminal. Meat is murder, bro."

Billy and Ezekiel took me under their wing and guided me into much healthier eating habits. They taught me how and what to eat, the nutritional value of foods like wheatgrass, sprouts, whole grains, and live foods. I was sold. I became a vegetarian. They also gave me a ton of weed to smoke and a place to stay for a while in their house on Page and Central. So I wanted to do whatever they said. Plus, I was happy to be a vegetarian; it felt good.

I worked hard, and played even harder. Later I met up with Bruno de Smartass (Stephano Georgio Gimilko DeMartis), and we started a no-name band with The Kid (Steve Martinez). We never played out but always went to punk shows at the Mabuhay (affectionately known as The Fab Mab). Bruno and I got a job on Sixth Street building this big S&M hotel. I was kept busy putting together these bondage beds. I spent all day installing leather stirrups, restraints, and straps into the beds and the chamber walls and laying horrible shag carpet. I was playing very little music. I just built bondage beds and smoked weed.

That's when I met my first real girlfriend, Theresa Herninko, a middle class Jewish girl from Philadelphia whose dad was an orthodontist. She was outspoken, short and strong, which is how all of my girlfriends have been since. We would hang out after work, drinking beer and sometimes going to the Strand Movie Theatre on Market Street, a funky old theatre where you could smoke. Or we would go to the Tivoli on 16th Street between Valencia and South Van Ness. All the punk rockers hung out there, and the homeless slept in the top balcony seats. Theresa was into these No Wave bands like Throbbing Gristle, Tuxedo Moon, Snakefinger, DNA, and New Wave bands like Crime, UXA, Devo, B-52s, and Bow Wow Wow. I was into these bands too because they were the new frontier, the newer, the weirder, the better.

During this time I met a guy named Indian, and we started a band called the Speedboys. They called him Indian because he used to wear his hair in two long ponytails, but he was really a Jewish kid from New York. He was really into martial arts and in later years had become a master. Indian was Mr. Hipster and always had slick clothes and looked really good. He was put together in a punk sort of way. He was a combination of bohemian, hippie, and punk, with a funky twist.

He always sipped on some kind of green drink, ginseng upstart, or royal jelly. He was a militant vegetarian, and he and I were a great match. He was always at punk rock shows and listening to music, but he would talk about James Brown, the funky this and the funky that, and hit it on the one, he'd tell me. We shared a vision of funky penguins clapping their hands on the side of the stage to the hardcore funky Speedboy groove. Visionary or delusional? He and I would get high and talk about starting a funk/punk band. He had a friend over at Iguana Studios, upstairs from the infamous Stud, a sometimes leather, sometimes disco, but always gay, bar. So we started practicing and came up with a set. Since Indian was a fast talker and scenester, he quickly got us gigs at the Def Club, Mabuhay, Sound of Music, Temple Beautiful, and American Indian Center with Dead Kennedys. I also did heroin for the first time with Indian.

12

We've Got a Bigger Problem Now

One night I was hanging at the Mabuhay and East Bay Ray told me Dead Kennedys were looking for a drummer. He had seen me play with SSI and Speedboys and knew I was a good drummer. The drummer, Bruce (aka Ted), was quitting—he was pretty fed up with Jello Biafra's snarky egotism. When Ray called and asked me to audition, I was shocked and surprised. They were a big deal. Their gigs were always packed, and they were played on KUSF college radio all the time. "California Über Alles" was already an anthem, and Jello had already run for mayor of San Francisco. Immediately I'm thinking there is no way I would get it.

Theresa encouraged me. "They're famous! You gotta go do it...*you better do it*," she said. But I stalled because I felt loyalty to Speedboys. Then one day I was installing some straps into the wall when "Holiday in Cambodia" and "Kill the Poor" came on the radio. One of the leather restraints snapped off as I was putting together yet another bondage bed at work, and I cut my finger.

"That's it!" I said to myself. "I'm gonna go fucking audition. I can either work in construction here or I can take a chance," so I went and auditioned.

After the auditions, it whittled down between me and one other guy. Quite a few people had auditioned for the gig. The other guy, Al from The Seizures, was a friend of Jello Biafra's from Colorado. Both of us auditioned again, with a song called "Insight." The drum part was fast and furious, just like I liked it. I thought I killed it.

Jello wasn't there, but East Bay Ray and Klaus said, "As far as we're concerned, you're in." Al and I came back and did it again with Biafra. The difference between us was like night and day. It was obvious to everyone that I was the one—my rhythm and energy was right and they knew it.

I don't know that I really knew it myself, though. Inside I thought I was perfect for DKs, but I was insecure because of my blackness. I didn't really feel that I deserved anything due to my old childhood experiences of racism and being treated like a second-class citizen. Unknowingly, I had begun to treat myself like that, taking a backseat in conversations with opinionated people. But when I was drumming, my talents shined through and spearheaded me past my insecurities. It pushed me to the point where I was raw and naked and I had to learn to socialize in different groups. I was still scared, but I felt the fear and did it anyway.

That was it, I started playing with Dead Kennedys. I kept my head down, put my back into it and it all came together. The first show was in San Jose; it was immediately gratifying. The scene was explosive, expressive, exciting, and evolving. The more the younger kids came to the scene it evolved from pogoing to a freeform dance where they'd bump into each other trying to get other kids into it. It was later called moshing or slamdancing—but with courtesy. If someone fell, you helped them up and the guys would watch out for the girls because they were part of the scene, too. Then some guy got the bright idea to climb on the stage, dance around, and before security caught him, dive back into the crowd. The crowd didn't let him hit the ground; they caught him. In 1980, stagediving was born.

Soon after I was in the band everything started moving very fast. We went into Hyde Street Studios and recorded "Too Drunk to Fuck" with "The Prey" on the B-side. While we were recording, I quit work on the construction of the Bondage Hotel and got a job as a bicycle messenger for Choice Courier, but I soon left Choice for a job at Arrow, which paid more money plus commission. You got a base pay, which was minimum wage. At the end of the Carter era, and the beginning of Reaganomics, it was $3.10 an hour. But the more packages you delivered, the more money you made. I worked spastically to maintain pace. Again, this was something that matched my energy level.

We had five speed bikes and little flip down baskets. I'd huff and puff all day, up and down the streets of San Francisco. All through downtown—Pine Street,

Broadway, Sansome, Bush, Kearney, the Embarcadero 1st, 2nd, and 3rd Streets, Market Street, Montgomery, and 555 California Street—straight up the fucking steep hills with mounds of boxes. So many boxes that you had to strap them down with bungie cords as San Francisco's wicked wind blew. Sometimes I couldn't see over the handlebars for the amount of boxes I had to deliver.

The bike messenger scene was really punk rock. We were the dropout crew, delivered shit all day smoking weed and drinking beer. We would all hang out on Sansome and California during our lunch break, lounging around and watching all the straight business people—the suits and skirts—going to work.

Sometimes I would hang out at Theresa's, but I eventually moved in with Klaus Flouride. He had a nice big flat up on Cypress Alley at 25th and South Van Ness. My room was off the kitchen, so I could hear everyone making coffee in the morning and raiding the fridge at night.

I was falling out, exhausted from working all day as a bike messenger and rehearsing all night. I wasn't really sure, and didn't care, what kind of money I was going to make with the band. That was the element of risk. You never knew if, or when, you were going make enough to survive but that solidified my love of music and my commitment. After all, this is what I wanted to do, what I had always wanted to do. I wasn't afraid of going broke doing what I loved—in fact, I didn't think about it. I'd lived in the streets before. I knew how to survive.

D. H. PELIGRO

My life was spent on the bike during the day and on my drums at night. Although I was tired, I did not feel pressured by it. Somehow I knew it was going to be all right. When we finally set up the national tour, I got to quit my job.

That first tour was fantastic, my real training ground for the road: the exhaustion, the long drives in a van from town to town, the exhilarating crazy energy before going on stage, and reciprocating energy as we played, not to mention meeting the fans who let us in to every punk rock party at a common squat in whatever town we were in. I don't know that all of me could catch up with what was going on, but playing the music felt phenomenal. We didn't have to deal with a lot of racist bullshit most of the time, although we would feel it around us when we toured in the South, or I would feel it. Real or imagined, it was there for me. We played all through the South: Atlanta, Knoxville, Mobile, Charleston, Raleigh, Winston, New Orleans, Tampa, Dallas, and all in between. Since we were playing for college students and punk rockers we didn't run into that much overt racism, but I was continually aware that just twenty years earlier I would have had to stay at a separate motel.

When we were on our second tour we all wore little pencil thin mustaches and soul patches. That was when punk rock was rigid about its dress code. The punk rock audiences hated it, so we kept doing it. We thought that was more punk than a Mohawk.

Going to Europe was a real treat. Seeing the architecture, cars driving on the wrong side of the road in England, and people with different accents depending on which country or township they were from, was so different to me. Sometimes, especially in Scotland, fans would come up and bark this gibberish that sounded like, "Hout Hout Hout!" They were just talking, but it was hard to believe they were even speaking English. I would think, "What the fuck are they saying?"

Throughout Europe I was in awe until, in England, we ran into racism that seemed worse than in the American South—mostly it came from the National Front. I remember one night in Leeds, in 1981, some of these skinhead National Front assholes got in and tried to start a fight. Instead of reacting to those assholes ourselves and playing into their hands, we got the crowd to control them. This was not the first time we used this technique. We stopped the music, and Jello pointed them out.

"See those assholes?" he said.

There were only maybe six of them out of 1,200. So when nobody joined them in their racist rhetoric, the crowd just pushed them towards the door. "Go on, FUCK OFF THEN!" the crowd said.

DKs were on the more intelligent side of punk, as were our audiences, for the most part. We made sure that bands aiming at the Nazi Punk market were not on the bill with us. While in Hannover, Germany, on the same tour, somehow hoards of skinheads, neo-Nazis, got into the venue with baseball bats. What really pissed me off was that they were sieg hieling to "California Über Alles." They were taking the song out of context, so we later came up with the song "Nazi Punks Fuck Off" The German Polizei set up camp right outside our dressing room. That was weird having these German cops dressed in full riot gear—helmets with face-shields, and tear gas canisters—sipping coffee outside our backstage door, just waiting to do what they do. At some point—in Bond, Frankfurt, Dusseldorf, Stuttgart, or Bonn, I don't remember because I was drinking a lot of German ale—in one of those cities, the Polizei escorted the skinheads into the paddy wagon while tear gas filled the corridors. I have a vague memory of wearing a "Nazi Punks Fuck Off" button-down shirt that had a swastika in a red circle with a slash through it. The German tour manager, Christian Ploppa, said to me, "You kant vear diz shirt in Deutschland."

"Oh yes I can!" I replied. I got some hateful looks that made me a little nervous, but it turned out okay in the end.

Another weird thing Christian told me was that the Holocaust never happened in Germany.

"Oh yes it did," I said, while we insisted that he take us to the Holocaust site in Dachau.

"Nein," he said. "Diz iz not in ze schedule."

"Motherfucker," I said. "You work for us. We don't work for you."

He complained that it was too far out of the way, but Biafra, Ray, and Klaus also insisted that he take us there.

I had a blonde girlfriend named Suzie who was Jewish. When we got there, she was crying her eyes out. We couldn't believe the size of the living quarters—or dying quarters, I should say—the lampshades made of skin, the blankets made from human hair, the giant ovens, the photos of emaciated men, women, and children with eyes devoid of hope, and the smell of death that had lingered for decades.

I looked at our tour manager and said, all smart-assed, "So if the Holocaust didn't happen, how is this here?"

He looked into my eyes, innocently stunned, then lowered his head and said, "Zis iz not in our history books."

"Well, maybe not," I said. I was shocked. It seemed like Germany wanted to erase this part of their history. Ploppa seemed to be genuinely ignorant. Maybe they tried to wipe it out for the next generations? I don't know.

I do remember staying in Berlin while the Berlin wall was up, though. Checkpoint Charlie was no joke. These Nazi border patrol guards were straight out of the SS. They took our passports and looked at me and started pointing at their eyes, screaming at me in German when they noticed I was with a blonde white girl who, by the way, looked pretty German—go figure.

We could see the Berlin Wall from our hotel room. It was about a block away. The wall looked liked it was about fifty feet tall to me; it was topped with loops of barbed wire. From our hotel room, we could see over the

D. H. Peligro

wall. There was a field, similar to a track field, and inside of it were rows of x-shaped wooden barricades wrapped in barbed wire. Several Germans and a few Dutch anti-Nazi punkers on our road crew told us that there were landmines buried in that field. There was a walkway on top of part of the wall, and we could see armed guards patrolling it. Some guards on the ground had German Shepherds. Everything about them looked very serious. I started envisioning what the oppressed people of East Germany looked like. I imagined them to be hunched over, malnourished, and devoid of any sense of future, life, or fun.

Later on, after we got drunk, Microwave, our roadie, and Chris Grayson, our sound man, started throwing beer bottles and full cans of beer over the Berlin wall trying to set off the landmines. This made the German Shepherds howl, bark, and froth at the mouth. At one point, one of the guards in the tower guarding the wall (from what? I don't know) pointed his gun directly at us. I was petrified.

The next night we played the SO36 club in Berlin. It was a different kind of club, more like a squat, run by a co-op. It reminded me of The Vats in San Francisco. Inside the club we walked through a thick haze of German cigarette smoke mixed with the smell of Pilsner—the perfect punk rock incense. There was music in the background, and lots of German chitter-chatter. As my eyes adjusted to the dark, smoky atmosphere, the first thing I noticed was a German girl squatting and peeing on the dance floor just inside the club. *Wow*, I thought, *look at her little pee-pussy.* Security was like, "Pussssst, Whatever." I thought, *Damn this is gonna be a great gig.*

Backstage, our dressing room was a small cylinder-shaped hole, like a crawlspace; you had to climb a ladder to get into the room. Once inside, it was pretty big. There was a table filled with beers, water, and orangensaft. On another table sat bratwurst, knockwurst, blutwurst, Nürnberger Rostbratwurst, frankfurters, and chunks of Limburger, swiss, and other kinds of cheese. I wasn't eating any of the sausage, but I did eat cheese at the time. MDC was on the tour, and they were all vegetarian, too. I usually ate and smoked hash with them. I thought it was fitting to hang out with their drummer, Al, who we affectionately referred to as "Auschwitz." It was a hot, sweaty, great gig—just like I thought it would be after I saw that girl's pee-pussy. I mean, shit. How could you have a bad gig after that?

In Stockholm, Sweden, we had to make a fast getaway as Biafra, in all his cleverness, found it comical to spray paint the DK logo on a mural of John Lennon inside the club. This was in 1981, just a few months after Lennon had been assassinated in NYC. It wasn't that we were so punk rock that we went around tagging DK logos everywhere we went. We didn't, although some of our roadies did. But I had to admit it was pretty punk rock of Biafra to just tag a big red DK logo right on John Lennon's face. So this was a slap in the face to the

Beatles fans and John Lennon supporters—they wanted to kill us.

They felt disrespected by Biafra's tagging, and there was an underside to the Swedish temperament—especially if you shit on the face of their Jesus. The security guards were huge bodybuilders, and they were pissed off. They surrounded us. Everybody was screaming. Microwave was in the middle of it; he signaled Tuna, our Swedish handler, to get the truck, and we got the hell out of Dodge. We bounced and left the DK logo embedded on the John Lennon mural.

13

NYC, Cocaine, Pussy, and Pancakes

On our second national tour, the shows in New York City were most memorable for me. We played Irving Plaza for two nights. The Sick Kids opened for us. I met their drummer, Becky Wreck. We would later become friends when she moved to San Francisco, and then in L.A., where we are still friends today. Both nights the show was packed. At that time people were starting to slamdance and mosh more and more. In the middle of the pack in New York was Jon Stewart, way before his gigs on MTV and *The Daily Show*. After our set John Belushi, Dan Aykroyd, and Michael O'Donoghue came backstage—I think Buck Henry was there, too. It was Aykroyd and Belushi's Blues Brothers period, so they were wearing long trench coats, hats, and sunglasses. John Belushi and Dan Aykroyd were big punk rock fans, and they asked if they could use a song in the film they were working on called *Neighbors*. O'Donoghue, Aykyroyd, and Belushi talked with Klaus and some with Jello. They got the rights and used "Holiday in Cambodia" in the film.

We were never the kind of band that hung out together all the time. Like family, we loved each other, but there was a limit to how much time we wanted to spend together. I was always the one who hung out afterwards and went my own separate way, partying. The Irving Plaza was one of the first of these nights. I was starry-eyed there in the Big Apple, and I knew there would be great drugs wherever I went. Sue Brisk came backstage with her camera. She was a photographer for some magazine, I think New York Rocker, and freelanced at the time. I had met her before when we had played Mabuhay with The Mutants, so she came over, and we started chatting it up. Since NYC rocked all night, I was down for whatever. Sue took me to my first New York glam party at Giorgio Gomelsky's loft. Giorgio was a weird Russian artist, filmmaker, actor, and music manager—he'd managed The Yardbirds—and was also a record producer. He knew all the downtown glitter rockers and had been on the scene for years, since before the New York Dolls and the Ramones. I'd never met that many Russians, but most of them I had met were rigid, stiff, and cold. Giorgio was a warm, inviting, accommodating, friendly, spirited guy. He was super-energetic, dynamic, and very talkative. Maybe it was all the cocaine.

Giorgio's loft was somewhere downtown, uptown, midtown, lower east side, I didn't know were the hell I was. But his loft was fantastic—concrete walls adorned with paintings, high-gloss grey painted floors, and a plethora of thick velvet drapes trimmed with white lace hung upon the entrance of every room and small den in the loft. There were women in tight, peg leg jeans and runny black eye make up everywhere. On every velvet couch lay an emaciated, coked-out model in some '80s fashion statement, sort of like left over Twiggys that had lost their way and found the coke.

"Got any blow?" they whined with a nasally tone.

I said no.

"You fucker, yes you do. I came all the way from Jersey for this party. Fuck you!" In their teetering heels and with their asses and tits hanging out, they would slobber over to the next guy, "Got any blow?"

I talked to David Johansen of the New York Dolls for a while at the party. He was there holding court in super tight little low-waisted white pants. I thought he was really stuck up and into himself. He confirmed everything I had heard about this scene, that these New Yorkers thought they were better than everybody else—more down, more punk, more funky, more chic, and that everything important only happened in New York. As if they were the start of it all, the center of the world. More like the assholes of the universe.

I felt awkward, and I didn't know what to do with myself, so I set my sites on the bar and to finding whoever had some coke. It was 1981. Somebody had coke. The little whiney bitches were right, but I sure didn't have any, and I wanted to fit in. I was still just a sniffer, but

D. H. PELIGRO

fully into it. Sue and I found one of her photographer friends, Richie, laying out rails at the bar.

High on coke, we stayed until about 5:00 A.M., then Sue and I walked back towards her place. We stopped in a park to have sex on the swing set before going back to her house and having sex all night. I could really pound away when I was high on coke. When I got up she made pancakes, and I went back to Amy's where I was staying.

I knew Amy Linden from San Francisco because she was in the band Vs with Indian on guitar, Ulga deVulga on bass, and singer Heidi Familiar. They had a revolving door of singers, and Amy was one of them. She would later become a writer and VH1 analyst. We couldn't afford separate hotel rooms, so I was sharing one with Biafra. I love the guy, but no way was I sharing a room with him again, so for the rest of our stay in New York I stayed with Amy.

I have never had what you would call an internal regulator when it comes to drugs or alcohol. I was all accelerator and no brakes. Sometimes the parachute just wouldn't open at all, so I was drinking and smoking way too much before going on stage. I remember leaning over in the middle of a set to throw up. Jello, Klaus, and Ray were serious and politically against all drug taking and decadence. I knew even then to try and hide my drinking and snorting—not that they didn't have their own things going on.

Ray was a player and always had lots of girlfriends, those that he met on tour and those that came to meet him backstage at gigs. We called them Ray's Pets. We thought he should have an all girl band of his ex-girlfriends called the Ex-Rays. He always was, and still is, a busy man that way. I've only found out recently that Klaus, too, got around with the ladies. I was too self-absorbed or spaced out to notice.

People often thought Jello was gay, but he wasn't—as far as I knew. He was married to Teresa Soder at the time. She had big tits—Jello did have a thing for big ol' titties. Teresa was a punker, one of the fashionable ones: cigarette holders and vintage dresses, a real scenester, and voluptuous. I don't remember his girlfriend after her except that she also had big tits, and she confessed to me later that she didn't like him very much. As far as I know he never cheated and only drank occasionally.

We all did coke one night in New Haven. Some dealer showed up and thought it was cool to whiff us all out before a show, but what a disaster. People in the audience knew we were on coke since some of them saw us backstage and heckled us for being fucked up.

Biafra said, "We don't need coke and neither do you." And he was right.

Jello was an attention/media whore. He would stay up all night talking, talking, talking with people in his room. I remember sharing a room with him in the early days of this tour and going crazy. All I wanted to do was get high, not listen to him preach to his audience. Biafra would make record and distribution deals with other labels, but the DKs are East Bay Ray's band; he is the one that put the ad in the paper that brought the band together. Really DKs was our band—Ray, Klaus, Biafra, and me. Each of us put in equal amounts of work, some more than others at times, but Ray was always the organizer. He was the bean counter, the moneyman, kept track of all the funds and later became the band's accountant. As all-business as he seemed, he has always been quite a ladies man. He always had this or that beautiful girl on his arm, and they always seemed to come out of the woodwork while we were on the road.

Ray is an interesting cat. He grew up in Castro Valley, California—the white part of town. His mom was from Oakland, his dad from Spokane, Washington and they met as college students at UC Berkeley. His parents were real San Francisco liberals. They were middle class but in the '50s and '60s they fought for civil rights. They were on a committee that fought red lining which was the way realtors and politicians kept black people from moving in and buying in certain neighborhoods. His father was a musician. Ray got his first guitar in high school and took music lessons. His father took him to see black musicians, and I remember him telling me about the impression Lightning Hopkins made on him. Ray moved to Oakland before most other white people lived in his neighborhood, but he never thought about it like that.

Klaus, on the other hand, has always had that little-old-man-absent-minded-professor style. He would forget his head if it wasn't screwed on straight. Klaus was

so absent-minded that one time he came to rehearsal without his bass. We only had a three-hour block of time, and Klaus shows up: "Oops, I forgot my bass!" It took him an hour to get back. "Oops, forgot my amp!" By the time he got back our time was up. Even now he loses his passport, and we all freak out.

Klaus is from Detroit and was a DJ at a college radio station before he moved to the Bay Area and joined the band. He is also an interesting and quirky guy. He managed to dodge the Vietnam draft for the war by being an obstructionist. He acted like a crazy imbecile, drawing on everything with crayons during his interview, pretending to be colorblind and deaf during his physical, and telling them he was a homosexual. He even went as far as to smear peanut butter up his butt before he arrived, stick his finger in there while being examined and then licking his hand and making a "mmmmmm" sound. The officer immediately picked up the denied stamp and slammed it on his physical forms. His father also wouldn't fight. He had been a conscientious objector during World War II.

Klaus has always been a loving guy and always looked out for my welfare. He would do things like make sure my car was parked legally and not out in traffic, as I would come home drunk sometimes when we were roommates on Castro Street. He would scold me but always in a nice, supportive way. "I don't think you should be drinking so much," he'd say. When I first started with DKs, Ray wanted to pay me less than the others, let me work up to full scale to prove myself, but Klaus insisted that I get paid the same. "He's working just as hard as everybody else," he argued.

Despite his image, Jello loved his fashion and was a real shopper. He had a shoe fetish and an obsession with vinyl. He especially loved pimp style shoes so whenever we were in D.C. he would get these crazy multi-color side-lace Denson Winklepicker shoes. It was cheaper to shop in D.C. than San Francisco so he also did a lot a thrift store shopping. I liked thrift store shopping. It reminded me of when I was a kid going to Veteran's Village, a St. Louis Goodwill, so sometimes I'd tag along with him.

When we first went on tour neither Klaus nor Ray would stay in a room with Jello. I didn't understand why, and since I was the new guy, I had the honors. That first night I learned why. Jello didn't take drugs or fuck lots of girls, but he always invited crowds of people into the room. He would hold court—just talking, talking, talking until 5:00 or 6:00 A.M. He wouldn't go to sleep, just talk shit all night long. This was really irritating since I was staying in the same room. Then, when morning came, Jello would never want to get up. He would scream and throw his Winklepickers at the door when the maid came, and he was always late for the van.

Sometimes, when the journalists were back stage interviewing us, my old shame would rear its ugly head, and I would again feel like a second-class citizen. I felt a little intimidated to speak my views for fear of saying the wrong thing, or not knowing what the hell I was talking about. I would begin to doubt that I had any views at all other than black ones, and that wasn't their focus. When the cameras were on I felt like I was at school being given a test in U.S. government.

"What do you think about Reagan's cabinet? Or Reaganomics?" I didn't want to just repeat someone or be a stupid drummer and give some phony baloney answer just to save face. Biafra seemed equipped to handle the media better, so we let him. He would dominate the spotlight whenever we were being interviewed. Neither Klaus, Ray, or I could get a word in edgewise, literally. It was all about Biafra. Talk, talk, talk and go, go, go, go. It's the case with singers a lot of the time. They don't have an instrument, but they have their mouth, so they use it.

By then I was also playing guitar, writing my own songs, and I was into the whole drug subculture. In my addiction at some point I felt better than the rest of the band. They were squares. I had to drink every day to stay steady so when I'd get in a sobering environment and talk about something that really could change the world I felt like a deer in the headlights. In some of our more sentimental moments, Jello would encourage me to speak my mind and try to give me support. "I think you know what to say, you just need to take your time and say it," he said. That was one bit of encouragement he gave, and he was right. I should've just taken my time to process my thoughts.

However, my thoughts were not as pre-planned and practiced as Biafra's. This and the conversations I had with Klaus were also a chance to expand my mind, open it up to new possibilities, to listen and find out what was going on. Still, Jello didn't give us any time to say anything. He could give interviews till five in the morning. After a while it was stuff I had heard over and over again—just torture. I wanted to stick knitting needles in my ears and gouge my brain out.

At our next show in New York, The Sirens and Bad Brains opened for us at Bonds in Times Square for two nights; the following week The Clash did seven nights there. We were all part of this brand new genre of music spearheading a new decade and a new movement that promoters and club owners were not familiar with. As a result, they didn't know the magnitude of the fan base. And of course they would always have too many security guys who would mistake fun for fighting. They'd see people slamdancing and think that they were beating each other up. It became our job to let them know the difference between fighting and moshing, and that the fans were just as important as we were and should be treated with respect.

I had not met Bad Brains before, but I had heard their song "Pay to Cum" on the *Let Them Eat Jelly Beans* Alternative Tentacles compilation. This was our first gig with them, and they were electrifying. H.R. was a true showman, like a black Iggy Pop. He came out with his shirt off, fully ripped, and did back flips, sending a seething cauldron of energy swaying through the crowd. His whole body was an electric current of rebellion. I remember thinking, *Wow, how are we gonna follow that?!*

As fate would have it, our set was simply smashing. After all, the crowd was there to see Dead Kennedys. It was my first tour of the East Coast, and I gave it my all. As did Ray, Klaus, and Biafra. When we were on, it was on—we opened the floodgates and drowned the crowd in political punk rock awareness, DK style.

14

The King of Afropunk

There was an instant bond among black musicians in the punk scene. We were brothers and sisters in that way. There were only a handful of us: Bad Brains, Fishbone, Eugene (the lead singer in Whipping Boy), Mike (Chicken Butt, the bassist from Jodie Foster's Army), the illustrious Snookie Tate, and me. We were pretty much it. We were all black in a mostly white world so we understood right away what we were dealing with. Or did we? It was a new scene. Sometimes we didn't know what we were dealing with. I didn't personally go around thinking "What am I up against?" I just played music because I loved it and let it flow.

I always liked Doctor Know, the guitar player from Bad Brains. He was really cool and laid back. So was Darryl, the bassist. I could tell that the drummer Earl and H.R. were real brothers because they squabbled in the way only family can. Bad Brains were a different kind of family than the DKs were. When our show was over we'd split up and go our separate ways. But you could clearly see that Bad Brains lived, ate, and drank together amidst the "I and I" Rastafarian vibe.

Maybe it is just different on the East Coast because there is less space, but just because someone has dreadlocks or is black doesn't mean I am going to agree with them. Sometimes I got annoyed with H.R. He is from D.C., but would endlessly preach in a Jamaican accent about the ways of Jah, Rastafarianism, and the evils of Babylon, speaking in what the Jamaican locals call a patois accent.

We did have the weed in common, and when they played with the DKs in 1983 in San Francisco they would come to me to cop. But I hated their intolerant macho bullshit mentality. H.R. would get stoned and pontificate, calling everybody a blood clot faggot. This was a problem when they were on tour with other bands, especially with The Dicks and MDC, because The Dicks' lead singer, Gary Floyd, was openly gay and Dave of MDC was pro-vegetarian and militantly gay. So when H.R. found out about them he started talking shit. Gary and Dave weren't big fans of H.R., but they felt comfortable talking to me.

Even though reggae and punk rock sort of go together, I thought the sexist, homophobic attitude that H.R. and a lot of Rastafarians had was stupid. Punk rock was supposed to be accepting of all people. It was a rebellion. Unwritten as the rules were, my interpretation was that we didn't hate on anybody regardless of gender or sexual preference. But we did hate the butt-licking liars like Jerry Falwell, Anita Bryant, Jesse Helms, Terry Dolan, Phyllis Schlafly, Ronald Reagan, Daryl Gates, corrupt cops, and the L.A. police state.

Being hated because of the color of my skin as a black child, I didn't feel the need to take that torch of hatred to the next generation. That's how we all got into the punk scene in the first place—because we felt accepted, not because of the color of our skin or our sexual preferences, but because of the music.

But still there was always a kinship between us. Darryl and Dr. Know have always been cool with me. I always got an especially loving "I and I" vibe from Dr. Know. We aren't close buddies, but we always give each other recognition. It's about loyalty, a brotherly loyalty. Like if it came down to it we would guard each other through thick and thin.

I saw Earl, Bad Brains' drummer, in Atlanta when my band Peligro did a show with Sylvain Sylvain of the New York Dolls. I spotted Earl while I was on stage, and I really felt his support. It was quite a compliment that he was there for the show and that he stayed for the whole thing. I'm sure he had other things he could have been doing. He was amazed that I was playing guitar.

Bad Brains asked Peligro to open for them at the Key Club in L.A. They were called the Soul Brains then because they had signed with Madonna's Maverick label and lost the rights to their name.

Eventually, H.R. started having some real mental problems. The last time I saw him was in 2002 when I was recording *Sum of Our Surroundings* in this studio in East L.A. It was a hot, hot summer, and the studio was in a rundown house in the ghetto. Nothing around but train tracks and warehouses. The studio was a real dump. It was run by these Mexican Rastas and their band Quinta Sol. There was garbage all over the place, beer cans, empty food containers, dirty clothes. The first thing we had to do was move all the trash out. The whole house smelled like weed—which I didn't hate, but I didn't appreciate it either because at the time I was sober. That meant no mind-altering substances for me—no weed, alcohol, crack, her-ron (my favorite). Couldn't have it. Any of it.

In the middle of this shit-storm was a couch. I noticed a guy sleeping on it and thought, *Now we have to get this bum out of here.* I warped in to hyper-mode—the clock was ticking, and I was paying money for this so-called studio, so I woke this bum up. As he sat up I noticed he was wearing a long black cape, holding a gold scepter, and wearing a crown with big dreads sticking out under it.

I did a double take. "H.R.?"

"Eh natty...hey boy...yeah, mon...wha' h'appn rass?!"

I didn't think he recognized me. "It's D. H. from Dead Kennedys."

"No, from the Living Kennedys, mon!" he said.

I had heard that he was having problems with either schizophrenia or bipolar disorder and was not taking his medication. He was in and out, sometimes lucid and on the earth, other times off in his own delusions. Homeless, he was bouncing from couch to couch. He was friends with Quinta Sol. He did some recording with them and he never left. I told him, "Man, we're

124   D. H. Peligro

gonna be recording our record so you can't be up in here right now, rass."

That day he hung around and smoked weed, sat out on the porch and talked to himself. He asked us if we had papers. He wasn't the rippling vibe of rebellion I used to know, the man who really influenced Henry Rollins and a host of bands around the globe. He had definitely lost bits and pieces of his mind. The next morning we came in and he was still sitting on that couch again, his head engulfed in a huge white cloud. He wouldn't leave, so we had to send him to the porch again. It was a well-shaded area, so I knew he was all right out there. It reminded me of the days I spent with Donnie Hathaway on the porch in St. Louis, watching movies, playing at the drive-in while Donnie mumbled to himself and smoked weed.

I did see H.R. again with P.O.D. at the KROQ Almost Acoustic Christmas Show in Irvine with my boy Fez. The last time I saw him we put together a band called Mr. Green with Norwood (Fishbone's Trulio Disgracias), Rocky George (Suicidal Tendencies/Fishbone), Hawaiian Lyon (Mr. Green), Travi, Philharmonic, Scientist, H.R., Grant, and few more. It was 2009, and a series of events went down, and I was strung like a Stradivarius and not at my best at the time. He however seemed to be doing much better.

15

Vegemite, Marmite, Starfruit & Jail

*I*n 1982, back at the DK ranch, after our American tour, we went into the studio at Target Video on South Van Ness and 18th Street and recorded the EP *In God We Trust, Inc.* It was unusually hot that week in San Francisco, and we were burning up in that little sheet rock room, drinking Budweiser. After recording the *In God We Trust, Inc.* EP, we went on to record *Plastic Surgery Disasters* then went on tour down under.

Our trip to Australia and New Zealand was memorable from the van to the flight. I always liked traveling with the road crew because I could drink and get high and felt like I didn't have to behave. On the plane I was hanging with Chris Grayson, our sound man and all around tech, and Microwave, our roadie. Chris lived across the street from, and worked at, the Mab. He was quite a fixture in San Francisco for a number of years along with his boy Patrick O'Pillage who later became our road crew guy as well.

Patrick—Trick Baby, as we liked to call him—was one of my roommates at Mission-A. He lived upstairs where all the ODs and carrying on would happen. Every other weekend there was paramedic pandemonium: sirens, stretchers, young EMTs with defibrillators, and the girls upstairs screaming, "Goddammit! I told you not to do that much! You should've let me go first!"

Once, Trick Baby OD'd. After the paramedic shot him up with Narcan, he came to, gasping for air looking at the EMT, eyes wide open.

"Welcome back to life, you were dead blue," the EMT said.

Trick Baby replied, "Fuck you."

Years later, Patrick moved in right next door to me and my girlfriend, Sherry, in Hollywood. We both got kicked out for not paying our rent and being junkies.

Chris was the Chili Peppers' soundman for a while until he ended up getting murdered over some drug deal. I don't know the details. I just know his body was found in a field with a bullet hole in it. *Fuck.* I loved that guy. We had such great times together. I still miss him dearly.

But back on the flight to New Zealand, I was sitting with Chris and Microwave. Ray, Klaus, and Biafra were sitting elsewhere. This was back in the days when you could smoke in the back of the plane, so that's where we were. The captain announced there would be complementary champagne and free drinks. So we started getting really ripped on the bottles of free champagne and beer. Chris was drinking rum and

Coke. I was drinking beer and champagne, and I got so tore up when they served dinner I started throwing food at total strangers on the plane. We were watching a movie so I thought it was funny to throw food at the movie screen. Later, when everybody was sleeping, I let out a scream like a wild, bellowing banshee, "Waaaaaaaaaaaaaaaaaaaa!"

People woke up like, *What the fuck? Is the plane going down? Oh my God, is someone dying?* I was out of fucking control.

About ten minutes later the captain came back and said to me, "You guys seem to be having a lot of fun, but we're getting some complaints that you guys are throwing food, screaming, and disrupting everyone."

So I said in my little boy voice, "I'm so sorry, captain."

He said, "Can you please try to hold it down?"

"Yes, sir."

"Thank you," he said and started to walk back to the cockpit. He got about six rows up, and I screamed in my drunk punk rocker voice, "So, you're the Captain, right?"

In his baritone Captain's voice, similar to a radio DJ, he said, "Yes, that's right."

I screamed, "THEN WHO THE FUCK'S FLYING THE PLANE?!?!?!"

He looked at the stewardess and struck his hand across his neck, saying that we were cut off. All three of us just started laughing at the top of our lungs, "Aaaaaaaa ha ha ha ha ha, daaaaaa ha ha ha!!!"

He was so pissed off, his face turned red as a cherry tomato as he walked back to the cockpit, still signaling for the stewardess to cut us off. After he'd gone, the stewardess asked us, "What band are you guys in?"

"Dead Kennedys," we said hoping to scare her off.

"I love DKs," she said. "The Captain told me specifically not to give ya'll drinks but here, don't tell."

We couldn't win for losing or lose for winning. So, we were smoking cigarettes, and Chris whipped out a huge chunk of hash and a bottle of Myers' Dark Jamaican Rum that he had to get rid of before we went through customs. We were so courageously crunked that we started smoking the shit right in our seats, bold as fuck. We all started acting like real assholes.

My personality completely changed when I drank. Not so much when I drank beer, but when I drank hard liquor it was night and day. I started yelling and hollering, making a scene like a damn fool. From then on Chris, Microwave, and I were dubbed the Trilogy of Terror.

We started off in Auckland, New Zealand, and then on to Wellington. It was not as eventful as Australia. It was beautiful nonetheless.

I roamed around Auckland on my own for a while and eventually stumbled into a biker bar (or, as they say, "bikey bar") filled with all kinds of Maoris, tattooed faces, leather clad cats chanting and getting drunk. I had on a motorcycle leather jacket and was blacker than any of them so I fit right in—except for my American accent.

It seemed sort of sad that there was all this beauty and culture, and these cats were drinking their life away. You could clearly see that they were there every night. They were so drunk you didn't know what these motherfuckers were going to do next. Most of them carried knives and would slit your throat over spilling their beer.

The bikey bar was a very sad, run down kind of cafeteria bar that you would only find on a sheep dominated island. The place had a few seats and tables and some standing bars. They served typical New Zealand bar food and Vegemite, cucumber, and tomato sandwiches with a Marmite option. Being in there felt like slow death in a concentration camp where old *bikies* went to die. I was so glad to get back to my hotel, where I hooked up with a dirty blonde I met at the Auckland gig.

Australia loved us. All of our shows were packed, the fans were great and the drinking was out of control. I drank (VB) Vick Bitter, and Castlemaine's XXXX, known as four fuckin' X. There was none of that Foster's crap—that was exported for Yanks. I sampled many different beers in many different townships and spent a lot of Australian dollars on cocaine.

Walking around Kings Cross one day, I met some Aussie birds. At that time, Aussie girls just loved, loved, loved a black man. I met Suzee, who was a real Olivia Newton John looker, and her four friends: Mandy, Mindy, Cheryl, and Josie. They took me all over Sydney, showing me the culture. We went to farmers' markets for fresh veggies and fruits, and Suzee turned me onto

D. H. PELIGRO

starfruit, which I had never heard of or seen before, then over to their friend's house for tea and hashish.

Suzee took me on many a cab ride all over town. We were at the Manzil Room almost every night sniffing up all my dough on coke. Fuck, I couldn't stop, and I couldn't get enough. One night at the Manzil Room we saw this rather large bald-headed guy with a leather motorcycle jacket and a beard. Suzie said, "Oh hey, there's Chris!"

"Who?" I asked.

"Chris Greaves, this Australian actor."

Chris was in Road Warrior, one of my favorite movies, so I was freaking out. I walked over, and Suzee introduced us. We hit it off so hard—we drank some ale, smoked some hash, and talked much shit. We went outside at about three in the morning so I could check out his motorcycle.

All drunk, I said: "Let me ride it."

He said, "Sure, mate."

I didn't think he'd let me ride it. I was pretty drunk, and I knew it, but I just didn't care. So I took off on his KZ1000, popped a wheelie, clipped a car driving on the wrong side of the road, came down off the wheelie, hit a parked car, and flew into the brush. Chris came running up to me. "Are ya okay, mate? By the way, we drive on the other side of the road here, mate...you're a fucking daredevil!"

Suzee took me back to my hotel in Kings Cross and rode me like a wild stallion. The thing about Suzee was that she was always ready to fuck—when I came back from the Manzel Room she was ready, in the morning she was ready, when I got out of the shower she was ready, when we came back from the farmers' market she was ready, when I went to get a pack of cigarettes and came back she was ready. She would fight off Mandy, Mindy, Cheryl, and Josie—she'd tell them to piss off. I tried to fuck them too, but she wasn't having it. She was a very possessive nymphomaniac. She rocked my world, Aussie-style.

But it wasn't always like that. In Melbourne I met a girl named Fiona. She was no frills, short cropped brown hair, but really nice. She was happy to take me sightseeing. Of course, I wanted to fuck her, but instead we hung out, had coffee, took the tram all over town. She showed me the sights, and we went shopping in Melbourne. Then we went to the Zoo. Afterward she walked me to my hotel, I kissed her goodbye, and I never saw her again.

Most of the younger guys in the punk rock scene were cool, but some yabo skinheads were fucking dicks—straight up racists. Queensland was the worst. The Queensland region was notorious in the 1980s as a really repressive, corrupt, and racist police state, run by Premier Joh Bjelke-Petersen. Beneath his repressive ignorance, the aboriginals had it especially bad there. They were beaten, raped, and killed by police all the time. Out of fear and stress many of them became alcoholics.

D. H. PELIGRO

I remember talking with Flea about it later, and he told me about one particularly bad experience he had there. He was in a cab, and the driver filled him in on Queensland race relations.

"Yeah, we keep our coons in line, over he'ah!" the cab driver said.

"What?" Flea couldn't believe he'd heard that.

"We keep our coons in line!" The driver said it again.

Flea immediately demanded the driver pull over and let him out.

Our opening band was a cow punk Australian band called The Johnnys who where actually really funny and friendly guys. We played for thousands of people at the show in Brisbane. Coming out of the venue I noticed that cop cars lined the street on either side. I began walking down the street, drinking a beer. "Hey, you, fuckin' Abo! Get over he'ah!" I heard a cop yell at me.

I thought, *Fuck you I ain't no Abo.* I just kept walking around the corner. The cop followed me shouting, "Hey you, come here!"

I walked faster around the block to the back stage door where the manager and East Bay Ray were hanging out. The fat cop came up on me, clanking his cuffs, hand on his gun. "YOU FUCKIN ABO! I know you hear me! You're being charged for disobeying a direct order!" Like I was in the army or some shit.

"Look, man, I ain't no Aboriginal. I'm American!" I said, as he was shoving me into the back of the police car. East Bay Ray began protesting while the manager showed the cop my passport and all these other papers. It escalated. They all started arguing back and forth. East Bay Ray was tussling in the street with the cops, and I saw them push him into the wall and handcuff him. I didn't have any handcuffs on so I kicked the back door open and jumped out. The door hit the cop in his fat ass and sent him flying onto the street. The cop was howling mad. "That's IT! You're going to jail!"

The cops took me to jail and threw me in a group cell. East Bay Ray was also taken to jail in another car. Brisbane was such a police state that they would regularly arrest groups of people. But this was good fortune for me, because I was thrown into a cell with all these punk rock girls who had just been to our show. "Thank you, God!" I told the cops. I was quickly surrounded by several adoring girls in hot leopard-print skintight pants, short schoolgirl skirts, fishnets, and bondage trousers. I was in heaven.

In the early morning, Bill Gilliam, the band's manager, and Klaus came to spring us. I said goodbye to all my new friends. As I was leaving the jail one of the cops who had arrested me stopped me.

"You in that band are, yeh?" he asked.

"Um, yeah, I am," I answered cautiously. Who knew what he was going to do?

"Well, go on over here, sign this, pay thirty dollars, and you can be on your way. And, oh yeah, give us an autograph, mate."

A number of us were released at the same time, and as we walked out a very sexy, petite girl with long blonde hair, leopard-print leggings, and a ripped t-shirt gave me her phone number. Right next to her number was her name, Aggie, think it was short for Agatha. The next day was my day off so I called her. She lived with her rich parents in a gigantic white-pillared house with a fountain in the front. We spent the day in her big soft feather bed destroying the pussy. She was like seventeen.

She said, "You were so drunk I didn't think you could go that long."

Right about then I went to the bathroom, and I had on some tight white pegged pants, no underwear, and I see blood. I'm like, "Damn, I think she cut my dick off!" I came back in the bedroom, and she had this shit-eating grin on her face, and she said, "You're my first."

And it hit me. I've just devirginized her. I got real nervous, and I said, " I gotta go to sound check."

"On your day off?" she asked.

I was in a panic. "I-I-uh...yeah yeah I gotta go." I went outside and realized I had no clue where I was. Since I didn't want to get arrested *again*, I asked if she could take me to the hotel. She said, "I'm a little sore but I think we can make it." So we jumped in the Holden and pushed on.

16

Chips, Special Brew, and Neo-You Know Who

*I*n England I truly felt like a rock star. We toured London, Leeds, Manchester, Liverpool, Leicester, Birmingham, Brixton, Wales, and Bath. In London, we stayed at the Virgin Townhouse, a combination recording studio and lodging at 140 Goldhawk Road. PiL was recording there at the time, and our record label, Faulty Products, had put us up there. Every morning they served a typical English breakfast: eggs, steamed tomatoes, and beans on toast.

I asked Penny, who was working at the Townhouse, what the strongest beer in England was. She replied, "Carlsberg Special Brew."

So I went to the off-license and bought a sixer. When I got back, Penny said "You're not gonna drink all that, are you?"

"It's only six beers," I said. I drank beer all the time, so it was normal to me. After about four and a half beers, I smoked some hash and looked up at Chris, our sound man, and saying, "I'm OK...I'm OK." I don't remember anything else.

Then Chris and Microwave picked me up and carried me around the corner and up the stairs to my room to put me to bed. Chris and Microwave had just cut off all their hair, and Chris wore an army coat with the Fear logo on the back with two F's—one facing up, and one facing down—which was very reminiscent of the National Front uniform. In his army coat with his dirty blonde buzz-cut, he could easily be misconstrued as one of the National Front boot boys. Micro also rocked a green U.S. Army field jacket. Penny even told me the next day that she thought I was being accosted by the National Front, two skinheads taking a young rasta around the corner. It must have looked strange. I think I did something else in a blackout, because I woke up in a pool of piss with management telling us, "You have to leave the Townhouse, now!!!" Just another day in the D. H. Peligro life.

England was a curious cacophony of new experiences: drinking international ales such as Newcastle, Carlsberg (*this time not the special brew*), Bateman's XXXB, and Woodpecker Cider; new English customs like smoking weed with tobacco and hashish; hanging out with our opening band, Peter and the Test Tube Babies; eating lots of greasy *chips* and other bad food; learning British slang; and sleeping with easy Brit chicks.

I was staying at Bill Gilliam's house in Parson's Green with his two daughters, Beth and Laura, and his wife, Mel. One morning I got some chick in the sack after a night of drinking at some British pub. We were sleeping in their living room and little Beth came in—she was about four or five—and she screamed and ran out when she saw us naked.

She went into the kitchen and told her mom, "Darren's got a girl in there and they're not even married!"

Bill and I would have these conversations about rastas, and he'd say: "People always say rastas are so spiritual 'everyteeng *Jah.*' No they're not. They're some of the most violent people on the planet. Take the Brixton Riots for example—bombing, burning, and looting. And whenever they have elections in Jamaica people get killed," he said.

Jerry said, "You'd be fighting for your rights too if you were constantly under the 'sus.'" The "'sus" was the British police force's right to stop and search citizens, mostly young black Dreads, Rastas, and Jamaicans, based solely on suspicion of wrongdoing. Similar to racial profiling in the U.S., like D.W.B (driving while black), and getting pulled over in rich neighborhoods because of the wrong skin color.

This was another moment of political awareness for me. At that time, Britain only had about four television channels: BBC 1, 2, 3, and 4. There was BBC radio 1 and 2. I always loved the John Peel show. To me, Europe was a lot more politically savvy than the U.S. People didn't have as many distractions as we did, so they talked about the issues at bars and pubs. Through these talks in the pubs I saw how people could disagree about politics without killing each other, though there were fist fights sometimes, mostly that was due to arguments over football.

Meanwhile, "Too Drunk to Fuck" climbed the pop charts on the BBC. They were nervous because if we had gotten to number one they would've had to put us on *Top of the Pops*, an unsecured television show, and they had so many problems with the Sex Pistols they were leery of punk bands.

I hung out with our tour manager and driver, Chris, and his wife, Carney, who wined and dined us. By that time my girlfriend, Suzie, had come over from Berkeley, and our British coke dealing friends in the States told her to call Sebastian. Seb was a queer art and fashion designer who invited us to some important person's birthday party. The roadies/loadies, Chris and Microwave, turned up their noses at anything called New Romantic or New Wave, but I was more adventurous and went to all kinds of parties in London.

Seb took us to this lavish loft with white silk, cushioned sofas, plush white rugs, fireplaces, and crystal glasses of champagne. The place was filled with beautiful women, actors, and musicians, all drinking, smoking, and snorting away. Early on at the party Suzie, my little fashion punk rock blonde, hugged up on me and took me into the bathroom. Sitting on the toilet she tapped out a line of coke along her thigh and handed me a rolled up five pound note. I snorted it up. Then she gave me the best blowjob I have ever had. But the highlight for me was the illustrious entrance of one legendary cool brother, Mr. Isaac Hayes.

Arriving late, he pushed open the door with his pointed black alligator shoes with gold buckles. He had a long, black leather coat lined with tan fleece, his signature huge sunglasses, and his bald head rubbed to a chrome quality shine. I started to introduce myself, but I had to wait as he had stopped and was clearing his throat as if to make an announcement. Since it was a dinner party he had brought the dessert, he told us, and held out two gorgeous banana cream pies, one in each of his huge, well-manicured hands. "Fresh banana cream pie, made with Devonshire cream in a delicious graham cracker crust," he boomed. I was so impressed. But all I could really think about was, *Who's the black private dick who's a sex-machine to all the chicks? SHAFT.... ya damn right...can you dig it?*

I regret to this day that I was too coked up to try the pie made by Mr. Hayes himself.

17

1984: *Rock Against Reagan*

*B*ack in San Francisco, Dead Kennedys rehearsed about three or four days a week for about three hours at a time, developing new material and then going on tour or playing small gigs. Musically, we worked out arrangements in rehearsals. In other bands the drummers typically twiddle their thumbs while waiting for the guitarist and the bass player to work it out. Not me. I was involved and throwing out suggestions left and right. Most drum parts came naturally to me and since I could play guitar and sing I did my part and then some. If I had a song that I thought would fit in, I would bring it in with all of its parts: guitar parts, bass parts, lyrics, melodies, and of course drums. It was very nerve-wracking since Biafra was so brilliant with lyrics, but then again so was I. He'd hum stuff and we'd have to figure out how to make it music, then transpose it up and down to fit the range of Biafra's voice. Biafra would come in with ideas, but he would have to process them through us. His timing was pretty off, from my point of view, and by the way he explained things it seemed as though they wouldn't work. First I'd try to understand what the hell he was talking about, and then I'd have to fit it into a workable time signature. Then we would start the transposing process again.

This was an intense period politically, and Biafra created quite a controversy. Reagan, a very shaky president, entered the War on Drugs while the government was giving money to the Contras in South America which in turn helped flood the USA with cheaper cocaine, creating the crack epidemic. This fueled the fire for Blood and Crip gang wars in the inner city. Reagan also closed many mental institutions, which filled the streets of San Francisco with untreated mental patients. Everywhere we played there was a huge police presence. I was sure the CIA kept tabs on us. I was getting stopped and searched and pulled over way too much for it to be any kind of a coincidence. I think the cops set me up on a weed bust in Hunters Point while I was doing a favor for a my friend, Wild Bill, an ex-Vietnam vet. Because of that I got a felony rap which I still pay for today. My record's been expunged so I can vote and serve jury duty, but I can't legally own a gun.

Dead Kennedys played Rock Against Reagan, a huge free outdoor show. There were police on all the roofs completely surrounding us. I didn't know what the fuss was about but there were a lot of people there. There was so much security that Biafra started shouting, "Look above you, see them all on the roof? That's the police state!" It was moments like this I saw what I was really involved with. It wasn't all drugs and parties, leather jackets with studs and bristles, mohawks, safety pins, B.O., and peg pants—it was Marshall Law seeping in and I would hammer the message via drumming, as if I was sending some secret African tribal message to everyone tuned into the vibe. I felt like I was high on fire. I would break my sticks during every song so I kept extra sticks in the lug nut on the kick drum. Some kids thought it was cute to jump onstage, skank around, and try to steal my spare sticks. I was playing fast, but it was nothing for me to reach out, grab the sticks out of their hands, and not miss a beat.

After *Plastic Surgery Disasters*, the punk rock scene in San Francisco started to heat up. It revolved around a few venues: Mabuhay Gardens, On Broadway, Valencia Tool & Die, The Farm, 10th St. Hall, Ruthie's in Oakland/ Berkley Square, The Elite Club (now The Fillmore), The Stone, Keystone, and The Vats. Temple Beautiful (which was later named The Temple) was closed by then—incidentally, this is where Jim Jones brainwashed people, and where they gathered before going to Guyana and drinking poisoned Kool-Aid. Punk bands recorded wherever they could to stretch a dollar. Of course, we recorded *In God We Trust, Inc.* at Target Video, *Plastic Surgery Disasters* with Tom Wilson at Mobius Music, *Frankenchrist* and *Bedtime for Democracy* were filmed at Hyde Street Studios in San Francisco. In Studio D, we recorded *Frankenchrist* with John Cuniberti. We also recorded *Bedtime for Democracy* with him in Studio C, and I think Gary Creiman helped out at some point. Gary also did the late night sessions with the Sluglords that I recorded with Bruno de Smartass (a.k.a. Steve DeMartis). The tracks I played on were "Yakety Trumpet" and "Free Food." I also did guest vocals on "Work For It"; if you listen closely, my voice is the first one you hear saying, "Uh...we're being taken for a ride."

Back in the early '80s, The Vats was part of the old Hamm's Brewery off of South Van Ness and 16th. It had been abandoned for a while and became a squat for punk rockers and general misfits. Someone jack hammered through the concrete wall and somehow got the electricity running. Bands came in and put carpet down in a few of the rooms to make rehearsal studios. Everybody used to go there, and I would hang out with all kinds of bands coming and going. It was an insane place. You would walk in total darkness, squishing through puddles of old beer left over from the brewery. I can still smell that smell today when I walk by an old dumpster. There were entire floors you couldn't go to—empty, scary, little cave-like rooms and then these huge vats twenty feet deep into the floor.

This is when I started getting to know Mark Byron. He was a real mechanical whiz at the time and had access to generators, which we needed at The Vats. So Mark brought in this 5,000 watt generator, and bands started playing outdoor daytime Sunday shows. Mark would pull up on his Harley with a skateboard bungee corded to his sissy bar and work the generator. Everybody got along for the most part. Mostly people were drunk or tweaking, but the cops left us alone, and for the most part the bands would play all day.

San Francisco is so small we just fit together in a dysfunctional kind of way. The crew from Texas and MDC were good friends with us for a long time. Al from MDC actually made the first DK logo that I had on my kick drum.

Later we became friends with The Dicks. Their lead singer Gary Floyd was a trippy queen. They played The Vats along with bands like Dirty Rotten Imbeciles (DRI), and we did the Rock Against Reagan tour in Texas with MDC and The Dicks in the relentless, sweltering heat and humidity of the Southern summer. After touring the South, we befriended east coast bands like Mission of Burma from Boston, Kraut from NYC, Bad Brains, False Prophets, Minor Threat, and Government Issue from D.C., and our Canadian friends D.O.A., Pointed Sticks, and SNFU. There were So Cal troublemakers like TSOL, The Vandals, and Circle Jerks who we also played with from time to time.

The homegrown San Francisco bands were the Sluglords, Frightwig, Hellations, and Flipper—one of the rattiest sloth-dirge punk bands ever. Flipper's drummer, Steve de Pace, was also in the legendary punk band Negative Trend with our friend Will Shatter. Steve and I later became roommates at Mission-A, as well as serious friends and partners in crime. Steve would go on to play with me in the Jungle Studs.

Also there was Bad Posture with Eddie and Emilio, some of the first Mexican punk rockers from Brownsville, Texas. They were always broke, bumming beer and weed, and we had to buy them strings, but they were great players, and they came as a pair. Bruno had a joke back then. They'd walk into the studio and we'd say, "What are Eddie and Emilio in a box?" Everyone knew. "A pair of brown loafers!"

Jeff 4Way was the singer for Bad Posture and wore about a seven foot tall Mohawk. No, my bad, he was about seven foot tall and wore a Mohawk. He got his name 4Way working security for Bow Wow Wow at the Kabuki Theater when someone gave him a four way hit of acid. The thing is, it's a four way hit. You're only supposed to take one, but no, he took the whole thing and lost his mind for a few days, hence the name 4Way. Bad Posture's hits included "Goddamn Motherfuckin' Son of A Bitch," "Signal 30" (which was also done by The Sluglords), and my all time favorite, "Time for Smack!" John Sidel was their drummer, and Emilio was the bass player; Eddie and Bruno played guitar.

Woody played bass in Sluglords, and most of them lived on and off at the House of Morons on South Van Ness between 15th and 16th streets. I spent most of my time there, and Woody would later be in the Jungle Studs with me. Tony and Fred Dickerson, Steve de Pace, and Bruno de Smartass were all in the Jungle Studs at one time or another.

I started my own band called the Hellations. I was the songwriter, vocalist, and guitar player. I had this girl, Megan, on bass, and this crazy girl named Jane on drums. Jane didn't do any drugs; she was just genuinely crazy and a real artist. She painted a gigantic mural on the outside of the house with various collages of the Beatles. Her room was filled with dolls and stacks and stacks of comic books. She would make these brilliant flyers, combining collages out of comic books and her own artwork.

Later on Tony C. and I organized the Jungle Studs with Steve de Pace on drums. We were just biting off of everything in our music. We tried to be a cross between the Time, Prince, and Van Halen but ended up sounding like Flipper meets Peter Gabriel. It was weird but it was fun and kind of funky. Fred Dickerson was with us for a while. He brought in a '70s rock influence; I had the punk aggressive vibe, Steve de Pace had this laid back, depressed Flipper beat. I tried to push up the energy, get Steve up to speed, but he just didn't play like that. I knew it was just a fun project. I doubted that it would ever be put out, but Alternative Tentacles actually did release the album in 1986.

Between 1983 and 1985 I lived at this scandalous little pad, 119 Central Avenue, right across from the Jimi Hendrix Electric Church Foundation between Haight and Page Streets. That's when I started using drugs full time. I lived there with this Danish girl, Karin, and a handful of other roommates. She had been there the longest, so it was like her place, and she was a big time speed freak. She had been an au pair, but I think she was way too shaky and high on speed to work with little kids. She married this gay guy, Steve, to get her green card. He came around and checked in on her from time to time, usually after she'd been on a speed binge, and sometimes would crash for days after. He just wanted to make sure that she was alive. People in San Francisco were cool like that. She started earning a living making studded leather bands, belts, and other punk rock gear. Up all night in the living room, eyes lit up like pie plates, sewing and hammering away. There were two other bedrooms. Mine was at the top of the stairs on the left. Junkie Julie from San Diego lived in the room up front with the bay windows. I wanted that room because my room only had one window that faced the alley. When I had sex with wayward Europeans, the sound reverberated through the alley. The next morning everyone would look at me like, "I know what you were doing last night..." But mostly, I just wanted the bay windows. They looked cool, and I could see what was happening on the street. So when Julie left I took over her room.

Mark Byron, who would later become a very close friend of mine, had the room next to me. After Sherry left, lesbian Robin moved in. At least, I think she was a lesbian. Mark fucked her sometimes, though. That's how it was; everybody was fucking everybody in San Francisco back in the day, it was a real frenzy. I was doing my share, but the girl I was seeing the most was

D. H. PELIGRO

this Swedish girl, Kirsten, although her Swedish friends called her Schosten. She was one of three Swedes, Monika and Petra were the other two, who lived up the street. They were also total speed freaks.

The three of them had come over as au pairs. Kirsten worked for some rich cat in the Berkeley Hills, taking care of his kids. He was never around—apparently he had gotten busted for importation of hashish, so he was back and forth from court and in and out of the Federal pen. So Kirsten had this huge place to herself, which was great because the house had a great pool and Jacuzzi where we hung out. She wasn't the only girl, but my favorite, and she would get a little bit jealous. But that was the free love vibe of the Bay area and the way things were.

I also hung out with the comedian Jane Dornacker for a little while. She lived right up at the top of Central Avenue as well. She was really into Prince. I loved her because she would always make me laugh. We'd be right in the middle of having sex, and she would just start talking about him. Her head would pop up. "What's all this about the castles and Corvettes?" She'd start singing, and the jokes would flow. She was also in a band called Leila and the Snakes who went on to tour with The Tubes. Then she had a morning talk show in NYC; she broadcast from a helicopter flying over the Hudson, telling jokes. She died in a helicopter crash in the Hudson River in 1986. I heard it on the news one morning. I just couldn't believe it; my six-foot lover was gone. I was floored and flabbergasted. It was like we were just fucking, joking around, and talking about Prince the other night, and then she was dead.

Well, while living on Central I hung out with Kirsten at the Swedish girls' house, who lived up the street from me, and a few doors down from Jane. Sometimes I would be on coke, but at this point I mostly just drank. I did more coke once Bart Pennington, the most scandalous motherfucker on the planet, got me into it. That fucker, he taught me how to shoot cocaine, which, in certain ways, fucked up my whole life. Bart's sole aim in life was to get high and stay high. He was thoroughly committed to drugs and especially dedicated to cocaine. Later I learned that as a child he had been severely abused and witnessed his mother killing his father. He was a very handsome dread, charming as a snake in the grass. He could con a thousand dollars off a girl in two minutes, and he did, regularly. He'd get the money and he'd tell them bitches he'd be back in a few minutes, and they believed that shit. All the European girls loved his lying, cheating, stealing black ass. Last I heard he had stolen from the wrong people, been stabbed and shot, and was in San Quentin, but was still alive. That cat definitely had more than nine lives. That's the thing about San Francisco, it's so small you can only get away with stealing and robbing, lying and cheating for so long. It catches up to you eventually.

Once I remember Bart coming into our house with a bunch of grams of cocaine. We started shooting it, but

D. H. Peligro

this batch had a weird, tangy taste to it. Coke usually does get in your gums and your nose like a blast of airplane diesel, but that batch gave me this screaming, buzzing, nastiness. It hit my blood and walls of sound began caving in on me. Who knows what I put in my veins? Rat poison for all I know. It didn't occur to me that I could die because back then that shit never entered my mind.

A roar started between my ears. Every millisecond it grew until it crescendoed into an *eeerrrrrriiiiiiiiaaassscccrrrraaaaa*...like the sound of a phase shifter, or like a fleet of scout ships from *Star Wars* screaming out of the Death Star in my head. I felt insane. This was the edge and I knew it. I kind of liked it, but I couldn't control it. This is where drugs can become wicked evil, and this is where you can cross the line where there is no coming back. That loud noise hovered in my head for what seemed like hours. In reality it was probably forty-five seconds, but when you're about to die shit starts to flash before you and time slows down.

The next day Bart was laughing. "Hah, hah, hah! I gave you the shit last night that sent you away." He had this voice that was airy and oily at the same time. Smooth and deceptively gentle. I remember thinking, "You're fucking laughing about that, man? I almost died."

Bart turned me on to crack, too, which was just hitting the streets at that time. We used to get what was called Ready Rock and smoke hubbas, rock with a straight shooter. Hubbas were everywhere. You would get a whiff of hubba while walking down the streets in the Fillmore. I started using more and more coke, Bart or no Bart, finding my own dealers. Thanksgiving of 1986 I remember some dude hustling, selling me a bag. "Hey, man, this is real turkey shit, real holiday cheer, muthafucka. This got that gasoline dope ain't nobody else got out here, muthafucka. This shit will get you fly," he said. I got really blasted that night, too. I had crossed over the invisible line. I could no longer call it casual using. Now it was not enough to just get a little high. I had to go into oblivion, the danger zone, right to the edge. I had no clue what I was, or where I was going. All I knew was that I had the responsibility every couple of months to go on tour with Dead Kennedys.

Since San Francisco was such a small town, if someone saw me high, one little word spread around the city like wildfire. There were really no secrets but a lot of rumors. I was at Capp Street for an Art event, and my neighbor, Nadur, had me up all night smoking crack with him. I didn't think not to go, but we were so high, licking our lips, grinding and noshing our teeth. All the San Francisco heads were there, even Dirk Dirksen who ran the Mabuhay Gardens. He walked over to me and said, "How are you?"

I couldn't get a word to come out of my mouth.

He looked at me, shook his head, and walked away. I knew Dirk had seen it all before. He was a big time producer in Los Angeles. While he was working on *I Love Lucy*, he came up with this stunt of dropping thousands of ping-pong balls on Lucy during a scene. But somehow

D. H. PELIGRO

golf balls were used instead of ping-pong balls; when they were set loose they destroyed the set and binged some of the actors and producers on the head. Lucy was pissed. After that, he was banished from Hollywood and moved to San Francisco where he became the legendary force behind the Mabuhay Gardens. He booked, hosted, filmed, and generally supported more New Wave, Punk, and Alternative acts than anyone else in the city. He was always willing to give you a chance.

On the other hand, Sebastian from The Dicks, who was a notorious speed freak, looked me dead in the eye and shook his head and walked away. If I could have gotten the words out of my mouth I would have said, "Fuck you, Sebastian." I'd seen him tweaking many, many times before and never said a word. So maybe they didn't like the fact that I was coked out of my mind, I don't know.

What I do love about San Francisco is that people would say hi to you all the time, anywhere. When I got to Los Angeles it was so different. People were much colder. I'd say hi to people and they'd basically say, "Go away, I don't have any money, ya filthy bugger!" Los Angeles was a very different place.

After I started shooting up coke on Central Avenue, it started to affect my career. Before that I was able to hide my drug use from the band, but it started getting harder to do. DKs had a tour starting in Oregon, and the night before I was supposed to fly out I stayed up all night shooting coke with Bart. By daybreak I had massive tracks up and down my arm, so I wrapped an ace bandage around it to try and hide them. I got to the airport late, missed the flight, and had to catch the next one out. I got into Oregon late for sound check, and I was a mess.

"What happened?" The band asked me, looking at my bandaged arm.

"Oh, I sprained my elbow." I told them some old bunch of bullshit and then killed at the gig as if nothing had ever happened.

Around that time, my roommate Karin got pretty deep into the crystal and started snorting up the rent money. Next thing we knew we were thousands of dollars behind in the rent. We tried to pull our way out of the eviction, we went through and appealed it, but we lost; so we all had to look for new places to live. Mark Byron bought a school bus with his brother and fixed it up as a living space. I loved to visit him there. I moved back to 2448-A Mission Street between 20th and 21st, the notorious Mission-A. There were storefronts on either side, and the entrance was a small door with a steep, narrow stairway that went straight up. I rented a room on the first floor in the back and another storage room off of the kitchen. I was lucky to be on this floor away from the other rooms on the floor above which is where the real madness went down. Not that my floor wasn't a glorious speed den with people running in and out all hours of the night, buying speed from the notorious Mr. Bo, who was the house mouse.

Mission-A was very transient. People came and went, and every punk drug addict musician in the city came through there at some time or another. Rachel (Mud Women/Flipper) and Dead Kennedys' ex-manager Che Che lived upstairs. Lisa lived in the back, and our crazy, junky stagehand Patrick O'Pillage lived upstairs.

In the room down the hall and at the top of the stairs was another brother, named Sweet, who ran the house. He was a major speed dealer; everyone on the scene went to him. Before that he'd been a Muni bus driver. I think he was tweaking one day and ran over some kid's leg in the crosswalk, so he lost his job and became The City's speed dealer. He and his sister Jennie had moved to San Francisco from Detroit. She had a little boy, Leon, and they were always around Mission-A. Sweet had a room full of stuff that he had traded and bartered for speed: a crazy collection of classic guitars, leather jackets, musical equipment, silver tea sets, old Ham radios, CBs, three-handled family gredunzas, and stacks of records. People would trade their entire record collections for drugs. There were random piles of gear everywhere: guitars, amps, basses, guns, microphones, tape machines, boots, skateboards, all types of shit.

Around that time, my old Yamaha motorcycle broke down and I saw a stolen, partly stripped-down newer bike abandoned near Folsom Street. Mark Warner from Mark Pauline's Survival Research Laboratories got some new forks and tires and built it up. We changed the numbers to match my old Yamaha and made a new rat bike. He had these mad mechanical magician friends who gathered together a group of crazy mechanic guys and built huge, gas guzzling, fire exploding machines. Mine was a Yamaha XS 650, painted primer black. It was the loudest rat machine you've ever seen or heard. They would put on exhibitions of their creations, which were uniquely SF events. These massive robotic machines, blowing smoke and fire. Pauline actually lost most of his hand building a bomb.

18

Lady Heroin, 1985

*N*adur, my partner in crime, and I started smoking freebase together, but we didn't know how to cook it up. Nadur's roommate, Mark, didn't smoke it, he always preferred his weed to anything else, but he had learned how to cook it up in the service from a bunch of football players while stationed in Hawaii. So Nadur and I would get some coke and call up Mark, "Come on, Rockmeister, cook it up!" I'd say. Mark would get a little mad, he always thought we called him just for his services. But we'd laugh and have a good time, Mark smoking his weed and drinking his beers, Nadur and I getting based out of our skulls.

Vito (Steve de Pace) and I had a serious *Miami Vice* delusion going on. We'd dress up in white or pastel suits, sniff a bunch of cocaine, drink a bunch of cocktails, and hit the streets like we were on an undercover mission. But we'd usually end up at some divey punk club, way overdressed and too coked out to stay for too long. For a while it was fun, but it soon changed. I began using coke more and more, though I was still drinking more than anything else back then and was not into heroin yet. I would use and drink more than anybody and still have boundless energy.

One day Mark, Vito, and I were hanging out. When we came home to Mission-A we noticed a package at the door. It was addressed to Margaret Masserman. "That's some girl who used to live here four years ago. She's long gone. Wanna open it?" Vito asked.

We took it into Vito's bedroom. When we opened it four plastic bags of white powder fell out. We opened one and smelled it but didn't recognize what it was right away.

"Damn, what is this?" Steve asked.

"It might be coke, it might be heroin." I said, "Let me go get a syringe and see what it is." Since I was now a shooter that's how I was thinking at the time.

Steve looked at me, "Are you crazy?!"

"No, man, take it easy, just sniff a little bit."

I mean, with heroin I could have easily shot up too large an amount and died. "Okay, I'm your Huckleberry," I said, then sniffed some.

"What the hell." Mark sniffed some.

The minute I snorted I began a good nod. "Wow, man, this is heroin." I grabbed Mark's hand before he could sniff another line. "Stop! Stop!" I didn't want him to die right then. "You've never done this before, don't do it! It's heroin!"

We had just received four ounces of pure China White. The three of us were partners in the discovery, so we gave it to Mark to hide in his school bus. I was

D. H. Peligro

paranoid. With that quantity there was a heavy penalty involved with the police or the people who were expecting it. So we had to lay low. Later we found out that the old managers of Dead Kennedys, Chris and Ken Lester, had sent it there.

Mark stashed it really well, but Vito and I took some to trade. We traded a bunch for a couple grams of blow and three hundred bucks. We were trying to peddle it out on Mission Street through some other connections. We tried to sell it, but everyone we knew was more into coke and speed than dope. Since Mark didn't like to use it, Vito and I divvied up our own private stashes, then we found a buyer for the bulk of it. We pretty much gave it away. It was so pure and we weren't really drug dealers. Just the potential repercussions of having an amount like that made me nervous. Although we sold most of it, that was the beginning of my relationship with heroin. I still just loved to drink, get all hyped out on the booze and coke, but later on it would get much much deeper. We gave Mark $600 bucks. Vito and I got about $2000 apiece from the heroin sales. With my few thousand I bought a brand new red Yamaha.

Before I bought the red Yamaha, I had the black Yamaha rat bike, and I went to an art opening on Sixth and Harrison. There was a lot of construction going on around there, and they had torn up the blacktop. Manhole covers were sticking out of the street. I had my eye on this beautiful Iranian girl, Gina. She worked at the I-Beam or Das Klub, one of those places. I knew her brother, Muhammad, and I'd seen her before. Plus I was drunk and comfortable.

So I swaggered on up to her. "Hey baby, want to come home with me?" I breathed on her. I had been drinking lots of wine.

"Yeah, let's take a cab," she said. She was a lot more together than most of us.

"No, you need to get on my fuckin' bike, come on girl, ain't no problem."

"I ain't getting on that bike with your drunk ass," she said.

I told her to meet me at my pad. Then I tore off, but since they had ripped up the pavement there were these spiny stalactites sticking out of the street. I punctured my tire on a stalactite, hit the manhole cover, broke my front mag-wheel. Bam! I didn't have a helmet on so the fall ripped the skin right off the side of my face, down my right arm, wrist, and hand. I hit my knee on the stalactites and ripped it down to the bone. I was in shock. I couldn't feel the pain in my body yet. From pure adrenaline and alcohol I hoisted myself up, picked up my bike, and tried to kick it over.

Gina was right behind me in the cab. She said, "Oh my God, are you okay?!"

I knew I was hurt but I said, "I'm cool. I'm just gonna take my bike and meet you at the crib."

Gina said, "Oh, no. You got to go to the hospital."

I said, "Naw, naw, I'm alright." I tried to start my bike again. The handlebars were bent sideways, and it

D. H. PELIGRO

wouldn't move. I threw it on the curb and looked at my finger—it was bent backwards. I looked at my knee. My jeans were ripped open, and the skin around my kneecap was torn away; it was exposed and gushing blood. I put my hand on my face; it was covered in blood. "Oh shit," I said, and fainted. Gina and the cab driver scraped me up off the street and took me to the hospital. I was in there for a month.

So many people came to visit. Bart Pennington came to visit me, brought me some beers and snuck some weed in. My coke dealer Ruben came and brought me some coke and one of his girlfriends. "You can have her," he said. Boy, she was a psycho. I fucked her in the hospital only once, then she started calling me up and raging in a loud maniacal whisper, "I know you are sleeping with other girls, I can see you! I have eyes everywhere. I know you're shooting coke. You're gonna die, Fucker!"

Jennifer, this Swedish model I was dating at the time, was my real girlfriend. I met Jennifer at some party of Ira's through Woody, the Jungle Studs bass player. Ira was this man about town who owned and ran a number of nightclubs. At that time he ran Das Klub, later the Oasis and Please Don't Sit on the Furniture. Jennifer was very clean cut and super pretty. I didn't think she would go for a guy like me. I always had a certain amount of charm to turn on and off as needed, and soon enough she had come over to the dark side. She always had that kind of look on her face, as if she was getting ready for her next photo shoot. At the gigs she would sit there, all stiff, looking totally out of place in her perfect little outfits. She was a little bit snobby and thought all the little rough neck punk rockers were beneath her. She tolerated them because she liked me, but she refused to come in when we were playing at The Vats and would wait in my Econoline. The Vats was dark, dirty, and incredibly dangerous. There were huge gaping concrete pits, each at least ten feet deep, with no rails or anything, and hundreds of raging drunk and tweaking punks thrashing around. The lights were not always reliable; we could be cast into darkness at any point.

The real punk rock girls were a special breed: tough, loud, and could drink and shoot drugs with the best of them. Most had tattoos all over and wore steel toe Doc Martin boots. One little gang called themselves the French Fries; they named themselves that because the dominant girl was from France. They hung out with Bob Noxious from the punk band The Fuck-Ups.

Anyway, these teenage girls, the French Fries, would come to Mission-A all the time to cop speed from Sweet. A couple of them started working the streets when they got older. I know one eventually died of AIDS. This was definitely not Jennifer's scene. She was more comfortable in the Euro-trash, coke-snorting club scene with the other fashionistas, though she didn't do any drugs or drink. She was so hot and so sweet with me. "I worry so much, when you drink and do the drugs, I hate the way it makes your beautiful eyes so cloudy," she would say in that sweet voice. "And I don't like that

D. H. Peligro

you're seeing those other girls." She asked me to marry her. I was twenty-four and certainly not about to get married.

Herb Caen actually once wrote an article about Jennifer and me for the *San Francisco Chronicle*. Jennifer had a new fashion spread each week in the *Chronicle*, so Herb's article was about the yin and yang of fashion and punk rock. He thought Jennifer and I were an unusual couple, that our connection was unlikely. But in San Francisco everything was likely.

When I got out of the hospital, I was on crutches, and I had to limp up the steep-ass stairs at Central Avenue. I couldn't walk for a while, and I was covered in lacerations that needed some time to heal. So I lay there in bed, getting people to bring me beer. One of the girls who worked at Rough Trade came and brought me coke. She was this long-legged girl from Vermont with braces and a skateboard. Later she would become Bart's girlfriend, and she was mine for a short time. She lived with Teri, one of the girls from Rough Trade Records. Their house was the spot to use for a while. Bart lived down the street in an apartment on Steiner with this young, light-skinned girl, Va-Jay-Jay. She got the name, and her apartment, from this drag queen who had kind of adopted her.

We got drunk and high and had sex a couple of times, but she had a crush on Bart. Both Bart and I were up to move in, but she only let Bart. She was a total heroin addict and loved to shoot up with me and

Bart. She gave us a little heroin for a little coke, and we had some scary parties there. She was seventeen and got really whiney and always begged for more drugs. I ran into her years later in L.A. She had been clean for quite some time, and we actually got to be good friends.

19

Pruno N' San Bruno

ed Hot Chili Peppers always called me when they came into town, and we'd hang out. I first met them in 1984 when they were playing at the I-Beam, and I had gone backstage. I don't usually do that, but I really wanted to meet these guys. I had on this suit, and I boldly marched backstage. Flea was pounding on his bass. I extended my hand and said, "Hey, man, I'm D. H. Peligro from Dead Kennedys."

Then Flea said, "Hey, man, I always wanted to meet you!" He was really friendly and had a very cool vibe. Jack Sherman was playing guitar with them at the time. Hillel was playing with another band. Cliff Martinez was the drummer, and Anthony Kiedis sang. Flea and I had an instant rapport, and we soon started building a friendship.

The next time they came to San Francisco they had Hillel back with them. I was at Mission-A, and they would all come over to my house to do drugs, hang out, and party, listen to and talk about music. Cliff wasn't really a drug taker. Flea would do a little bit and go, "Whoa! That's enough." But Anthony and I would go crazy. It was as if he was the spark and I was the flame. He could use as much as I could and was actually much crazier.

Once I took him with me to my friend Gyorge's crib to get some coke. Gyorge was this Hungarian artist cat who lived right down the street from Central Avenue at Oak Street. He had really shitty coke, actually, but he was close by. He was really paranoid and absolutely forbade anyone to shoot up in his house. But I made the mistake of giving Anthony his bindle before we left. I turned my back for a minute and Anthony disappeared.

"Don't bring that guy back here anymore!" Gyorge yelled.

"Why?" I asked.

"Did he shoot up in my bathroom?" Gyorge asked.

"No, man, why?" I said again. I didn't think he had time to do that.

"Yes, he did. I saw him!" Apparently Gyorge had spied on Anthony shooting up through a window on the side of the bathroom. Anthony denied it, but all his coke was gone. And he was tweaked, so I'm sure he did. Gyorge had some shitty coke anyway. He must have stepped on it with some quinine/baby laxative, because it made me shit all the time, and when you shot it, it left a pile of residue on the spoon.

When the Chili Peppers came to hang out in San Francisco I always liked talking shit with Flea. I really admired his musical ability. He was no ordinary punk rocker. We really pissed Mark off. He was living off and on in the school bus and Mission-A. He had to get up and go to work, and we'd be there passed out all over the house. He started screaming from the bathroom in the morning. Flea had puked up all over it. "You son of a bitches! Who's puking all over the bathroom!" He was already upset from all the crazy drug use going on at Mission-A. I calmed him down. Flea was so cool. He went in there and cleaned that bathroom until it was sparkling.

It was getting really crazy around Mission-A. People were overdosing constantly. In a one-week period the paramedics came three times. Most of what was happening was upstairs. At least we were on the first floor, but Mark was really sickened by all of it. After a dozen or so episodes of crazy shit he had to move out.

One night we were sitting around and heard this thump from upstairs. One of the guys on the second floor overdosed, and the paramedics came in, busting the door down. Mark went up to see what was going on and saw this guy, Tracy, laid out on kitchen floor. His lips were purple, blood everywhere. Tracy was a fixture at the Mabuhay and another DK roadie. The paramedics gave him an injection of adrenaline, and he jerked up suddenly after being on the edge of death. Mark came back downstairs really shook up. He was traumatized. He was really angry and told me he couldn't hang. "This is bullshit!" he told me. It was even getting to be too much for me.

I ended up moving to Hunters Point for a while to get away from it all. Hunters Point was the black ghetto and very rough back then. There was a fair amount of traffic at my loft, people hanging out and using. The Swedish girls and their friends came over regularly. With all these white girls coming in and out of the place the police had their eye on me; they probably thought I was either a pimp or selling drugs. Actually, it was the Swedish girls who had all the drugs. They were my delivery service.

One day this dude came up to my door dressed like a house painter and asked me if I he could buy some weed. Being so gullible and trusting, I thought I had seen this guy before, somewhere, but couldn't quite place him, and people were coming and going so I didn't think much of it. I called up Wild Bill and got this painter an ounce of weed, pinching some out before I sold it. I wasn't too savvy to the drug scene, really. I thought I was doing this guy a favor. But when I handed the weed to him he pulled out his badge. "SFPD!" he shouted and pulled out his gun. He pointed the gun at my face and shoved me against the wall then handcuffed me.

At the same time a herd of undercover cops busted in behind him, guns drawn, and they searched my whole house. We all got busted. Wild Bill was there, so he had to go to jail with me. Spongie, my roommate, hadn't even done anything or been involved at all, but he had to go downtown, too. I got charged with hand-to-hand sales for selling drugs to an undercover cop.

When I got out of jail, I was on probation, and ended up moving back to Mission-A and soon got up to the same old shenanigans. I was on summary probation and I didn't think I had to check in, but one day I got pulled over on my red rocket. The cops told me I had a federal hold, no bail, and said I was supposed to be checking in with my probation officer, which of course I hadn't been. I didn't know anything about that, nor was I paying attention when I got sentenced, so I rolled the dice, didn't think twice, paid the price, and got snake eyes.

The cop was a woman and said, "Now, you're not gonna fight with me, are ya?"

I said, "No, ma'am." I think she had a beef in the past with other cats because she was a woman and guys would beat her ass before backup arrived so she said, "Now if you have anything on you tell me now, they will search you again at the 850 Bryant City Jail."

Now, I had heard things before and gave my dope to cops before, and the cops tagged it on with the rest of the charges. I told her anyways that I had some weed on me in my pocket. She let me park and lock my bike, handcuffed me, took the weed out of my pocket, and kicked it under the bike into the sewer.

My probation officer was Jeannie Nunley, this stern black woman. She was the kind of black woman that would get on your ass, just like my mama. "I know you've done some great stuff and played this music that has influenced a lot of people," she said. "Now, I don't know what the hell you doin' living back on Mission Street. You back in the belly of the beast, just wasting your gifts and talents."

I didn't know how she knew who I was. "I'll try to get you out of trouble this time," she said.

I told her I was planning to move to L.A. "Your probation is up soon and then you can do whatever you want," she said.

But until then I had to sit in jail. They took me first to 850 Bryant, the San Francisco jail. 850 Bryant had some characters: there was a geeky, creepy black Christian guy. All he did was read the Bible and try to preach to us. He wouldn't shut up. Then there was Jean, a psycho, outrageously gay guy. They sent him away to the psych unit in Atascadero after he got in a fight with skinny little big mouth Billy, the biggest shit talker and instigator on the cellblock. Jean beat Billy silly because Billy tried to boss him around and take his candy and chocolate bars. I don't think I had laughed so hard in quite a while, funny shit.

Jean was always in my face, "Oooh, you so pretty, nice and dark chocolate. You look just like my friend Trina," he said to me.

Now that doesn't really bother me, but you know in there I had to harden. "How you gonna let him talk to you like that?" Billy whispered in my ear, trying to instigate some shit.

"Get off me, man!" I said to Jean as I jumped off my bed and flexed on him.

He ran away, but Billy chased him, and they got into a fight. Jean was much bigger than Billy, who was a skinny little thing, so this was true comedy. Billy tried and tried like a little dog but could not wrestle Jean down. He kept on trying, which was so hilarious even the guards were laughing. We all circled around cheering them on: "Yeah Yeah, get that nigga, get him! Kick his ass Billy, get that nigga get 'em!"

I can laugh now, but it really did seem like life and death in there. There were some big guys in there waiting to be transferred upstate to San Quentin for some heinous shit. The preacher wouldn't tell me what they were in for, but I was sure that one of them murdered his family.

After three weeks at 850 Bryant they moved me out to San Bruno. I looked up as they were processing us in, strip-searching us, and saw three or four tiers of nothing but criminals. I didn't know how long I was going to be there, nobody told you anything. I got thrown in the cell with this guy, Steve. *What in the hell am I doing here?* I remember thinking. I was a misconstrued misfit, but not a criminal. I had never been to prison. While I was inside some career criminals would say, "Yeah, nigga you belong here. You belong in jail. You gonna be here for a long time."

But I never thought so. I think they were just trying to scare me, bring me down to their level. I remember the noise, the chatter, and the idiots in there. I asked Steve, "What do people do in here, all day and all night?"

Steve had a suggestion. "We'll mix up some Pruno, man." Pruno is a home made jailhouse moonshine made from kitchen scraps. So we saved up the sugar, the bread, orange peels, apple peels, whatever we could steal out of the chow hall. We got an orange juice container, put it all together with some water and kept it hidden under the bunk. But I didn't get to drink the Pruno or even finish making it.

One day at chow time they brought food into the communal day room, which also served as the chow hall; it was the area right outside the two-man cells. This was where everyone ate, hung out, played cards, watched television, and did scandalous shit. Some Mexican cat took an orange off a Colombian guy's tray and crash! Bam! Boom! A full-blown riot, just like that. Trays, food, feet, fists, and shanks were flying, and I thought, *Holy shit. Am I gonna make it out alive?* Sirens roared and everybody hit the floor. The Sort Team came in to break it up, then—*slam*—we were all on lockdown. We stayed on lockdown for the rest of the time I was in the joint.

One day the guard came around and said, "Henley! Roll it up! You're out of here!" I was only in two weeks that time, though once I moved to L.A. I would do a couple weeks here and there for heroin possession.

I went to court in San Francisco. I had a battery of lawyers, and I remember I paid them $1,000 cash each. "I don't care if you're the next John Lennon. I don't believe you are going to stay out of trouble," the judge said.

After that, I moved back into Mission-A, but things were not the same, and they were getting worse. There was friction in the band over the Giger artwork, "The Penis Landscape." Jello wanted to use it as the album cover for *Frankenchrist*. We thought he was going too far, and Jello was getting really hot about his artistic freedom and his integrity, this and that and the other; it was all about him. He can be a pretty controlling dude. The ultimate decision of the band was that we would put it in the insert, not the cover. Things really started to unravel when a sixteen-year-old girl gave the record to her thirteen-year-old brother, and her parents got wind of it. They filed suit. Alternative Tentacles was raided by the San Francisco vice squad, and we were charged with distributing pornography to minors. Amidst other band friction this was a new and large thorn in our side. In 1986, we decided to break up. We recorded our last record, *Bedtime For Democracy*, and we played our last gig in March of 1986 at UC Davis.

After the band broke up, I had little money and no direction, which is a lethal combination. The artist in me was warning that now I really needed to scrimp and save because I didn't know what was coming. The band was gone, and I really didn't have anything happening. I played in a couple little bands and worked on some other projects with people, but mostly I was smoking a lot of crack, shooting coke, and smoking crazy amounts of weed. When the Chili Peppers came to town in early

1986, we were hanging out, and Flea asked me, "So, what are you doing musically, are you playing with anyone?" He was always intense, enthusiastic, and so direct. "You should move to L.A. There's a lot of work down there." He was so wide-eyed, matter-of-fact. I always admired that in him, his single mindedness. He would become one of my closest friends.

Of course we had that San Francisco antagonism to L.A., but Mark Byron and I had been talking about the same thing, getting away from the nowhere drugged-out Bay Area scene. So Mark and I decided to make the move. He packed up his school bus, and I drove Mark's funky Dodge van. We caravanned down south to sunny So Cal, stopping only in Big Sur to smoke some crack. Mark of course didn't smoke any, he just puffed his weed, but I was buzzing my brains out for the rest of the trip.

We were parked at the beach near the water's edge. I went down to look, and there were a couple of massive elephant seals on the beach. They looked so big and bold in the morning light—especially after I had been up all night smoking crack. My heart was pounding. I looked at them, and they growled as if to say: *Don't. Fuck. With. Me.*

As high as I was, I had to touch them. It seemed like they would be slothful, slow-moving creatures out of the water, but when I went to touch one he whipped his two-ton body around quick as a rattlesnake. He snarled and bared his teeth at me as if to say again, *Don't. Fuck. With. Me.*

D. H. PELIGRO

I jumped back and screamed, "Mark!"

"Oh man," he said. "Look how big they are!"

"Yeah, and they're mean, too. They're pissed off," I said.

"Don't mess with them," he said. "Man, leave 'em alone."

Since I was still high on crack, and my heart was racing from the fear of being crushed by an elephant seal, I figured I'd better leave them alone. So we went back to our caravan and pushed on.

20

Jane Says

Mark's 1969 Dodge school bus had been remodeled into a mobile home by its previous owners. It said OUR PRIVATE COACH along the front and was fully equipped with a kitchen, two full beds, a twin bunk, toilet, and a shower on the other side. He had welded a five-foot long platform on the back for our motorcycles. I was driving his Dodge van, towing my 1958 yellow Karmann Ghia with burnt-out brakes. At night I would move into the school bus, which was like our little home.

On one of my previous visits to Los Angeles I had met a stunt man, Chris Neal Rommelmann, and he let us park the van outside his house on Curson between Santa Monica and Romaine, down the street from Melrose. That was before Melrose had become overrated, over-hyped, and over-priced. Chris's pad was called the Wheaties House because there was this huge billboard with a Wheaties ad on it that stayed there for years. Chris Neal was from Brooklyn, but he was friendly and cool like the kind of guy you'd meet in San Francisco. He'd say, "Yeah, bro, my house is your house. Come on in."

We called him Chris Neal because there were so many Chrises, Kevins, Johns, and Marks. There was an empty lot right next to his place where we parked the bus and then ran some water hoses from the Wheaties' kitchen into it. But I would often sleep inside the house, as Chris and I were tight. It was a total party house, a little like Animal House. Chris had snakes, spiders, dogs, cats, motorcycles, and bicycles everywhere. His sister Nancy and her boyfriend, Tim Sampson, lived there, too. Tim was the son of Will Sampson, the actor who played Chief in *One Flew Over The Cuckoo's Nest.*

It was so homey with Nancy always cooking and baking. The Wheaties House was a real underground actor/musician center, and everyone hung out there. It was a festival twenty-four hours a day. We would throw huge barbeques that lasted all day and into the night. Hillel Slovak would show up from time to time. His brother Jamie didn't drink but was there every day with his own bong. He bought and sold weed, and he was always ready to give us some choking bong rips.

When Jamie talked to me he always tried to cop a black lingo and stance. When I met him he told me that he didn't drink but he did say, "Wonna bussa joose." I tried not to laugh, but it slipped out just a bit. It was uncomfortable for me at first, but I got used to it. So I was able to sit and talk to him without laughing in his face. If that's the way he was, then that's the way he was. I accepted him.

Hillel also had this stutter; nobody fucked with him about it, except me, and only because he was so insecure about it. The first time I heard him speak I laughed. I can be real callous, immature, and a little stupid sometimes. I laughed because when I was a kid my neighbor Henry Head had a bad stutter, and Hillel's stutter reminded me of Henry. Flea saw see me starting to laugh and flipped out, gave me a scolding. Flea freaked out because he was really protective of Hillel. I didn't know that they were Fairfax High School buddies. Still, it was funny to me. Hillel was an amazing and talented person. He was a mastermind behind his shy demeanor.

The Wheaties crew was Chris Neal, Donnie Triumph, CC Grime, Totus the Fly, Dougie Fresh, Sick Nick, and me, DHP. We were too cool for school. Nightriders. Daywalkers. Twilight tip-toers. L.A. dudes. Some of us wore our motorcycle jackets covered in studs and our tight peg leg black jeans. Some of us rocked old, torn Levis covered in oil, dirt, grease, and grime because we were always working on these magnificent machines at Chris's pad. There was a full shop in the back of the house with tools, lifts, hoists, jack-stands, and spare parts everywhere. Everything a growing boy needs to keep his bike at top speed.

I was brought in as one of the gang maybe because of my Dead Kennedys status.

Los Angeles clubs were jumping at the time and Chris Neal was a popular doorman, so we got in free wherever we went. We were out at the clubs every night.

D. H. PELIGRO

John Sidel ran most of the clubs: Power Tools, Funky Reggae, Botswana, Smalls, and Variety Arts Theater. There was so much creative energy, and everyone was forming bands. I was drumming in a band called Cat's Cradle with one of the DKs producers, Geza X, along with Katie and Debbie Patino. Geza had produced some of the bigger Dead Kennedys songs like "Too Drunk to Fuck" and "Holiday in Cambodia." He came in to work on another for *Plastic Surgery Disasters*, but we didn't use it in the end. I also did some fooling around with Flea and Anthony. We called ourselves Slap Happy at first and later became The Three Little Butt Hairs: Flea on bass, me on drums, Anthony singing. We played mostly at this hang out joint called The Lhasa Club. We did punk rock medleys. We'd do a Black Flag song straight into a Dead Kennedys song into another familiar tune. It was very unfocused but fun. Mostly we just enjoyed going out and getting high and playing together.

Two other guys, Dougie and Nick, also lived at the Wheaties House. My drinking and drug use increased. Dougie got me back into crack for a while. After that it was all about the pipe. Like always, I tried to hide just how much I was using. When Dougie, the rest of the fellas, and I were out at the clubs at night, Doug and I would sneak away and smoke crack in the alley or a nearby parking lot. Then we would saunter back in, all sweaty, like nothing was going on. Or at least that is what I thought.

At the house I would get up early in the morning, go buy beer, and drink about two forty-ouncers before anyone else was awake. I pretended to be perky, happy, and energetic, but I was really just drunk.

One day Dougie was sitting on the couch nodding out. I said, "Whatchew doin? MAN! Give me some!" He wasn't handing it out, but he took me to Giuseppe. Giuseppe looked like a cliché Italian mobster: hair slicked back, shiny alligator shoes and all. He was the main dealer for that scene. He was always the man with the stash. I had no idea that I would have a long relationship with Giuseppe. He looked me up and down. "Not a cop, right?" he said in his Italian accent. Once he checked me out he sold me some China White cut with Fentanyl which is what I would use until I started shooting up and going downtown for cheaper dope.

As Giuseppe handed me my bag I flashed back to the first time I had ever used dope. It was with Indian, at his apartment, philosophizing about guitars, way before that huge package of China White was delivered to Mission-A. Even then I had a premonition that it was going to take me down, but I didn't listen to that inner voice. I never listened. I had no idea of all that goes along with getting high. No idea of the kind of life-sucking shit I was about to go through for what would feel like the next million years. I could have saved myself a lot of suffering, but I was the same impulsive, self-destructive kid who threw himself off the roof just to see what would happen. The same compulsive kid that,

D. H. PELIGRO

after he had broken all his bones, would jump again and again. Change would come, but it wasn't in my pocket yet.

At some point I moved back into the school bus, and this is when I met Sherry. She was a friend of Karen Cantor's, one of the little girls that would hang around when I briefly lived in L.A. with SSI. Sherry was a sweet nineteen-year-old girl from the valley—long legs, big breasts, brunette, and not only beautiful but a lovely person. She worked at Flaming Patti's. I would show up at her work in my hot leather pants, leather jacket, and high top sneakers looking like a rock star. I would saunter on in and order a veggie burger. I was not really hungry, but I just wanted to be near her, or at least in the same space. We were friends first, talking for hours in the living room. We started fooling around, and pretty soon she became my girlfriend. We had sniffed some coke together, but it was only later that we began to use heroin hardcore. I was living in the bus with Mark, and we were tight friends, but once I got together with Sherry we started drifting apart.

I got sick of living on the bus and wanted a real place to live. There was a room opening up at the house where Karen Cantor lived so I moved right in. It was 365 Wilton, where Perry Farrell of Jane's Addiction lived. Jane, the inspiration for the band's name and their song "Jane Says," had just vacated the room I moved into. She went to Spain or some shit. That room must have had a curse because it was where I officially became a junkie. Carmen, the woman who moved in after me, got strung out, too. I knew some of the other girls who lived there as well. There was Karen and Danusha, who later married Fishbone's Dirty Walt.

I didn't know Perry at all when I moved in. He was in Jane's Addiction, and they were in the process of getting signed. I had heard a bunch of buzz around them, but I hadn't really heard their music. My relationship with him was never that deep, not that heavy. I kept it that way with them. I never wanted to get too involved in their personal lives or them in mine. But he and Mark Byron were close. Mark was uncomfortable parking outside of the Wheaties House as it was getting too hot between the neighbors and the landlord complaining to Chris about the bus being parked outside the house.

Perry had turtles in the back yard, and he liked to grow vegetables. His tomato plants were pathetic; they were getting cooked in the L.A. sun, but it was fun to watch him try because he was so into it. Mark, Perry, and I would sit around, talk about the garden and the turtles. I learned about all the different types of turtles and tortoises. When I moved in, Perry had these henna colored dreadlocks with rings in them. I thought they were kind of funky. He said they were inspired by some African tribe. I thought, *That's a white boy thing to have some fantasy about getting back to some kinda tribal roots.* He would dance around like a cave man. I didn't think he had a rhythmic bone in his body. Although a lot of people really liked Jane's Addiction, I wasn't a big fan.

There were a couple songs here and there I liked, but mostly I thought it was bullshit. I did admire Perry for his hustle, that he did all this work and research when he was trying to find a producer. He would go and get every album that he liked and thought was well produced, and then he would write or call the producers. I felt bad that I didn't like their sound. I didn't tell him. "Some people," he said, "don't like us because we're not all hard all the time." I could see that he was sensitive about it, so I didn't express my opinion.

While living at the Wilton house I started hanging tight with Flea. We got to be good buddies at the Wheaties House, and after I moved in he came over to the Wilton house almost everyday to hang out. We would kick it all day, and then at night we would go to Power Tools or another club. Sometimes during the day we would go for a hike in the Hollywood Hills, or we'd go to his place, and he'd tell me these Hollywood Hills stories. He told me about a monastery behind his apartment on Gower. He would just look me dead in the eye with those child-like blue eyes, all white around. He would open his mouth really wide and always carefully enunciate every word. "Dude. They never leave that place ever. Never, ever, ever, dude, never." They were cloistered monks and nuns that could never leave.

One day, we climbed to the top of the Hollywood sign. I climbed up the O, and he climbed up the H. "When we get to be big rock stars we're gonna buy a whole letter, dude," he said. I would believe whatever he said. I'd always believe him because he was so sincere and adamant. Some days we rolled around in his copper colored beat up Dodge Dart. We'd go cruising down Hollywood Boulevard window shopping for shit that we couldn't afford. Some people knew who we were from the music scene. More people knew him than me. If we struck up a conversation half the day would be gone.

Melrose was a cool hang out before it became what it is now. Sometimes we'd see Anthony running around with his girlfriend, Jennifer, who was one of the dancers at Power Tools. We never had any money, and we never bought anything except some things from Aardvark's Odd Ark. I still have a picture of Flea and me in a pair of $10 shorts I bought there and wore forever. Then we'd split a bean and cheese burrito. I would smoke some weed and offer it to him but he didn't really smoke. He had always been a lightweight. He would have one or two beers, but I always wanted to keep drinking, so I would try to sneak away from him to drink.

Sometimes we'd go over to Flea's mom's house. Flea's mom was always really nice, really cool to me. I first met her when I was still new to L.A. Flea was always getting on her case for smoking and drinking too much. Considering what it was like with my mom, I was amazed that he got away with talking to his mom like that.

She actually really liked me. Later on, after I got strung out, I never felt like she judged me. I felt like she was always pulling for me when I was trying to get clean. "Oh D. H.," she'd say in her Australian accent. "You're

gonna be all right. I think you can do it. You can get straight." I also liked his sister Karen. They were people that made an impact on me, a real loving family. Flea stayed the same even after he had blown up and lost that tore up Dodge Dart.

Later on, when he was rolling around in a Jag we would take the same drive only this time up to his beautiful new house in Los Feliz across from the Frank Lloyd Wright building up there.

"Dude," he'd say, "Ya can't do this in a Dodge Dart," as he took the sharp corners at 50 mph. "This ride handles better in the dark."

Jane's Addiction rehearsed there at Wilton Street, so Dave Navarro and Steve Perkins were there all the time. Even though I wasn't that into their sound I really liked those guys. They were just these wild, ratty kids from the Valley. Navarro was sporting those '80s long rocker locks and piercings. And I really liked Steve Perkins, a curly headed funboy who could play his ass off. When they were at the house they would come knock on my door, spend some time. We would talk about music, this and that. I turned them onto to the Chili Peppers. One day when they came to visit me I was rocking out to *Freaky Styley* on my little cassette player. "What is that?" Steve and Dave said, so excited. I said, "Red Hot Chili Peppers!"

"I've never heard of them," Steve said. He stood there for a couple of minutes and listened. Then he just looked at me with his big, bushy hair and said, "Wow."

I was really happy for Jane's Addiction when their album did well and they started to blow up. One New Year's Eve at The Scream, Steve Perkins was playing the steel drums and asked me to jump up on stage and play "Jane Says" with them, kind of interesting since I was living in Jane's room at the time. He kept motioning me to dynamically come down because he thought I was playing too loud for such a soft song. He seemed a little worried that maybe I didn't know the song, but I did and it was sounding good.

When the show was over, Dave came backstage. He was really pumped. "Wow, did you see those fuckin' people out there? They loved us! Fuck!" He was ecstatic that they had come into their own and had their crowd behind them.

I detected a subtle egotism in his enthusiasm, as if it had already gone to his head. I had seen this before, but I didn't think too much about it. It was exciting. The music scene in L.A. at that time was vibrant. Punk Rock had opened new horizons for performance artists, playwrights, comedians, lots of shit all over the place. *Rock City News*, *Scratch Magazine*, *LA Weekly*, and a few others were some of the voices of the scene. L.A. had a legacy with punk rock, ska, rock, and metal; we all made a lot of noise. We were part of something so big, and we couldn't see it at the time.

When I first moved in at Wilton I was mostly smoking cocaine. I could afford to use because I had money from my Dead Kennedys royalties coming in, and they were pretty decent for my meager lifestyle as I wasn't paying taxes on them. I knew one day all that was going hit the fan, though. By the end of my time at the Wilton house I owed $80,000 dollars in taxes and eventually they froze my checks from Alternative Tentacles. Shit was still hitting the fan. I used to cop my powdered coke behind Sears on Santa Monica, take it home, and cook it up myself. One day, I turned Perry onto crack in that house.

"Perry, you gotta try this stuff."

He took a puff. He was like, "Wow..." Then he said, "Isn't it bad for your throat? What will it do to your lungs?"

I didn't think about it. I really didn't care.

At some point I started using heroin more and more. For one thing it was easier and safer to cop. Giuseppe delivered to the door, or I would meet him on some secret corner, which was better than what I had been doing—prowling around in the night, on dark streets trying to buy crack or some of that *her-RON*.

21

Disorder South of the Border

*O*ne day in early 1987 or 1988, Perry, Flea, Mark, and I all decided to take a surfing trip to Mexico. I didn't surf really, but I was always in the water paddling around and giving it the old college try. Flea and Perry were established surfers and Mark was pretty good, too. I went mostly because I knew drinking and carrying on in Tijuana would be a blast.

"Let's go! Jump in the bus, dudes!" Mark Byron said. So they threw their boards in and we screamed out of the driveway in his old tricked out school bus. Perry loved this school bus and wanted Mark to drive them in it on Jane's Addiction tours. It's a good thing they didn't, considering what a nightmare that bus turned into on this trip.

Driving into Rosarito I think we blew a gasket. Smoke was billowing out over the road. A group of Mexican guys were running along on the side of the road with guns, cursing at us. "Hey, Gringos!"

The boys and I got nervous so Mark drove faster. "I think it's a good time for everybody to go surfing," I said. We had lost the Mexican men, so Mark pulled off the road. Perry and Flea grabbed their surfboards, and I came along, lighting a joint, watching them go in and do some light surfing. Mark was trying to fix the engine, and he managed to button something up, but it wasn't really fixed, so we limped through these brutal hills in Mexico, the bus still smoking like a pig, and finally made it to Rosarito and Ensenada.

Mark tried to fix the bus, and we partied with some surfer fools from San Diego; they ate fish cocktails, and we all drank margaritas. When we finally got to the beach, the first thing we did was jump out and grab some chalupas, a couple beers and some tequila, then we made a bonfire. Some surfer dude, Clay, who we had just met on the beach had a monkey. Perry, Mark, and Flea thought it was funny that he had a monkey on his back, so we brought him onto our bus. We hung out playing with it until some asshole lit some fireworks and scared the monkey so much that it shat all over the bus.

Perry, Mark, and I were drinking like fish and smoking a ton of weed. I was not strung out yet so I could still do a little dope and be cool for the week, although I was pretty much always drinking and smoking. Flea would drink just a couple of beers, smoke a little weed. He wasn't a saint, but he wasn't like us. That made sense because Flea always had to deal with Anthony's addiction.

Anthony's on again/off again binges would just throw a ton of shit up in the air and stress Flea out.

Anthony had skanked out the year before, getting absolutely strung out and disappearing on drug runs for days, missing rehearsals. I remember a gig in Long Beach where he just didn't show up. Flea kicked him out of the band.

Around that time, the Chili Peppers—Jack Irons, Flea, and Hillel—held auditions for singers. I auditioned and wrote some lyrics to one of the Peppers' empty music tracks—I called the song "American Cheese." Anthony was M.I.A. and hadn't written anything to the track yet. After I auditioned, some guy with a grass skirt and a mohawk came in and just started screaming, "Whaaaaaaa!" Flea closed auditions because he could see it was pointless. About a month later Anthony went into a thirty-day rehab; that was enough for Flea to take him back. When he was back in the band, Anthony wrote "Fight Like A Brave" to the same track I'd used for "American Cheese." It became his out-of-rehab fight song.

Back in Mexico, we partied all night and into the dawn, sleeping on the ride back into Los Angeles. Poor Mark was the only one who could drive so we slept like babies as he was sweating up and down them hills in that fucked up bus. Later he told me he had bad food poisoning which gave him the runs so he stopped every mile or so to shit and throw up.

Mark, Sherry, and I took another trip to Mexico that was much more dramatic a few years later. By this trip both Sherry and I were strung like a couple of cellos in the L.A. Philharmonic. I didn't know how to tell Mark that I couldn't be away from my dope for a whole weekend, so I tried to bring enough with me to be all right. We decided to drive down in my muscle car, a bright yellow 1969 Road Runner I had gotten from my brother, Bruce. It was already souped up but just needed a little tinkering because it had been sitting for a few years in my mother's front yard.

Before we went on the trip to Mexico, Mark and I flew to St. Louis to pick up and fix up the Road Runner. My entire family met us and everyone thought I was so cool coming to town with my own mechanic. Mark and I stayed under that car until I couldn't take being in depressing St. Louis and around all my family any more. Mark loved my family, and they loved him. We came during a family reunion; all my relatives from Mississippi and Chicago were there. That's when I asked my Uncle Sam, "why didn't you tell me about my biological father?"

His reply was, "Boy, ya look jeh like 'em." And he said no more.

I didn't have time to have any feelings about that. I just wanted to get out of there, away from my family; I could only take so much. I felt like I was reverting into little Darren who had left years ago. But mostly just being there felt suffocating, like I'd become stagnant and should've been doing something more.

The car was a 383 Plymouth Road Runner with a four-speed stick with Hurst linkage—very hard to find

parts for. We had to order parts and wait for a couple of days. When we got the parts we got to work. We put in new spark plugs, an electronic ignition, a new fuel pump, hoses, an alternator, battery, oil, and a brand new Holly 750 carburetor with Edelbrock intake—which works best on a 383 Road Runner. The pistons were board thirty-over with a Godfather racing cam and Hooker headers. Damn, I spent a lot of money on that beast. Still, the thing often wouldn't start, so when we drove it across country back to L.A. the starter would crap out, and we'd have to pop start it.

Let me tell you, a 1969 Road Runner is a metal monstrosity—very heavy. So pushing it was no joke. I was tuckered out after a couple of times trying, and I'd get fucking angry. I said, "I should just burn this muthafucka. Fuckin' Bruce...my brother gave me this motherfuckin' jalopy."

Mark would look at me with his big cow-eyes and say, "Why bro? We should just take our time and fix it. No biggie take it easy."

It seems to me now that he was trying to teach me some patience and tolerance. The car wasn't rebelling against me, it just takes a lot of time and money to own and operate a '60s muscle beast. Somewhere in my punk rock speediocracy I'd forgotten that.

We kept driving, camping out along the way with the Road Runner breaking down frequently. Once we got it going, we tried to keep it running, jumping out only quickly to pee and buy food. We drove crazy fast

D. H. Peligro

across the country, sleeping in the car, pushing it in the morning to get it rolling. I was so relieved when we got back and immediately called up Giuseppe.

When we got back to L.A. I had it painted and cleaned the original cow print interior, and Mark had finished some other motor work, so now it was the loudest, hottest, flashiest, canary yellow Road Runner you could ever imagine.

I later learned that it was originally Omaha Orange with a white racing stripe wrapped around the trunk, one of only five ever produced in that color with that interior. In hindsight I should have just left it as it was, or repainted it the original color and kept the stripe.

Mark, Sherry, and I went on that second trip to Mexico. If you know anything about the Mexican police you know driving a canary yellow, freshly painted muscle car was a really stupid idea. We rolled into Tijuana, little kids trying to sell us chiclets gum and everything else under the sun. We drove past a group of guys waving guns and flashing badges at us as we stopped to get some beers. Two cruisers with their lights flashing pulled up on us. "You just blew through our road stop. You drove right through. You were supposed to pull over," they yelled, as they got Mark and me on the car spread eagle. They frisked us, flipped our pockets, pulled everything out of our wallets and then found a little baggie with crystal meth residue in Sherry's purse.

"I can throw you in jail and confiscate your car...or, my friend," he rubbed his thumb against his index and forefinger making the money motion inches from my nose, "we can work something out."

Mark pulled me aside and whispered in my ear, "Dude, they want money."

I thought, *Fuck! I need that money for dope.*

Sherry was freaking out. We would be in deep shit if we got thrown in a Mexican jail. I was hot as a junkie's spoon as we looked through our stuff and gathered together our money, about $500 bucks. I quickly stashed $300.

The cop came back over. In his broken English and Mexican accent, "You have de money?" he asked. Seeing the money in my hand, he handed me our driver's licenses.

But I couldn't do it. I jumped back in the car and stuffed the money back in my pocket. The cops started punching at me through the open window and pulling at the door and trying to open it, but the door was locked. Then he pressed his gun into my cheek. That did it. I handed over our money.

Fucking bandito, we knew it was a scam because one guy asked for a million dollars, and the other guy whispered in his ear one hundred each, corrupt-ass bastards. So we gave them $200 and they let us go.

After that we were totally depressed. But Mark had stashed $100 in his sock, and I still had three hundy, so we stopped in Rosarito for something to eat and to get a hotel. The same thing happened again before heading back. We got raked over the coals again by Mexican

Federales, as corrupt as the day is long. Same deal. Two hundred dollars to pass go.

Nobody talked all the way to the U.S. border. "Do you have anything to declare?" asked the border guard at the checkpoint.

"No, no," we insisted. But all they saw was a red-eyed black man with wild dreadlocks, an emaciated brunette chick with big tits, and a weird looking little geeky white guy in the back seat with a brown, curly mullet and a big smile on his face.

"Pull over to the secondary inspection check point." the border guard said.

"Hey man," I said, "we just had the worst time of our lives. We were pulled over by Federales and they took all our money. They punched me and stuck a gun in my face, c'mon, man, we just wanna go home."

"Pull over to secondary inspection," the guard insisted. I thought: *Well, fuck you.* I looked at Sherry. She looked at me and said, "Don't do it."

There was a distance of about 300 feet between the first stop station and where we were supposed to pull over. I was so angry that I didn't even think about it. I dropped that fucking car into first gear and barreled straight ahead through the S-turns and was rolling, but not for long. We got up to about 99 mph before we were chased down by ten border guards. I thought, *Shit. The gig's up.* Then I just gave up and pulled over.

"You stupid asshole, I told you not to do that! What the fuck do you think you're doing?!" Sherry lost it. "I can't believe you. Why would you do that?"

The Border Patrol guards took us into custody and confiscated the Road Runner. They put each of us in a separate room for interrogation. One by one they grilled us and grilled us and grilled us until they were fed up. They strip-searched Sherry so, needless to say, by the time they let us go she wasn't talking to us. Finally they just cut us loose without the car so we had to take a train back to L.A. Sherry was so pissed. It was a long train ride. It took me months and months of letters and appeals to get my car back. They hadn't found any weed because we had smoked it all up by the time we hit the border. The first thing I did when I got back home was borrow some money from Danusha and call Giuseppe.

22

★

Into the Grip

I remember that first horrid day that I woke up truly dope sick. It was a beautiful spring day in early May 1988. I was lying next to Sherry and woke up in a pool of sweat. My entire body ached. I felt queasy and sick to my stomach and anxious. The world was gray to me and all I could think about was dope.

Wow, I thought. *I'm a junkie. I may have to do this every fucking day.* I knew it was the only thing that would stop the sickness. I knew that I had no choice. I had to call the dealer and quick. Sure enough, as soon as I snorted some I felt great. But it still wasn't that bad yet. I could still spend $60 and be satisfied with a little quarter gram of China White. I wasn't shooting up, and I still had my cars, motorcycle, drum kit, and guitars.

It was just one month later that Hillel died. I wasn't tight with him, but I knew and respected him. Flea came and told me. I saw the look on his face—he was devastated.

"Hillel died," Flea said. "And Anthony's missing."

It was like two huge missiles hitting Flea in the gut. I felt for him, I really did. But since I was using, I had to stay shut down. I couldn't afford to be too affected by Hillel's overdose, or I would have to face my own addiction. So I got callous.

Oh well, too bad. After all, he wasn't really my friend, was the lie I told myself. But it was because all I wanted to do all the time was go and get high. So I acted like an asshole: selfish, shallow, and silly. At the funeral I was nervous and just plain scared. I was asked to be a Pallbearer with John Sidel, Flea, Bob Forrest, Pete Wiese, JK, and Hillel's brother Jamie. All of us were rocking yarmulkes. Anthony was not at the funeral. He was still on his drug run. As we followed the casket from the funeral home to the gravesite all of his family was sobbing. After the ceremony we went back to the home for the reception. Everyone was to go back to the family's house afterward for what Flea told me was a shiva.

"What's a shiva?" I asked Flea. He told me about the Jewish ceremony to honor the passing of loved ones. The idea of going to the shiva and actually having feelings made me crazy, so I started making a joke of it. "Yeah, I'm gonna go rock a shiva. Yeah."

Flea told me to shut up.

I was so out of line. I opened my mouth and shit just spewed out—not to hurt anyone, but to make light of an uneasy situation. Everyone was completely torn up, and there I was with no compassion, unable to feel. I wasn't the only junkie there feeling that way. "Let's go get high afterward," someone said. Norwood, Flea, and some other folks went to the family's house, but a group of us, instead of sitting shiva, went and got high with the Diva...Lady Her-ron.

Norwood was really affected by this and really pissed off. He felt that we could have been the ones who gave Hillel his last hot shot. A funeral for a talented man whom so many people loved. A man who died of a heroin overdose, and what do his friends do? Go and do the very thing that killed him. It was only later that I could let myself feel the tragedy of it. I hope he would have understood. We couldn't face those feelings at the time.

I knew that Perry's girlfriend, Casey, was also using. She would occasionally buy from Giuseppe. One day Perry told me I was paying too much. Giuseppe was asking $60 for half a gram. He told me that you could get it much cheaper downtown, and he told me where. This dope was different. This was Mexican black tar, not the China White I had been snorting. When I started getting it downtown Sherry and I smoked it at first. I thought that it wasn't as strong as the China White I was used to—and it wasn't. Perry assured me that if you shot the tar, it was just as good. He said we could get our rigs down there, too.

"Sounds like a plan," I said.

"Darren, don't shoot it up. If you do, you will never stop. Never," Sherry told me.

I had shot up a couple times, but after my time shooting coke with Bart in San Francisco I wasn't really a fixer anymore. For one thing I never had great veins.

But I crossed that line and would not come back for years. I copped down on 6th and Union near the KFC. It was dodgy to cop down there because it was three blocks away from a police station—not very smart. Still, there was always a host of dealers, border brothers, eses, and eighteenth street gangs who ruled the area. There were turf wars between the freelancers and the gangs—everybody wanted a dollar. I didn't give a shit about any of that. I just wanted my dope.

23

Black Rock Coalition

*E*ventually Sherry and I had to move out, so we moved into Barrows Street, right off of Fairfax on Carthay Circle. This was the Fishbone house. Dirty Walt had the room across the hall. Norwood's ex-girlfriend, Sandra, shared a room downstairs with Rick. Danusha moved in and would later marry Dirty Walt. Angelo had the room right next to mine. Norwood was living nearby in a house with Bob Forrest.

I truly love the Fishbone guys. They are like brothers to me. I met them in 1985 when they did a show in San Francisco. We hit it off and became fast friends. Whenever they'd come to San Francisco we'd hang out. They all had such a strong bond with each other, were so locked in together as people. Especially the brothers—they knew what the other was going to say and they'd finish each other's sentences. They were a real family.

Fishbone were fantastic performers and talented musicians. They fused ska, funk, and punkish rock in a very soulful way. They also had a horn section; not very many bands had saxophones in those days. It was a brilliant combination. Angelo was one of the most soulful singers I've ever heard in my life, a truly brilliant front man.

Norwood and I hung out after I moved to Los Angeles. Often Norwood, Pete Weiss, Bob Forrest, JK, Flea, Anthony, Hillel, and I had BBQs over at either Bob Forrest's house or the Wheaties House.

There was a time in the 1990s when Fishbone were contenders along with the Chili Peppers for the crown of L.A.'s alternative sound. Both bands were doing something totally different. The Peppers were rebelling against all those white hair metal bands with the feathered mullets and emaciated bodies, like Mötley Crüe and Poison. The Peppers created their own look. They were all buff, athletic, and playful—but also sexy. They always played with their shirts or pants off which could be risky and unacceptable in certain cities. They were true to the funk, and recorded with George Clinton. Eventually they created their own look, which the record companies love. As off the wall as they posed, they always had the potential to appeal to the massive audience and their manager, Lindy Goetz, always made sure of it. As Mark Byron says, "They always were a white boy band, even if they flirted with a black sound."

It wasn't like Fishbone wasn't known worldwide. They had a huge overseas audience. They merged a variety of styles and made this thing that had an impact on some major parts of the world, but they never made it commercially. They did have some stuff that played on the radio, which is more than Dead Kennedys ever did.

"Holiday in Cambodia" wasn't really played anywhere but on college radio, and we never crossed over to the masses on the Top 40.

Fishbone never crossed over to the Top 40 either. I think it had to do with their management. Nobody was aggressive enough to really fight for them and make sure they got the recognition they deserved, or to at least get credit where credit was due. They were an integral part of the L.A. scene, and risk-takers coming from Inglewood and Compton. There were no other freaky black American men playing that kind of funky ska. It made them kind of outcasts in the music world.

Fishbone didn't rebound from their pitfalls like the Peppers did. I think the industry didn't support them as much, and their battle to survive was tougher than the Peppers. Plus, black experimental musicians have always had a hard time supporting each other. Instead of coming together they feel like they have to compete for a very small niche market. I think this is what Living Colour's issue was as well.

Fishbone imploded eventually. Kendall went crazy and left. Chris Fish, their keyboard player, left. He started using heroin and coke, got strung out, and started stealing gear from the band and pawning it. At one point after that he was playing with Jerry Cantrell from Alice in Chains. I think he must have done the same thing to them. "He's no longer with us," Jerry said, in a cold voice, when I went to see them at The Palace.

Angelo, Dirty Walt, Norwood, the bass player, and his brother Fish on drums kept the thing going. Dirty Walt hung in there for many, many years. He was always the chill character, smoked out all the time with his parachute pants and his high tops. But when Fish left the band, it started to fall apart. I think if they had held it together they might have blown up. But once you lose that anchor, it just isn't the same.

This was one of the reasons I didn't join them when Norwood asked me to. Plus I had the heebie-jeebies about working with that big a band of black people. I was scared of black family drama. That's why I ran away from St. Louis. Everyone has drama, it's a universal thing, but there is something unique about black drama. It is always really intense and hardcore, like people are reliving the violence generations have suffered under slavery and racism only now they take it out on each other.

What happened to Kendall is a perfect example. Kendall was Fishbone's first and deepest loss. Those guys had been friends since junior high, and Kendall was an essential part of the band. He brought something crucial to them. He was not a phenomenal guitar player, but a very good one, and he was the band's unofficial spokesperson. He was an amazingly smart cat and wrote most of their songs. So that's what made his nervous breakdown especially sad. With Kendall in the band they probably would have made that record that would have taken them over the top.

Kendall was a really hard drinker, and his breakdown essentially began when he quit drinking Wild Turkey. His girlfriend had told him she wouldn't marry him as long as he was a drunk so he went straight. But feelings ambush you when you've been working hard to keep them down.

He had a really harsh, cruel, traumatic childhood. His father had done horrible things to him. I think all his childhood abuse and grief for his mother's death caught up with him when he stopped drinking. The last straw was his girlfriend's second rejection because she didn't believe he would stay sober. I had met his girlfriend, and I didn't know that any of this had gone on. In my childish, jokester demeanor I thought it would be funny to leave her a message in a demonic voice saying, *"Hi. This is Satan, and I've come for your soul."* I left the message; she freaked out. Then she told Danusha to make sure I never called again. *Ever.*

Anyway, Kendall was down in the dumps so he started calling his grandfather, a minister in South Carolina, seeking spiritual advice. Of course his grandfather told him to turn to God, and his family started crowing that he was coming back to Jesus.

He joined this crazy church and participated in some pretty extreme rituals. I guess his father caught wind of it and started calling him. His father, like his grandfather, started a cultish Christian compound up in Northern California. Kendall was vulnerable to that crap and started talking with his father nine, ten, fourteen hours a day on the phone. All of a sudden he loved the man whose guts he'd hated and who he had worked so hard to avoid. Pretty soon his father had him fasting for twenty-four hours and then praying for twenty-four hours straight. This went on for weeks. Eventually he wasn't eating or sleeping. It was classic cult brainwashing tactics.

He got more and more bizarre. You couldn't tell if he was ranting about his earthly father or his father in Heaven. He started telling the rest of the band that their music was demonically influenced and that his father was going to come and write songs with Fishbone. Then he started hanging out with his brother. Both of them had obviously been fucked up by their father's hardcore extremism, but it was a tragic cycle. Kendall's grandfather had done the same thing to Kendall's dad. Kendall's father was just repeating the pattern of abuse almost exactly the same way. I only learned later that his father had also been a musician and was in Love, the first black psychedelic band.

Right before his first tour of Europe, Kendall's father forbade him from going. He said it was against the wishes of Jesus, so Kendall didn't go. Instead, he went into a psychotic tailspin. Up for days and days, he finally went berserk. He started seeing swastikas moving under the paint on the walls in his apartment. He was chasing the swastikas, hitting the walls with baseball bats, knocking the chandelier off the ceiling. Then he cut open Kendall's waterbed and baptized his brother's

D. H. Peligro

wife. He went driving backwards through the streets of Hollywood in his Cadillac. At one point, Kendall threw out all his records, telling Norwood that it was all devil music.

Norwood wept as he told me that his Al Green, Marvin Gaye, Gladys Knight, and Donnie Hathaway records were wet and broken on the side of the road. Meanwhile, Kendall got on the plane to go to his father's church in Northern California. Norwood heard from his brothers in L.A. that shit was crazy up there. They told Norwood that Kendall's father was running a religious cult—that he had three wives and was molesting his sisters, which, as Norwood told me, was in line with what Kendall's childhood had been like. Norwood and his brothers called Kendall.

"Kendall is dead," his father replied. So Norwood decided to go up and snatch him away, put him in the hospital, do an adult intervention, as an L.A. psychiatric team called it. Norwood went up there with two of Kendall's brothers, burst into the compound, and snatched Kendall out. It was a real fight. Norwood had to put Kendall in a chokehold. They could have got him out, but family conditioning is a fucked up, powerful thing. Instead of helping Norwood the brothers turned on him, so he had to let Kendall go. The district attorney then pressed charges against Norwood for attempted kidnapping. They had a six-week jury trial, and he got a full acquittal. Kendall's father used him until all of his fat royalty checks dried up. When the checks shrank he kicked Kendall out. Last I heard, he was drinking and partying somewhere in L.A.

Angelo, the lead singer of Fishbone, is a special cat—but very strange. Flea told me before I really knew him that he was a little weird. I didn't know what he meant until one day Flea, Angelo, and I were hanging out, and Angelo started coming up with the wildest out of the blue shit. "I wonder why we're here, what we would look like if we were from outer space? Are we just monkeys in the evolution of man? Are we even here? Are we even having this conversation right now? The stars, they're sitting in the sky but they're billions of years old. Are we the stars that have already exploded?"

It was weird, but it did get me thinking. Most of those guys came from Compton and Inglewood, but Angelo lived out in the valley with his family. The first time I went to visit him I was amazed. I didn't know black folks had it like that. One day they threw a pool party, and I went with Flea. One of Angelo's cousins took a liking to Flea. She was older and real tall. "Ooh, you got some pretty eyes," she cooed, looking straight into his big china plate blues. Now that's a straight up black pick up line. Her mouth said, *You've got some pretty eyes*, but her body said, *I'm going to fuck you tonight*.

I remember feeling proud of Fishbone, a bunch of brothers expressing themselves and making it. I felt that way about Living Colour, also—24/7 Spies was another black rock, metal, ska, punk, hardcore band from New York. They had boasted, "We're everything Living

Colour wanted to be and everything Bad Brains wish they were." I thought that was just like a slap in the face, like they viewed it as a competition, like there wasn't room for everyone at the top. That's the same kind of shit that pulls us apart instead of bringing us together.

The first time Living Colour came to Los Angeles, Flea and I saw them at the Roxy or the Whisky. I can't remember which. "Damn, Flea, they're good, huh?" I said when I saw them doing their thing.

He agreed, but said, "I don't like all that shredding guitar playing." I thought it was genius, some of the best shit I ever heard. And I was really very proud to see black folk up there playing like that, but I didn't have the courage to relate that to him. How can you tell a white person that you are really proud that it's a brother up there playing like that? They might not understand. And it's weird to put a label or a color on anyone playing music to me.

When I was in Brazil or in other places in the world I never felt like I had to separate my loyalties like I do in America. America is still so full of this stupid narrow-minded shit. Guys are listening to hip-hop, and it's cool to talk like this and dress like that, but they don't want to fucking know what it is really like to be black. These same young guys don't know that rock was a white boy biting the blues.

White rock musicians visited my Uncle Sam Carr back in the day: Mick Jagger, Jimmy Page, Eric Clapton, all kinds of people. My uncle won a bunch of international awards for his music, the Jack Handy Award, the King Biscuit Award, and now the city of Clarksdale, Mississippi has a designated Sam Carr Day. But who knows about it? Some rock guys have heart; the good ones recognize where they got their stuff, and I give them great respect. I've had my best conversations about different kinds of blues, Chicago blues verses St. Louis blues verses Mississippi Delta blues, with white musicians. They understand and truly appreciate musicians like my Uncle Sam. But even so, he hasn't made any money from it. Where is his mansion in Beverly Hills?

L.A. was fun back in the late '80s and early '90s in many ways. We were spontaneous; we could just hang out, jam, and come up with some great music. That's how it often was back then with all of us. Norwood, Flea, Anthony, and I had a jam/recording session with Brett Gurewitz of Epitaph Records and Bad Religion. This was when Flea and I were hanging out all the time. Anthony had gone on one of his drug binges and been missing for a while. Whenever he came back into the picture after these binges, instead of confronting his problem and telling us where the fuck he'd been, he'd act all serious. "Let's just get together and go record a song," he would say, like we were the ones holding things up.

So we went over to a studio that Brett had before Epitaph was even started. We had no guitar player. "Where's the guitar player?"

"Dude, it's not gonna have any guitar," I said.

Flea said, "Dude, it's gonna have double bass!" Norwood started slapping and Flea started slapping. Pop-slapping bass was a style which hadn't really caught on, especially in the punk world. It was these two basses slapping over each other. It seemed like competition, but Norwood was so slow in his movements, very Norwood about things. And Flea was always really, super hyper. It was perfect. We just started jamming and called it "Coalinga." Anthony wrote the lyric out really quickly. It was about some girl who left him in Coalinga. (Coalinga is this horrific cow field and slaughtering factory right off the 5 Freeway. We used to call it Cowschwitz or a Cowcentration camp. You always remember Coalinga driving back and forth to San Francisco by the smell. By the time you look up to see where the stench is coming from all you see are miles and miles of cows being brought to slaughter. It smells like hell even when you roll up the windows.)

Flea told me another story about Coalinga. When he was in the band Fear, and they wanted to be harder-than-thou punk rockers, they pulled over right past Coalinga, jumped the fence and went into the stinky ass cowshit field to drink beers. One of the guys from Fear commented on Flea's Jimi Hendrix tattoo. "Yeah, I see you got that big strapping nigger on your arm," he said. That's when Flea quit the band. "Fuck you, I quit." I can just hear him, speaking all clearly, with his big, wide, over-enunciating mouth.

Jamming with Norwood, Flea, and Anthony was always fun. It was second nature to me to play power funk and make it rock, and it was always something I wanted to do. I could just jump into a Chili Pepper or Fishbone groove with no trouble at all.

24

"You're A Pepper!"

I was living on Barrows Street with Sherry, where I was really strung out, but I guess I looked like I was maintaining. Flea came over one day, "So, what are you doing?" He meant musically. I hadn't been doing much but playing with Geza X in Cat's Cradle.

"Just hanging around," I say.

"Well, wanna join the Chili Peppers?"

I honestly said, "Well, I don't know, I'll think about it."

"Well, I was hoping that you could show up at three o'clock today!" Flea said all matter of fact, as if he had this plan for a while before he asked me.

So I said, "OK." I went over and I jammed with them. And, *boom*, I was in the Chili Peppers. I had sold my original drum kit when I was living with Perry, which, in hindsight, was stupid because that was my original DK drum kit. I borrowed Jack Iron's drum kit when I joined the Peppers.

It was a delicate time when I joined. Hillel had just died, Jack had quit, Anthony had barely gotten out of rehab and was just days clean off a hardcore run. So part of the agreement set for me to join the band was that

I would not use drugs or drink around Anthony. Flea said, "Don't do any drugs around him, don't smoke any weed around him, don't drink any beer around him." I was already strung out and knew it would be impossible, but I agreed. I think now that maybe in the back of my mind I expected that if I got bad they would give me the same kind of break they had given Anthony.

We immediately started rehearsing and playing shows and touring. I was kicking the whole time. It felt like Caltrans was drilling holes in my lower back with a jackhammer. I was hot, I was cold, sweating, freezing, shitting, diarrhea, my skin crawled as if there were a million bugs beneath it. I couldn't bear to think about taking a shower—the coldness, the wetness, the feeling of water on my skin felt like each drop of water would attack my central nervous system. The water was too hot, the water was too cold, the water was too wet. This is all the shit my mind told me. Of course, when I took a shower, it wasn't that bad. It actually felt good. It felt good to escape the grips of the detox process, if only for a minute. I wretched with anxiety and felt as if the world was going to cave in around me—and I hoped it would.

However, at show time it was different. I loved playing so much I could forget the pain. "All right! Let's go!" I'd shout. That hour on stage was great, but the other twenty-three hours of the day were fucking murderous. Blackbird McKnight, the amazing guitarist from Funkadelic, had just replaced Hillel when I joined. We went up and did a bunch of Northern California dates: Santa Clara, Oakland, and other spots. We came back, and they didn't want Blackbird in the band anymore.

"He's not a Chili Pepper," their manager Lindy Goetz was saying. "He's too fat. But you look good, you're not overweight. You're a Pepper!" I remember him saying that shit to me. "You're a Pepper, man! You're a Pepper!"

In my opinion, we do this shit for the music, not for some centerfold in Drummer magazine. *So what now? Had we become everything we hated? No better than those hair metal bands we used to talk shit about?* That's what I thought, but I kept my mouth shut.

I knew this really young guitar player named John Frusciante. I had met him at the Wheaties House. He was dating Sara, an ex-girlfriend of Chris's, but they were all friends, so it was cool. He was only eighteen years old but an amazing guitar player. At that time he was playing in my garage band with some Musician's Institute (MI) cats. He was also playing in Thelonious Monster with Bob Forrest. John and I hung out a lot and soon became friends. He was a huge Chili Peppers fan so I introduced him to Flea and Anthony. They loved him and asked him to join. After he joined the band it felt really good for a while. I had history with Anthony, was close with Flea, and was friends with John. It felt like a new home.

We had some very good times, and I loved being on stage with them. The costumes and theatricality were really up my alley. We got these fabulous costumes from a prop house on Fairfax that we wore when we played at the John Anson Ford Theatre. Anthony was the Tin Man, Flea was in this mad Shazaam costume, John was Superman, and I was a bumblebee. My costume had these huge antennae and six arms so every time I raised my hand up to hit a cymbal they would get caught or hit another cymbal on the other side of the kit and cause this visual flurry of limbs and drumsticks running amuck. The multiplicity of arms seemed to have a mind of their own.

The band got very close. Flea gave me the nickname Dirty which people still call me today. Some of my peers from back in the day call me Dirty, Dirt, Dirtmund, Dirtmund 9, Dirt Dawg. We had little jokes, you know, I'd always do this thing and bust out singing, *I'm in the mood for love, simply because you're near me, funny, but when you're near me, I'm in the mood for love.* I'd do it so often that sometimes when we were on stage Anthony would say, "Dirty!"

"Yes?" I'd say.

"What are you in the mood for?"

Then I would bust out into full song in front of this massive crowd of people. That night at the John Anson Ford Theater I was in the bee costume and as I was singing that song I felt as if I were ready to pollinate the crowd, like they were some kind of special flowers.

Being in a band as big as the Peppers, you have to conform to what the band wants. They wanted me to play slower. That was alien and hard for me. When drumming you can play ahead of the beat, behind the beat, or you can play right on the beat. I tended to rush it, push things just a little ahead of the beat, especially on songs that I really loved like "Police Helicopter" and "Get Up and Jump." I would try to slow down, to an extent, but I heard in my head what I thought the drum parts should sound like in the song. Sometimes it was because I would get so excited; it just sounded so good we should push it to the edge. I would automatically feel, become all instinct, and speed the song up even more—all arms like a Dancing Shiva. I wouldn't even think about what I was playing, and really didn't have to. It was just natural to me. They would tell me I was playing too fast but to me in a live show the songs should be more to concert speed than sound like a fucking record. Whether they liked it or not I would hear things differently. So I just put my chops in there.

Sometimes they'd just look around, disgruntled. "What was that? Why would you do that?" Flea would ask. Sometimes if I missed parts or plowed through them, Flea and I would get into it. He started getting on my ass. "Slow down this part," or "You missed this part." He analyzed everything. *Go fuck yourself you little control freak*, I would think. *You asked me to join this band and now you don't like my drumming?* But I wouldn't say anything or display my feelings.

Now, being a guitarist and vocalist in my band, Peligro, I know what he meant. I tell my band mates to slow down in this part, and that the groove is way out of control on that part, and to come down dynamically here, and so on. At the same time Flea taught me a great deal about music and musicianship, it just took me a while to learn the lesson. His work ethic was something I had never experienced before. In Dead Kennedys when I came in to rehearsal I didn't have to work as hard. Sometimes I had too much information and I had to dummy up. Plus, ferocious punk rock came so organically for me.

In the Peppers I had to tune into their vibe more instead of listening to my own head. We were friends first when we'd hang out and climb the Hollywood sign or go window shopping on Melrose, but this was work. In the rehearsal studio Flea was another guy—all business. "Speed up, slow down, you missed this part." He made me work by the clock. He taught me about the advantages of warming up; in my arrogance I thought I didn't have to. I'd just get up there and start playing. I do have an ability to just snap into performance mode, but learning how to warm up really made the shows a lot easier. I didn't all of a sudden come alive in the third song or the middle of the set; I came out with fire because I was warmed up.

Flea also called me out a couple of times and said I didn't study the music enough. "Mommy, Where's Daddy" sounded like a lackadaisical, easy song to me without any intricate parts. Listening to it before rehearsal I had just glossed it over, thought I could knock it out. I didn't notice it was a real metered funky New Orleans groove. Flea was right to scold me. He'd always go on and on about jazz, Art Blakey this and Charlie Parker that. I was never schooled in jazz. *That shit is for old people*, I thought. I figured when I got old I'd probably get into it, but I learned to appreciate it more through him. I started to let new stuff filter in. I'd become a little jaded punk, forgetting that how I got in punk in the first place was by having an open mind.

I noticed when we were on the road all the boys had black music to listen to on the bus like James Brown, Sly and the Family Stone, Stevie Wonder, The Meters, P-funk, and all this other funky stuff. I had bands like BulletBoys, L.A. Guns, Metallica, and D.R.I. With the exception of the Beastie Boys and Fat Boys, it was all rock, rock, rock. Anthony looked through my stuff. "Where's the funk?"

"It's right here, man, in my arm," I said. I had no problem playing some of the funky stuff. I felt it was already inside me so I didn't think I had to practice it. I came from the ghetto. Funk, R&B, and Rock were all a part of my childhood—that's shit you just don't forget. Besides, when it came time to play some funky stuff it was always there. When I was a kid, Bruce Wade and I were always down with playing something rock but funky. Most white boys back then would try to get funky, but they were thinking too hard instead of feeling the soul of the music. They were stiff and rigid and not very funky at all. But there were exceptions, like Tommy Bolin and Average White Band. And Flea is fantastic; he really respects music, and he slapped that bass like

Louis Johnson of the Brothers Johnson. Flea is the force behind the early Pepper sound, funk fused with rap, punk, and pop.

There was an absolutely absurd and hilarious situation with Anthony before I was in the band. It was 1985 when the Peppers opened for Run-D.M.C. at the Warfield. At that time, Run-D.M.C. was the hottest fucking thing on the planet. The Peppers called me when they came into town like they usually did when in San Fran, so I showed up to sound check. George Clinton had just produced their last album so Anthony was feeling full of soul—or himself—because he went up to Jam Master Jay, who was standing backstage, and started into this rap. Now, I know how black folks are so I was thinking, *don't do it!* But I didn't say anything. "Hey, I've got this new rap, man," he says and goes into it before Jam Master Jay can say a word. "They call me the Swan cause I wave my magic wand and I love all the women to death / I party hard and pack a mean rod / knock you out with a right or a left!"

Jam Master Jay was quiet. He was patient, then he folded his arms in a B-Boy-Public-Enemy-D.M.C. stance, and he had this incredulous look on his face. He looked at Anthony like, *Man, who IS this cracker fool trying to bite some old used up raps?* Without saying a word he gave him a wilting look, cold, hard as hell. Then he turned and walked away.

D. H. PELIGRO

Although there were tensions, I enjoyed working with the Peppers. I worked on most songs that were recorded on *Mother's Milk* except "Magic Johnson" and one or two others. I wrote the lyrics to "Stone Cold Bush" and worked with John on the arrangements. John and I had started working on the song together in my garage at Barrows Street right before I joined the Peppers. I wrote the bridge for "Sexy Mexican Maid" which was my interpretation of a lick that I heard from *Don Kirshner's Rock Concert*, which is now "Funky Weatherbean" on my new record.

With John in the band we did a tour across America for a couple of weeks. Being strung out and on the road is a nightmare. You can't get any dope, so I was kicking my brains out. I was feeling like dog shit. I had bugs under my skin and felt like everyone was looking at me with binoculars. So when I saw the road guys were smoking weed I couldn't help myself. I had to do something to feel better. So I smoked some pot with them, grabbed some beers out of the Winnebago and guzzled them down. Anything to just feel a little better—and it worked for a while. It definitely helped but the sickness was always there in my bones and gut.

When we played Oakland I knew my former partner in crime, Wild Bill, could get me some dope so I jumped out as soon as we pulled in and called him up. We went to cop, but Wild Bill's friend, No Culture, was taking forever to get there with the dope. I had to wait and wait for the connection. I knew I was late for sound check, but I had to get fucking well. I missed sound check completely. When I finally got to the gig I was high as a kite. They were so pissed. Flea went off on me. "You motherfucker! I told you not to do this. That was the only thing I asked. You fucking missed sound check. You've been drinking beers for breakfast, smoking weed for lunch, and I specifically asked you not to smoke weed in front of Anthony. You're kicking in the back of the bus, flipping, tossing and turning all night. You're fucking up, man!"

He was really screaming at me. But I couldn't even hear him. All I knew was that I wasn't sick any more. He made it clear that this was my last chance. "If you keep getting fucked up we're going to have to find someone else," he said. John was taking their side too. In my addict mind I thought, *How dare you!* John and I roomed together, and he had been my new friend in the band because my friendship with Flea had changed to more like an employee/employer relationship. My addict mind said, *You have the nerve to take their side against me?* Again, I said nothing.

But now John was asking me, "What are you gonna do on the road? What's gonna happen when you can't get any dope? You don't need that shit." Little did we know what a hardcore drug addict he would become. But at that point John was brand new to the world. We all called him Green Horn. *I got you into this band*, I thought. He had no idea how I was feeling and how sick I was, but boy did he ever find out. I started getting that old defiant attitude. I didn't care about the house rules.

D. H. PELIGRO

It was too late anyway. I was strung out. I couldn't stop, even in those moments when I wanted to.

As soon as we got back to L.A., I called up Giuseppe to get some dope. It was a beautiful L.A. summer night in Carthay Circle. I had to go to the nearest ATM machine, which was in Beverly Hills, because the Peppers didn't pay in cash like all the other bands I had been in—they paid in checks. As soon as the cash was in my hand I jumped on my motorcycle. I started speeding down Wilshire and ran a stoplight. My driver's license was suspended because I had so many tickets on the motorcycle and the Road Runner, so when I heard sirens I panicked and gunned it.

I was out of my mind. All I knew was I had to get away. I had to get this dope. I had to get this dope *in* me; that was my top priority. The second was that I knew I was going to get thrown in jail if they caught me, and I would be sick; I didn't want to kick in jail. I powered around the corner trying to lose them and when I looked back I saw the cop car fishtailing sideways. I heard the roar of the engine, the screech of the siren as he tried to catch up to me like we were in a Michael Bay film.

I sped up a one-way street the wrong way across Wilshire into oncoming traffic. Cars whizzed by as I zigzagged in and out of oncoming traffic, swerving to avoid them. I jumped the curb, spun around, and somehow got back on the right side of the street. It happened so fast I hit all the sprinkler systems, so my back tire was wet. I knew if I hit a curve I was done for. My mind flashed back to when I'd wrecked my bike in San Francisco—my broken finger bent backwards, the bone sticking out of my knee through my torn jeans, the skin ripped from the side of my bleeding face—I looked back again and saw a helicopter light ten times brighter than the mid day sun.

"FUCK!" Game over. I had to pull up on the sidewalk or I would have killed myself skidding out.

The cops grabbed me and slammed my head down on the cement. One of them pulled me onto the sidewalk. "Freeze. Don't move. Take the keys out of the fucking bike and get on the ground."

I looked back. I could see smoke everywhere. Through the smoke I saw three squad cars and four cops pointing guns at me. When I turned back, I felt a boot on the back of my neck. I heard a crunch as my chin was ground into the sidewalk and split open. They handcuffed me, took me to the Beverly Hills police station. The cell they put me in was the cleanest jail cell I've ever been in.

The cop looked at my passport. "Have you really been to all these places?"

Well, yeah, motherfucker, I thought.

After six hours Sherry showed up to get me. When the cop saw this tall leggy white girl come to get me the cop started leering at her. "Like it kinky, huh?" he asked her.

Soon after this I showed up for a band interview with *Spin* magazine gowed out of my gourd. I remember

D. H. PELIGRO

my Road Runner parked half on the sidewalk, half on the street. During the interview I think I mumbled some things here and there, mostly nodding out in front of the guys, the cameras, and the interviewer. Flea called me the next day. "Man, you were pretty fucked up. Dirty, I'm sorry man, that was the last chance. We're gonna look for another drummer."

"No, no man. I'll go to rehab. Please. I'll do whatever it takes."

"I'm sorry. You know I love you but we can't take the risk after all the shit that's happened. We're gonna get somebody else," Flea told me.

"No, no wait, wait," I said as he hung the phone up. I was really hurt. For the longest time I had been trying to run from my feelings, block them all out with drugs. But this was one moment when I couldn't keep them down. I hung up and started crying. I couldn't believe I'd let them down, let myself down, let everybody down. I felt like shit. Like killing myself. I was hurt and sad, but I was also angry. They had abandoned me, betrayed me in my moment of need. I was resentful. Fucking hypocrites. They had taken care of Anthony, given him a million chances. Everyone was supposed to tiptoe around him, make his wellbeing their top priority, and he was only barely clean this time, for only a few months. I had been there for him, so these motherfuckers should help me. *I have a problem, I need some help. What happened to brothers taking care of brothers, no matter what?* I took the classic addict's way out. Instead of taking responsibility for my actions, I took it as the chance to shoot as much dope as I could get. I was blaming them, but I was also blaming myself. *There's no use. I am a fuck up forever. Fuck this whole life, just fuck it*, I thought. In a twisted way I was also doing it to punish Flea and Anthony so they would have another death on their roster, which made no sense. The person I was punishing was myself.

All the anger and shame that I had been running from since my childhood came back with a vengeance. It had taken over. It was like my father and my mother had picked up the strap, the cord, and whipped me to get those feelings out of themselves. I took the whip from them and continued where they left off. Now I was wearing the victim's skirt.

The next time I saw Flea was at Dick Rude's place. Right after Flea told me to leave the band I spent a brief time drumming for the Too Free Stooges. The Too Free Stooges was Dick Rude, Manny Chevrolet, Zander Schloss, Martyn LeNoble, and me. Dick asked me to get him some dope, so I was at his place dropping it off. I thought I was getting it for Dick, but he turned around and handed it to Flea who proceeded to make some fat lines and snort them up.

I couldn't believe my eyes. I was furious. *You're buying dope, the same shit you kicked me out of the band for? And using me as your connection? That's not fair!* I thought. I didn't say anything but was steaming inside.

I look back now, and I can see how immature and selfish I was in my addiction. I know now that I was

D. H. PELIGRO

looking to keep my resentment going. It was a perfect excuse to keep using. So I did.

While I was in the Too Free Stooges we went to Vegas to open for the Peppers. Next thing I see is goofy Chad Smith, their new drummer, drunk off his ass. How can *he* drink but I can't drink? Flea can do dope but I can't do dope? That was a perfect excuse. Of course I went back to my room and got as high as I could. I just wanted to go home.

A few days after we got back to L.A. I went over to Dick's house for rehearsal. He came in with a sad look on his face and said, "Dirty...um...we gotta get a new drummer."

I said, "What? What the fuck?"

"Yeah," he said. "Zander and those guys...you know. I'm sorry man. I'm just the axe-man."

Lately Zander had been on my ass, "Play like this, slow down here, slow down there..." He thought I played too fast and too aggressive.

Same old story, I just couldn't hear it. I was totally ego-driven and angry so I had refused to cooperate and slow down my playing. I didn't even know I was doing it; I was incapable of conceiving and conforming to the band's needs. I really did love those guys and their music. On my way home I was crying and panting so hard I could barely see or stay on the road. Sometimes I felt so stupid. Did I fit in anywhere, with anything?

The minute we got back to L.A. from Vegas, my girlfriend Sherry and I copped. Sherry was quickly joining me in my self-destructive decline. The more dope I did, the more she did. At first she was just smoking and snorting it. She wanted me to fix her, but I wouldn't do it so she taught herself. Pretty soon we got kicked out of the house on Waring and June. It was about the fourth place we'd bounced in and out of since we moved out of Perry's place around two years ago. We put as much of our stuff as we could in our Volkswagen van. Sherry drove that and I drove my Road Runner. We agreed that we had to kick since our lives were unraveling.

We managed to rent this smelly little place on Bellevue in Silverlake, and the first thing we did was to go to an outpatient clinic in Glendale. They gave us three days worth of meds and specific instructions on how many to take and when to take them. They gave us a plan for how we would kick, solemnly counting out the pills we would take for each day and returning every three days for more. But one morning, I woke up at three in the morning crawling out of my skin and took every last pill, including Sherry's. Sherry was at work with all the keys to the Volkswagen bus, but little did she know I had an extra set of keys to the 1969 Road Runner. I was still sick and very woozy and I got a bright idea to cop some dope on Sixth and Union before she got back from work.

So I went and fired up the yellow beast and took it towards the 7-Eleven on Virgil then all the meds kicked in at once and I blacked out, lost control of the car and smashed into a 1979 Mercury, or Granada, or some shit

D. H. PELIGRO

car. I hit it at about fifty mph. My mouth hit the steering wheel, knocked out my front teeth, broke my nose and split my lip. I was in shock. The cops were everywhere. An ambulance came, good samaritans came out of their homes, "Are you okay?" they asked me. Someone went and got ice to put on my face, because my mouth and nose were bleeding so much. What a mess I had made again. Now it was no longer about any band; it was about me trying to get clean and sober, and I couldn't even do that without making a mess.

I walked in a daze, not sure where to go. My friend Louie lived nearby. I was in pain now and really needed some drugs. Louie always had some weed.

"Louie, I just crashed my car, man," I said, blood dripping out of my mouth. "I really need some weed."

Louie was disgusted, but he handed me a pipe. The smoke actually hurt my broken nose and mouth as I blew it out. But I kept smoking it anyway. Louie walked me back to the crash. There was my classic car, my pride and joy, the car I had spent $10,000 rebuilding, totaled. I'll never forget the look of scorn Louie gave me.

25

Morally Bankrupt/ Condemned to Death

After I crashed the Road Runner I went into my first rehab. I called up the Musician's Assistance Program, and they set it up for me to go into Tarzana Treatment Center. Sick and shaking herself, Sherry drove me in the Honda CRX to the rehab, checked me in at the counter, and waved goodbye. Orderlies stripped off my clothes, left me naked in a room, and then a big male orderly conducted a thorough strip search on me, sticking his finger up my asshole looking for dope.

Back then Tarzana had a huge male dormitory with twenty-two guys in a room all kicking dope—sweating, sniffling, snoring, farting, tossing, and turning. There was only one shower and one bathroom that everyone had to share. Every morning we all lined up for our methadone. Tarzana was one of the first rehabs to take in people with HIV, so there were a few guys there with the virus and a few with full blown AIDS. It was 1988. They were still figuring out how the AIDS virus worked. At Tarzana they gave them a cocktail of around twenty to thirty pills per day as well as protein shakes to help them gain weight. This was a real wake up call for me.

There was some scary tension as the big macho guys coming in from prison clashed with the little dope addicts with HIV. After two weeks of methadone and therapy groups I wanted to go home, but every morning we would have morning mediation and talk about our feelings. Then we would have an AIDS 101 class where people came to tell how they got the disease. They told stories about sharing dirty needles, unprotected sex, rape, prison rape. The stories were mind boggling for a little punk rocker from St. Louis, but I knew I was one of them—that it could happen to me. We also had a nurse tell us where to get clean needles, and how to bleach our works, as bleach killed the AIDS virus. She also showed us how to use condoms properly—and, of course, abstinence was always best.

We also had multiple groups on how your brain operates on drugs with words like dopamine and serotonin. I just wanted to take a nap, I was overloaded and not sleeping at night.

I ended up leaving against medical advice. Sherry was really happy to see me, as she had been off dope also so we decided to do something normal like go to a movie. But before we even made it to the theater I gave her the *I want some dope* look, she gave it right back, and it was on. Back to Sixth and Union. Oh shit, heroin is so good after you haven't had any for a couple of weeks. That one night, just that quick, we started the vicious cycle all over again.

Wherever we went, we took our dope habit with us. We developed the daily dope frenzy—cop, shoot, cop. Dealers made house deliveries to us at all times of the day. I was going through my royalty checks well before the end of the quarter. Rent was late, lights and power were getting turned off. I started selling all of my instruments starting with my classic guitars, a 1977 reissue Flying V, a 1960s Mosrite bass, and a 1956 Gibson Les Paul Junior that I bought for a hundred bucks from Anthony of the Wounds in San Francisco. I sold my 1970s Hagstrom Swedish bass, my nine-string Framus guitar I'd bought from East Bay Ray, my Yamaha FJ 600 motorcycle, and my record collection. Finally, I sold my Pearl drum kit that I'd bought off Jack Irons from the Chili Peppers.

When my stuff was gone I sold everything else, Sherry's guitar, the stereo, her record collection, the TV, whatever was around. Waking up in the morning with the jones on me, I would put whatever was left to sell in the back of the Volkswagen and gun it to the pawn shop.

Sometimes when we were in the valley copping we would go to our friend Larry's to get high. Larry was this mellow hippie stoner dude from L.A. who I briefly lived with when I was in SSI. He always had vegetarian food in his fridge and would tell tall tales of his travels to Amsterdam and smoking hash at the Melkweg (Milky Way). He also had a huge, successful scrap metal business. I worked for him for a while picking up scrap metal and delivering to a recycling plant. Then we would cop and go back to his place. We ran into Kevin, the old guitar player from SSI, and he was strung like a string of train cars from the locomotive to the caboose. Larry was a coke smoker, but Sherry, Kevin, and I quickly turned him on to heroin.

He got strung out immediately. He'd had a huge, six-foot tall safe full of guns and weapons, rifles, shot guns, semi-automatic Glocks, Brownings, Walther PPKs, you name it. As his habit grew he started to sell and trade his guns with drug dealers for dope. Eventually he sold his entire gun collection, which had classic collector guns and street sweepers. He wound up selling all of his belongings, including his business, which he sold for about $30,000—a mere fraction of what it was worth.

Before he had sold all his guns he came up with an idea. "Let's make some quick money," he said. "All we have to do is knock off some 7-Elevens and convenience stores, it's real easy."

There was no way I wanted to risk going to prison, but it was all right with me if Sherry wanted to do it. So they started robbing convenience stores. Sherry was the driver and Larry the gunman. He would burst in, waving his pistol, pistol-whipping anyone who gave him lip. Back at the shit hole I would be sitting by the window with the lights out waiting for them to come back, intense with dope cravings. The sound of the car pulling up and the keys jangling was music to my ears.

Sherry was impatient because she wanted to go first, but so did I. It was always a battle. The first time she fixed herself she overdosed. One day I came into the room, and she was lying on the bed, so skinny and wan, weighing about eighty pounds. Her lips white, her skin blue. I realized in that moment that she was maybe the only woman I had truly loved, and that she was about to die. "Fuck! Don't die on me!" I cried. I picked her up and got her in the shower and screaming, "Don't you die on me!" I slapped her till I finally got her to come to.

She came out of it, as if nothing had happened. "Darren, let's go to the park!" she said.

I was thinking, *no, I don't want to go to the park. You were dying and it took me twenty minutes to revive you...no I don't want to go to the park.* And that was how our life was. One minute we could be overdosing with a nice pile of dope, the next we could be splitting a popsicle for dinner.

One day I heard the helicopters circling our apartment. I knew it was for us almost immediately. Earlier that day Sherry and Larry had done a big robbery. I heard the jingle of the keys when Sherry opened the door. She had a few balloons of dope and coke in her hand. Dope was in the red balloons, coke in the green ones. Sherry went into the bathroom to fix. I was in the living room. After a few minutes I heard the sound of helicopters. I looked around and saw the shadows of people moving into tactical positions outside my window, the silhouettes of guns in their hands. I heard cop radios blasting. Then Sherry came out of the bathroom drooling, oblivious to what was going down outside.

"Sherry, the cops are here!" I said.

"What?"

The cops kicked open the door. "LAPD!" Six cops and two detectives with guns drawn burst into our living room.

We could barely move off the couch. We just watched as the cops tore through all of our stuff. It's a real rollercoaster ride when you're doing speedballs. The euphoric phase-shifting-sizzling-coke high hits first, then the heroin rolls in and drops you like a lowrider into that who gives a fuck zone of altered reality. They could have taken me to jail, or to Hell. I didn't care. I was high and nothing really mattered. The cops didn't even bother to try and detain us as we were limp as rag dolls anyway.

Apparently, the police had followed Sherry and Larry from a convenience store, busted Larry, and had now come to arrest Sherry.

As they knew that Sherry was the driver and Larry the gunman, they put her in a cell and interrogated her for hours. They tried to get her to roll over on Larry. She was scared, and they threatened to give her seven years for accessory to armed robbery, so she cracked. She snitched him out. She gave them what they needed to make a solid body of evidence against Larry and to lessen her charge.

Her parents freaked out. "That damn D. H. got our daughter strung out and doing armed robberies," they said. Her father was really pissed. He said lots of things to me that weren't very nice.

Sherry went to jail for a short amount of time, but all I could think of was that with her gone, there would be more dope for me. She called me regularly from jail and got out around thirty days later to go into the drug deferral program. For her it only took one time. It was 1992, she spent eighteen months in impact, and it completely changed her life. She stayed clean, started doing real work on herself, and got back to being the girl she had been or truly was.

I stayed in my self-imposed prison-hell. Because I hadn't been paying rent the sheriff finally showed up. "You are evicted. Get whatever you need, but you got to go," he told me. "You're out."

I tried to act surprised, but I couldn't fake it. I knew the jig was up. I handed him the keys. A few days later I snuck in the back window with some works and an issue. I fixed sitting on my mattress; it was the last of my worldly possessions, the only piece of furniture left.

I had met this girl Jill through some tweaker acquaintance. She had a crib up on Sunset behind The Comedy Club next door to the Hyatt. It was easy enough to move in with her, so the next day I did. I became her man-toy till she got tired of me. She moved into a huge drafty loft downtown. I lived with her there on and off. I had become an official couch surfer with a P.O. Box. I got a $10,000 DK royalty check, and the money was gone within a month. I was lying to myself that it was all part of the plan to get off the shit. *Fuck, when would it stop? Who was I kidding?* I was dead already and didn't even know it.

Since I had sold my guitars and my drum kit, I became a singer. I was the new singer in Reverend Jones and the Cool Aid Choir. I didn't dig the name so I called Jello Biafra and asked him for some ideas about names for bands. He suggested Chocolate Dinosaur, Al Sharpton's Hair, and a few other obtuse names that I can't remember. We finally settled on Al Sharpton's Hair (ASH) and eventually became Peligro.

Dawn, a friend of Sherry's, introduced me to Tools who played guitar, Pat who played bass, and the sixteen-year-old drummer, Andy, who still lived with his parents. When I am using I have no pride, no ethics, no heart. Andy looked up to me and wanted to do the same things I was doing. I turned him on to dope so that I could con him out of the money his parents would give him. Then I would coax him into stealing things from his house to pawn. I watched him OD more than once. Andy started hearing voices in his head, walking around, muttering under his breath. The voices in his head told him that he was to kill his stepfather. As Andy's schizophrenia came on he went from a clean-cut kid with acne to a bugged-out-dirty-haired-dreadlocked-psycho-white boy in a couple of months. The heroin was his way to self-medicate. But then he started getting violent with me and accusing me of plotting to kill him. I had to get him in a headlock and call his parents.

A good six or seven years after the headlock I saw Andy downtown at the dope spot. He was copping some cheeba and so was I. I was waiting for the guy to come back with my issue. I recognized Andy by his walk and his dirty-dirty-dreadlocks. I looked up. Our eyes met. I looked down. He was obviously homeless, and I had a home to go back to after I copped. I didn't want him to ask if he could stay with me because it would be hard to refuse him. I still loved the guy. But those kind of people come over and they never leave. Besides, I had taught him how to steal so he'd probably steal all of my shit. So I just hung my head down and put up a wall. He paused when he passed by me, but the corner was hot, there were cops everywhere, so he just pushed on up the street.

Several years later I heard he died of an overdose downtown.

In 1990 or 1991, Al Sharpton's Hair needed a drummer, so Tools got George, an Armenian guy from the valley. My money had run out, and I had no place to stay, so I convinced George it was just a temporary run of bad luck, and he moved me into his place. He and Tracy lived in the house and had day jobs. At first I planned to use the time to write some songs and focus on music. I did this for maybe the first week. I stayed there for a year, and then I wound up back on the street.

I got paid royalty checks every quarter but the money was gone after the first few weeks or so. I'd party for a few weeks, feel fine, chipper, lots of energy; then I'd be sick for months just scraping by trying to get well. I thought smoking crack would keep me from getting strung out. I hooked up with a girl named Deidra who was jumping in and outta cars on Cahuenga sucking dick for drugs

D. H. PELIGRO

and smoking crack with her girlfriends. They were all willing to share their earnings with me. They loved me and they were always horny, but for some reason I didn't want them to know I was a heroin addict. I thought they might lose respect for me. Although I never judged them for doing what they did, there was always some stigma about needles in comparison to crack pipes and alcohol. It's all the same to me, but I'm mostly alone in that thinking.

Around that time I started stealing CDs and stuff from George and those guys, selling bits and pieces of their musical equipment. I found a gun and thought about robbing some convenience stores like Larry and Sherry. But all I managed to do was shoot a hole in the ceiling. I was under the illusion that I was going to stop using any day, that I was going to get back on my feet and start playing music again. I would be sick for a couple of days and get well, get sick, get well, get sick, get well, round and round like a pack of angry ants.

I had run out of veins so I started skin-popping dope. That's when the abscesses began. The bacteria would build up underneath the skin and turn into a pus-filled bubble. I didn't know what it was the first time I got one. When I squeezed it, out came the foulest smell, like a pile of dead dogs. I squeezed it some more to get all the pus out. It hurt like hell so I had to do some more dope to not feel the pain. Whenever I had an abscess I would get this taste of bacteria in my mouth. It tasted like a combination of cold metal, phlegm from a bad flu, and what you'd imagine an old maggot-crusted dog carcass roasting in the sun for two weeks tastes like. When I got that taste in my mouth, that's when I knew it was time to get down to the pet store and purchase some pet antibiotics. The fish stuff was the cheapest. Then I would resume popping in the same places in my leg, thigh, and buttocks.

At night, so George and Tracy wouldn't see me high, I would go over to Dave's house. Dave was a guy I knew who had a crappy band and liked me to come play bass, even though I was completely strung out and pretty useless. One night I picked up the bass, got into my rock stance, then suddenly I felt something wet roll down my pant leg. I was so disconnected from my body I didn't even realize I had a huge abscess in my hip. It had busted open and a huge chunk of flesh fell out, rolling down my leg and landing—splat—on the floor. I was so out of it that I didn't give it two thoughts; I didn't care.

Dave almost threw up, but soon collected his courage. He went into the kitchen and put on a pair of big rubber gloves. "I don't know if you have AIDS or what," he said, picking up the lump of flesh and putting it into a plastic bag. "You need to go to the hospital now."

I told him I would go right away but wouldn't let him take me. I didn't go; I went back to George's. It was around 11:00 P.M. He and Tracy were asleep, so I went into the living room, where I'd been couch surfing, and shot up some more dope instead. I didn't even look at the huge open sore on my leg. I just got some gauze to

D. H. PELIGRO

cover it up. I didn't care if I lived or died. In fact, death would have been preferable.

Instead of dying that night, I waited until George and Tracy went to work the next morning, and I shot some more dope. I lucked out and found a vein to hit. I was coming out of the bathroom then I just passed out on the floor. I'd wound up with cotton fever. When I came to I was so hot I took off my clothes, but then I couldn't stop shivering. I remember, vividly, lying there on the hardwood floor, curled up naked in the fetal position. I would have cried if I could, but I couldn't stop shaking. I finally passed out.

George came home from work and found me there. He looked at me and said, "Yeah muthafucka..." He bee-lined to the chest of drawers I had near the kitchen. He found a drawer filled with bent and blackened spoons; and box of a hundred syringes among dozens of old, dirty rigs, clotted with blood and tar residue. "I should sock you!" he said. "Get out!"

I put on some clothes and stumbled out. I had nowhere to go so I just sat down on the curb. I was losing so much blood that I passed out on the street. This lady who lived in the front house took pity on me and let me sit in her back yard to escape the blazing, brutality of the hot sun.

"You need to get to a hospital," she said.

The insanity of the disease is unbelievable. Again, I decided to get some dope first. After leaving her yard, I caught a cab and checked into a seedy hotel on Hollywood

Boulevard so no one could bother me. I came to, dizzy, wrapped in blood-soaked sheets. I finally decided it was time for me to get some help, which sounded easier than it was. I went to Queen of Angels, and they said, "Get the fuck outta here, ya fuckin' junkie!" At least that's what it sounded like to me. More than likely they said, "We can't take you, you have no insurance." I went to a bunch of different hospitals. Even the Free Clinic wouldn't take me because my wound was too big, and they told me to go to County Hospital. I finally collapsed in the street. An ambulance brought me to County Hospital. They had to let me in then. After four days in the emergency room, and after the doctor cut out all the necrotic tissue, I had a hole about the size of my fist in my hip. I could see through to the bone.

Over the next week or so they kept the wound in my hip clean with a wet-to-dry process. The nurses put the wet gauze in a solution then packed it into the wound, let it dry, then they snatched it out—you had to, pulling it out slow was unbearable—which took away all the dead tissue. They did this twice a day. It was excruciating; I would scream so loudly they had four male orderlies, three nurses, and the doctor hold me down and put their hands over my mouth to muffle me. I was so strung out that the pain meds weren't doing that much, and the hole was just too fucking big. I dreaded the twice daily cleaning and packing process; even the tape they used to secure the gauze would rip off hair and bits of skin from my leg. The whole area was a tinderbox of

D. H. PELIGRO

pain. The horror, agony and anxiety made me crazy. I had a morphine pump and regular hits of Valium and Demerol, but I could still feel every little thing. Every movement equaled pain.

Six weeks later they discharged me from County. When I got out I stayed a couple of months with a friend of Sherry's in West L.A. I met these cats, Danny B. and Lazy, who took me to some of my first NA meetings. I started to get clean. My hip was still healing, so every day I had to pack the wound with gauze, clean it out regularly. After about a week or two I finally broke down and got some dope. My justification was the pain, and I told myself I deserved it because I had suffered so much.

Everyone knew I was going to use, and I was considered really bad news. Sherry was in Impact at the time and Scott, a friend of hers, warned her to stay away from me. Everyone expected me to die any day now, but some people helped me. Danny B. took me to meetings and let me stay on his couch. "Don't steal anything," he said. Sometimes he took me to work with him so he could watch me. Overall he was a pretty good guy doing what he could to help a brother out.

A few weeks passed, but I still couldn't stop using. Finally Danny B. said, "Man, you gotta go."

I was driving around in this beat up Honda Civic, sometimes sleeping in my car, sometimes in some seedy hotel. I wound up in a hotel on Ventura Boulevard and shared a room with a skinny white boy, Eddie, who came from Florida to fulfill his dreams of becoming a famous actor. He became a Hollywood hustler. I could only afford a single so we slept in the same bed. He didn't try to fuck me or suck me; he only did that for money. Once again, I hit bottom. I was out of money and found myself at Sherry's door again, asking for a handout.

She let me stay, and I got sixty days clean. Then I relapsed. "You can't stay here, you gotta go," she said. Again. She told me about Union Station Foundation, a homeless shelter in Pasadena.

So I went there. During the intake they interviewed me to see if I was an addict or an alcoholic. Those were the magic words, if you didn't admit to being one or both they didn't let you in. They served three meals a day, feeding anyone who wanted a meal. If you wanted lodging, you had to admit you were an alcoholic or a drug addict, which still didn't guarantee you a bed. Sometimes they didn't have enough space for everyone who qualified. A woman with a kid would definitely get the space before anyone who was alone.

Once you got a bed, to keep it you had to follow their curriculum. You had to attend three AA meetings a day; you couldn't sit around there the whole time. They only let you in for sleeping at eight in the evening. You had to be up, ready, and showered by seven in the morning. We had individual areas petitioned off around our beds for more privacy. There were little drawers beneath each bed where you could leave your stuff, but you had to be out all day. You had to be looking for a job or picking up donated clothes. Basically, you had to be out doing something to better yourself.

D. H. PELIGRO

Volunteers came in to cook the meals. All the homeless people would line up for free food. Every day I had to tell them I was a vegan, that I couldn't eat meat or dairy products. I started talking to this pretty half-Asian Christian girl. I was thinking of ways to get in her panties, but she started spitting the word of Jesus. Turned out she was a volunteer and a hardcore born-again Christian.

"Have you been saved? What do you want to do about your problem?" she asked me. She was such a hardcore Christian that she made a pact with Jesus to be of service, so she slept in the shelter with us for a week. She drove everybody crazy with her Jesus jargon. But she sure was hot. If Jesus had lived in her pussy I would've been all about it. She made sure I got my vegan food; that was good enough for me. I wanted to fuck her, but I didn't want to hear all about Jesus.

Randy, this African cat who was living in the shelter, said he stopped smoking crack and cigarettes. He had seventy-two days clean. I thought that was miraculous. "How did you do it?" I asked.

"I surrendered," he said, "I threw my hands up. I gave up everything I thought I knew. Just gave myself to God."

I couldn't conceive of that at the time. Every time I relapsed I thought of Randy. This guy was giving me something that I wasn't able to grasp at the time, but over time it started to make more sense.

It soaked in when it soaked in; I wasn't ready for it yet. I started thinking of ways I could just leave and come back to the shelter. I went to my P.O. Box, and, miraculously, I had a check. I figured I'd cash the check and chip a little cheeba and shuffle on back to the shelter. Juwan, Butch, and Tony were some of the holier than thou ghetto brothers there. They were ex-Muslims from the Nation of Islam—funny how they could pray six times a day, then smoke crack and find fault with me for being on the nod at a meeting. Nobody else knew or cared that I was high, not even the facilitators. They didn't give a shit. But Juwan, Butch, and the gang would say shit to me, "You gotta turn yourself in man. I saw you man, you was high. You was noddin' off."

"Man, fuck y'all," I said. "This is my program, mothafuckas."

They said, "Naw, this is an honest program, *mothafucka.*"

After a few days the guilt started to eat at me. I started to cry and went to Bill, one of the counselors. I said, "Man, I've been using."

Bill hung his head in disgust. I think he thought I was a good guy, and he didn't want to throw me out. "Aw, D. H. You know the rules. You have to sleep outside the shelter for a week or two and show us that you really want it. I'm sorry man. You can eat here, but you can't sleep here. Now roll your shit up, you gotta go."

I slept outside the shelter in my car for two days. It was unusually cold and rainy for Pasadena in December. One morning I woke up and thought I had a cold, but it was a bad case of the fuck-its. So, I left the shelter

D. H. PELIGRO

and went back to Hollywood. I ended up staying with a Dominatrix hooker named Kiki on Hollywood Blvd. and Orange. I was a little high, but I believe I had met her a few years earlier when she was one of the Jane's Addiction dancers. Anyway, I traded my Honda Civic for a Dodge Colt and kept it parked next to the dumpster in the alley behind her place. I would go sleep in the car while she turned tricks. Her pimp was this tall, black, pockmark-faced-jerry-curl-wearing-skinny-little sleazeball who came around every week. He always had crack and always begged us for some heroin, but almost every time he used he overdosed. After he had gone blue on us a couple of times we learned to only give him the tiniest bit, but he would still OD. So we'd pick him up, throw him in the bathtub, put some ice on his nuts. Why we saved him, I don't know. We hated this motherfucker; we knew he was ripping us off. He'd sell us tiny kibbles of crack for twice the price. I knew where to get it cheaper, bigger, stronger, but it was a hot zone, and you could get arrested easy. So, to play it safe, we just bought our crack kibbles from him and bitched about it.

One day, Mr. Pimp insisted on another hit and overdosed in my car while we were waiting for Kiki to turn a trick. "That's it," I thought, "I'm not savin' yo ass this time." I reached over, opened the door, and kicked him out of the moving car. He came to clutching the door as I drove off.

"Why you doing this to me?" he whimpered as he hit the ground still holding on to the open door.

I just reached over and slammed the door on his hands. He rolled over on the hard concrete, looked up at me, whined, and passed out.

I abandoned him there in that empty parking lot. Then I drove a few miles away, parked, and turned on my little battery powered TV to watch the football game. Looking back I can't believe how little respect I had for my life or anyone else's. I eventually drove back around, and he was still there. He lifted one hand up and raised one of his fingers as if to say, *I'm O.K.* When I told Kiki she went to see if he was still there, but he was gone. We never saw him again.

Kiki was still turning tricks. She hated her life and what she'd become. She was far, far away from the respected dancer she had once been. She was now just another Hollywood whore. Sometimes she would take off all of her clothes and sit on the sofa with her arms wrapped around her knees and her pussy hanging out begging for any kind of real affection. She'd look up at me with her big cow-eyes and beg me to fuck her. "Please, Dirty, please," she said.

I was too strung out. The love of my life was lady heroin; I didn't care about fucking. I just couldn't give her what she needed. We'd all felt this way, sick of this life, and hoped that it would be over soon. Only Kiki did something about it; she pulled up a hundred ccs of the uncut cleanest dope she could find and pushed it into her vein. Her eyes went black, her skin went blue, and now she's gone forever.

D. H. PELIGRO

When you are hurtling downhill it gets worse faster and faster. Pretty soon I was in a scene I didn't want to be in. I went to the Bart Methadone clinic on Hollywood Boulevard and Cahuenga for a twenty-one day outpatient methadone detox. I told myself I could kick, but I was also using. At the methadone clinic, where you meet all lower forms of scum, I ran into a guy I'd lived with and used with before, a guy named Mark, a real lifer. He had every kind of government scam you could think of, Medi-cal, SSI, GR, welfare, you name it, plus his mom was an old Jewish co-dependent who would give him money sometimes. I knew him from the first time I had been on the methadone program. So, this time around I told him I didn't have a place to stay but I had money.

His eyes lit up a little bit, he grumbled, then he said I could stay with him for a little while. He had an apartment on Ogden in West Hollywood. Our daily routine was to get up at 5:00 A.M., go to the methadone clinic, score crack, Klonopin, and Valium, then I would crack a couple of King Cobra 40s and get back by 6:30 A.M. so we could get fresh, hot, sesame rolls from the Russian bakery. There was always a parade of freaks coming in and out of his apartment in West Hollywood; they were mostly gay dudes.

Reggie, one of the freaks in this parade, was this queen who hustled gay men for money and crack. He was like a gay pimp, really, hooking rich guys up with the young Hollywood hustlers. One of his regular clients was a very wealthy Australian man. Reggie told me I could make money if I just went up to this guy's house with him.

"Well, what would I have to do?" I asked.

He said, "Just hang out. He likes young black boys. You're cute. It's easy money."

Plus, he told me there would be plenty of drugs. So I went with Reggie to the guy's mansion in West Hollywood. It was a luscious place, full of sculptures, paintings, and tapestries. He took us into his bedroom. The hardwood floors were painted luminous ivory, the walls deep burgundy, and beside the far window was a huge canopy bed draped with gauzy silks in shades of chartreuse, purple, fuchsia, and lavender. I sat on a nearby chair next to a table covered with crack, a pipe, and bottles of booze. I immediately started smoking and downing Hennessy while Reggie worked. They were so into it they stopped noticing me so I took the guy's wallet while they were distracted. Finally they came up for air. "Will you join us?"

Tweaked out of my mind, all I could think of was if it would get me more drugs. I would do anything. I grabbed a condom and put it on, even though I had total coke dick—my dick shriveled into its turtle shell. As soon as I looked up at them I freaked out, put on my clothes, and started to leave, but not before I asked for my money. He gave me forty dollars with a disgusted look on his face and said, "Don't come back."

26

Gripping to the Grave

I went back to Mark's a couple of days later. I stopped down the block because his house was completely surrounded by cops. The next morning I found out at the methadone clinic that he had done a big shot of coke and his heart just exploded. The first thing I thought about was not the sadness of a life lost, but how the fuck I was going to get in his house. I had sold him a gun, and all I could think about was how to get in and find it before the cops did if they hadn't already. Mark also had a chrome shotgun, and I wanted that, too. I had no place to live, but I wanted that chrome shotgun.

Walking the streets I had what alcoholics refer to as a moment of clarity. It was as if the entire world stopped, went silent, and I stood there looking at where I was standing, what I was doing. This is bullshit, I thought. So I called up my Mom and my sister Dianne. I told them I was desperate, strung out on heroin. My mother and sister told me they would check out the rehab situation in St. Louis. As soon as I knew help was on the way my moment of clarity faded and the courage it took for me to ask for help dwindled into remorse. I was ashamed and didn't want to go see my family in that shape. But I figured I would just stay in St. Louis for a while.

Back in St. Louis I got on a methadone program. Normally a methadone detox lasts about a month. Because I was from out of town they said, "Not only do we not give out as high of a dosage as you're on, a hundred mg, but we can only dose you down for a week." As your methadone detox progresses the lower your dose, the sicker you get. They started me at sixty mg and said all they could do was lower my dose by ten mg a day over a five-day period. I thought, *Shit is about to go down. Here comes the serious sickness.* If you've been on methadone for six months, to your body, it's the same as being on it for two years. I know, I'd done it before. Methadone gets in your bones and starts to eat away at your bone marrow, so your detox has all the classic symptoms of kicking heroin—only ten times worse. Back pains, profuse sweating, insomnia, insomnia, insomnia—I didn't sleep for nearly month—not to mention vomiting, diarrhea, anxiety, depression, and chronic fatigue.

So I called up the rehab, DART. It was the ghetto-est of ghetto rehabs I had ever seen. It was filled with ex-cons. Everybody was black, except Henderson, a classic alcoholic complete with the shakes; Mary, who worked as a tech; Josh, a guitar player; and a toothless, scraggly-haired lady, Lynn, who worked in the kitchen. They dosed me down for three days, but then I had to kick it cold turkey. "We ain't got no meds for you. You shit it out like you shot it in," said Helen, a plump, dark-complexioned nurse.

I was shocked at the horrible food they gave us. "I can't eat this! I am a vegetarian!" I insisted. I was a California junkie who stuck by the motto Health Food and Heroin. They looked at my scarred up arms and skinny legs and laughed at me. "Uh huh, Precious...you *really* know how to take care of yourself. Shut up and eat, or don't."

I talked to Lynn the cook, and she said I would have to talk to Mike, the head administrator. Mike came down to talk to me. He was a short, slim black cat with round glasses, a buzzed and tapered, freshly-lined haircut, altogether a conservative look. He wore khaki pleated slacks, tan hush puppies, and a tan and black plaid shirt with a solid black skinny tie. As Mike and I kept talking I noticed he had a serious stutter. "You were in D-d-d-d-Dead K-k-k-k-Kennedys," he said. "You're famous. We don't get many celebrities in here."

It had been a long time since I thought of myself as a rock star. Mike never judged me, he just loved me and said, "I'll go to the health food store and get you some vegetarian stuff. I'm a vegetarian, too."

I thought, *Awesome, thank you, God!* Now I could eat. If I could hold it down.

Then Mike asked, "You're from L.A.?"

"Yeah," I said, "but I wasn't born there. I'm from St. Louis."

"So you know Fred?"

"Fred Dickerson? No shit. Fred works here?"

"Yeah," said Mike.

Fred was the cat who had convinced me to come to California in the first place. I didn't want Fred to see me like this, but when I did see him, it was like old times. He called me by my old nickname, Headly, and brought in an old Jungle Studs record we had recorded together to show off to the techs. He seemed very proud of it. He had become very pro-black at this point, and he'd give me long speeches on blackness. He also brought in a *Billboard* book that had me listed as one of the top drummers that had influenced bands like Pearl Jam, Nirvana, and hundreds of other bands.

Woody, our bass player in the Jungle Studs, told me that Fred took it really hard when the Jungle Studs broke up. Now Fred had the upper hand since he was a tech-nurse and I was a patient. He felt it was his duty to scold me.

He said, "I'm not surprised you're here, Headly. You were always in the fast lane, running with the fast crowd, doin' the fast things. I always knew you were gonna crash."

He was right, but I didn't want to hear it. It's funny how your friends can see things in you that you can't see in yourself. No matter what, I still loved Fred. I loved him for what he'd done for me, how he'd sparked a fire under my ass to get me to come to San Francisco, and opened me up to a whole new world.

After about a week and a half I was still feeling sick. I went to the counter to ask for some help from Ms. Joyce, a bullying tyrant fireplug of a woman with huge '70s style glasses and an orange afro, who worked at the nurses' station. Instead of giving me meds she started telling me about how she kicked heroin cold turkey and how she was from Detroit, and if she could do it so could I.

After three weeks I started to feel a bit better. Two new arrivals from the penn were Jerry Wiggins, who we affectionately called J-Wig, and Eugene Culpepper. We called him Coldpepper or Pep. J-Wig did twelve years for attempted murder. Pep was about 6'3". I think he did four years for domestic violence and aggravated assault. Once I asked J-Wig, "Man, you did twelve years in the penn? No time off for good behavior? No half-time?"

He just hung his head with a look of defeat and said, "Yeah man. Twelve calendars."

Shit. He was only thirty-two. You could see that the correctional system had stomped a mud-hole in his ass, completely broke his spirit. He stayed close-lipped about his crime, but he followed every rule in DART. When brothers complained about rules he said, "Man this ain't shit, this is easy time."

Every night we would talk twenty-nine miles of shit before we went to sleep. With four guys to a room everybody had to outdo each others' stories.

A guy named Vince had the most wicked story of all. He said, "Ya know how to rape a guy in prison?"

It got real quiet. I said, "Uh, no, how?" as I scooted my butt up against the wall.

He said, "First, four dudes hold him down. Then you take a mop handle and shove it in his ass and twist it around until you hear a snap. Then you know you've ripped out the *grippins*...THEN you rape him."

I was like, "Oh my god! Really? Shit." It was hard to get to sleep that night worrying about my grippins. The next day I wrote a song with the lyrics: *When I get out gonna be no slave gonna keep my grippin's to the grave... grippins to the grave...grippins to the grave.*

Later on Vince dated my sister. When I saw him with her I could only think about the grippins. Vince had too many baby mamas calling him up, so my sister finally kicked him to the curb.

The protocol at DART was morning meditation, breakfast, chores, and all day groups. We had to do chores. The bathrooms, the dinning room, television room, dayroom, group room, and the bedrooms had to be cleaned every day. There was no eating and drinking in the bedrooms, but with a bunch of cellmates for roommates somebody was always smuggling some Zoozoos and Wham-Whams in the bedrooms for late night munchies. Roaches feasted on the crumbs and scuttled around the rooms while we slept. You always had to have some house shoes or shower shoes to get to the bathroom, which was another dangerous place to go at night because we were near the Mississippi River where the cockroaches grow big as mice—it was a real cradle of filth.

I refused to work in the kitchen because they served meat every day. I opted for clean-up coordinator. I had a

D. H. PELIGRO

clipboard with a list of everyone and their chores, which were rotated weekly. I had to check everybody's chores and make sure they were done, then check them off my list. If they weren't checked off my list, I had to turn them into any one of the techs, which caused a lot of static as the prison brothers didn't want to do their chores. Since I was friendly with everyone, they thought they could take my kindness for weakness. They didn't know that I was from St. Louis just like them. They thought of me as a California boy so I had to assert some authority, and they did not like that. That position made me learn to not take shit so personal.

At DART I spent my free time in the corner of the room listening to music and writing songs while everyone was watching television. I was writing and listening to Megadeth and the *Last Action Hero* soundtrack. As far down the scale as I had gone, I was still full to the brim with ego. I resented having to do any of the inventory writing that they made us do. *I shouldn't have to do this.* I thought, *I should be writing lyrics. I have important artistic work to get done. Don't 'cha know.* One day when I was listening to and jotting down the lyrics to "Angry Again" by Megadeth, I didn't know how to spell some words. Now me, I'll just ask somebody, like a little child does, "How do you spell that?" I asked this guy James how to spell "contortionist." He jerked his head back and said, "DAMN! What the fuck is you' writin'? Ol' Satanic-ass nigga," he muttered. "I don't know, man, here's a dictionary."

James was cool, but like so many people in the Bible Belt he was afraid of things he didn't understand. I realized then that I left St. Louis and had worldly experiences that these guys would never have. Part of me thought I was better than them because of the places I'd been, the things I'd seen, and my musical accomplishments. But I wasn't. After all, I was back at DART.

I started feeling sorry for myself and resentful. I mean, why was I the one in rehab? Dave Mustaine was as big a junkie as I was. I knew because I had gotten high with him. How'd he get a record deal, and I was suffering in this funky, stinky rehab? Maybe it was because he had surrendered and I hadn't yet.

27

Quest Mataquaisie

After a month, I came out of the rehab and moved into my mom's basement for five months. I really wanted recovery, and I walked that line, went to meetings everyday and my aftercare program religiously. I knew I was beat. I really wanted to get my shit together, start making music again. I had made a good friend, Mary, who was one of the techs at DART. With her encouragement I began to write music again. She had a little eight-track recording studio, and we started recording. I bought a white Stratocaster from the pawn shop and a crate amplifier that I still own today. Later I bought a jazz bass.

The first thing I did in my mom's basement was to relearn and practice playing guitar. My sister groaned and told me to get back on the drums, but I was stubborn. With Mary and the help of her friend John Kristofferson, we made a full demo of all my new material. First, I laid down the tracks individually: drums, then guitar, bass, and I put vocals over the top of that, then we'd mix it. Some of the material was revamped versions of songs I had done with the Hellations, Speedboys, and SSI. My main goal was to get my own band together when I got back to Los Angeles. Many of the songs I wrote in that basement were on the first album I made with Peligro. My ambition and drive slowly returned. I started to feel that old fire in my belly, that electric inspiration and the drive to make it happen.

I was also doing some intense soul searching at the time. What is this thing called spirituality and where could I find it? Mary told me she knew of a medicine man named Scotty. He was a long-haired freaky white boy from Chicago who had all these weird stones that he would make pipes out of and go on long hikes. He would hold up his Native American objects to the light and give us reverent lectures on the native gods. He'd already done his vision quest earlier, and that's when it was revealed he was supposed to do the Sun Dance ritual.

My understanding of the Sun Dance ritual was that he was to smoke the peace pipe and make offerings to the four directions including the sun and the sky. Self-torture was part of the ritual. The flesh of his chest and feet would be pierced with hooks from which he would hang. The pain was part of the rite, a sacrifice he made for the good of the tribe.

One day Mary took me on a trip to meet Scotty and another friend, Chuck, up in Joliet, Illinois. Scotty told us we were to meet a very powerful medicine man, that we should be honored to be able to visit him. We went to a small house in the countryside. It was Tracy Lost-

Bear's house. Tracy's grandfather was eighty years old, in a wheelchair, and on a respirator. They called him Grandpa, and he lived with Tracy. We waited on the curb while Scotty went over and talked to him in a native language then he let us inside.·

In the back yard there was a teepee made from bits and pieces of used plastic and canvas held down with rocks. Scotty was running things and began digging a hole. We gathered rocks and Scotty had us place them inside and outside of the teepee in a special order. We had to walk around the circle counter clockwise so we didn't interrupt the spiritual flow of energies. Scotty started a fire and put the rocks in it with a pitchfork. This was to be Scotty's first pour, the first time he was allowed to pour water on the rocks during the sweat lodge purification ceremony. After they'd heated we placed the hot rocks in the teepee then went in wearing loincloths.

We followed Scotty in his chants. "Mataquaisie," we chanted, thanking the Great Spirit and passing a pipe of medicinal herbs around. As I took a puff off the pipe a huge cloud of blue smoke came out of my mouth. I knew no one else saw this; it was a powerful experience. It really felt as if the toxic devils that had been running around inside of me were released. Emerging from the teepee we lay our faces on the cool earth, and I felt the black, still night surround me. I felt held by an indescribable being that let me know it was okay for me to be here, on the planet. I felt a sense of purpose and destiny. It felt like I was communicating with an entity—an amoebic, amorphous presence. This was my first spiritual journey and perhaps the strongest connection I have ever felt with a higher power. I was able to let go of my mother's God, the bleeding Jesus on the cross, and feel my own conscious contact. Then and only then would the old man in the wheelchair talk with me; he held me in his gaze, talking to me without words. My experience that night in that funky, hot teepee is what I remember as I pray and meditate in the steam room of the YMCA today.

With the money I saved not paying rent and not buying drugs, I bought a brand new 1994 Mustang. I had been talking on the phone with Sherry quite a bit. She was clean, doing really well, and we still had love for each other. So I called her up and suggested that we take a trip together, just drive across country, see America, share some clear, sober time together, and she agreed. She came first to St. Louis and hung out for two days with my family. Being together again was awkward, but we had to make plans for the trip so that gave us something to do rather than dwell on the past.

We were intimate the first night on the road but it felt cold. I was fresh from rehab and really horny, but it wasn't like it used to be when we were both high. She was reserved, and I felt really self-conscious and unsure of myself. I was much more relaxed and comfortable in the days while we were driving; it was much easier than being intimate. We remembered that before all

D. H. Peligro

the using we were genuine friends, that we liked each other's company. We talked a lot about being clean and sober, about appreciating our new lives. We spent two weeks on the road. We drove through the Black Hills of South Dakota; Jackson Hole, Wyoming; the Grand Tetons; Yellowstone National Park; the Badlands; Bryce Canyon; and Zion Canyon.

We drove through the desert for miles and miles. I imagined what it was like when it was Indian Territory and how land would have been when Indians lived there.

As we drove, surrounded by the beauty of nature we felt the wind and the sun on our skin. Light beamed into us and we, in turn, beamed it onto each other. It was wonderful. With the weight of the monkey off of my back I was finally able to enjoy life. But it was not all dreamy. Sherry put her sobriety first and was not willing to take any bullshit from me.

We drove across back to Los Angeles. Sherry had a nice place in Pasadena, and I assumed she would let me move in with her as I didn't have a place to stay, but Sherry was for real. I couldn't stay with her, and she would only talk to me if I went to meetings. For two weeks I stayed part of the time with her, part of the time couch surfing until I found a place in Koreatown.

28

Up the Downward Staircase

While in St. Louis I had sent the demo I made with John and Mary to Jello at Alternative Tentacles. I was still with Alternative Tentacles and had carte blanche to at least get a record released with them. After I moved back to Los Angeles, I talked with Jello. "You need a band," he told me. He was right, although my huge ego told me it was fine the way it was.

The first guy I asked to join was a fantastic drummer and old friend, Atma Anur. We got one of Atma's former band mates, Diz, to play bass, and that was that. I didn't know Diz, but I had met Atma in 1981 through Matthias Mederer and David Weiss at Hyde Street Studios. He was pure metal; he played with a pre-Megadeth Marty Friedman in Cacophony. Atma was a rock by numbers kind of guy. He talked and analyzed too much. At one point Atma ran his mouth so much that he got kicked out of Journey. He had the audacity to criticize and correct Steve Perry, who was known to be a dictator.

Peligro rehearsed in Los Angeles and then arranged a way to get up to San Francisco to record. It felt great, being full of my old energy and fire, able to scream and yell at the world again. Our crowds were small but people did come out to support us. I was glad to see Dr. Know and the Fishbone guys come to a gig we did at House of Blues. After we did the Peligro record we joined the Social Chaos tour, which included D.R.I., D.O.A., The Business, The Vibrators, Lower East Side Stitches, One Way System, T.S.O.L., and a few other bands.

Tight-ass Alternative Tentacles didn't want to give up any money to help me out with tour support and management even though Dead Kennedys accounted for 70% of the label's record sales. "We don't do that," Jello said in his high-pitched, nasally voice. So the record was released with absolutely no publicity or support. Both my band members had wives and kids and needed to get paid. I was going out of my mind trying to make it all work for everyone. I was completely obsessed with getting the band up and able to support itself. All I thought about all the time was money and tours. The band, and my way, was all that mattered. It became more important than recovery. I became self-willed and didn't put as much as was needed in my sobriety. I was going to meetings, but I was not reaching out. I did not open up to people and let them know me. The only thing I thought mattered was my need to be famous.

My back was hurting, and I told myself it would be all right to take some pills for the pain. There was this infamous bakery on Beverly where I knew they sold painkillers smuggled in from Mexico. I started taking Mexican diazepam, thinking, *Fuck it, ain't nobody gonna know.* In a matter of days I was back downtown copping heroin.

One day I went to Sixth and Union and bought a veinte of cheeba. I went back to my little place in Koreatown and shot it into my right foot and BAM I went out. When I came to my right leg was swollen up to five times its size and I couldn't move. I freaked out and I called Pete Weiss. "Pete! Help me out, Pete. I... fell downstairs and broke my leg," I lied. He came and picked me up in Flea's multicolored Mercedes, and that's all I remember as I passed out.

Somehow Pete got me into Cedars-Sinai, and they rushed me into I.C.U. When I came to my eyes were hot pinpoints of pain and my vision was blurry. I tried to move, but I couldn't lift myself up, and I couldn't feel my right leg or foot. When my vision cleared I saw that I had tubes running in and out of my arms and legs and a pulse monitor gripping my right index finger. I was covered in sweat, and my hospital gown clung to me. My leg looked fat and wrinkled, like it had elephantiasis. I panicked. Would I be able to play drums?

A nurse came in and checked my IV bag of pain medication, then a tall, spidery white doctor entered the room. "Hi, Mr. Henley." His voice was tired and dismissive. "Let me fill you in. You had a massive heroin overdose. Somehow, I don't know how, you've survived. We don't know what the long-term effects will be, but it does not look good. You have sciatic nerve damage and you may never be able to use your right leg. You also have

D. H. PELIGRO

what's called renal failure, I am sorry to tell you. That means you'll need a kidney dialysis machine, maybe for the rest of your life. First visit will be this afternoon, okay?" He paused, staring at me. "Was it worth it?" He sighed and left the room.

I would've cried, but I was too fucking sad for tears. The diagnosis was that I had Compartment Syndrome in my right leg and that my kidneys had failed. When I OD'd my brain told the rest of my body I was dying and my organs started shutting down one by one. Fluid collected in my right leg beyond the capacity of the connective tissues that surrounded the muscles to contain the swelling without muscle and nerve tissue starting to die. When I came to all the blood rushed back into my system, but it was coagulated so it hit my kidneys like mud on a screen door and my kidneys just shut down. On top of that, just as crucial, I had nerve damage from my neck to the bottom of my foot. The only treatment for Compartment Syndrome is a fasciotomy. Basically, they sliced into the sides of my leg, splitting apart the connective tissue that encased my muscles so the fluid could drain out of them. There was so much muscle and nerve damage, if left untreated my leg would have been amputated.

After the surgery, my leg atrophied to the point that it was half the size of my other leg. Even to this day I still experience pain, numbness, and electric pins and needles in my leg, and my foot will never be the same. There's less springy recoil in my foot when I walk, a necessary thing for drumming that I have to compensate for when I play.

As I drifted in and out of consciousness, another nurse came in, climbed on top of me, knees on my chest to pin me down, grabbed a foot long needle and pushed it into my chest. She had to probe around first, and I felt like I was meeting my death on the end of a Samurai's sword. She sighed in satisfaction as she hit the right spot and connected the central tube line directly into my heart. I was flooded with unbearable pain. "What the fuck is this for?" I asked.

"Just lay still," she said brusquely. "You're going into kidney dialysis. It will be a while." I had three competing sites of pain. As well as the tube into my heart I had a catheter in my dick, and my leg was hot and throbbing like pins and needles yet numb and able to feel all the pain. It felt like days before they came and wheeled my gurney down to the kidney dialysis floor. I felt like I was truly in a *Night of the Living Dead* movie.

The dialysis room was dominated by a huge, silvery-white machine, which sat in the middle humming and buzzing. It was lined with a series of pumps, filters, and tubes ending in needle points, like a huge Giger painting. There were people laying everywhere around the room, all of them skinny, weak, and sallow; it was pretty clear that this machine was what their lives revolved around. I lay perfectly still on the gurney in a paper robe, covered only by a thin sheet. The machine began to pump, sucking the blood out of my body and sending it through a series of filters.

D. H. Peligro

As I watched my warm blood go into the machine a deep frigid frost completely filled my body, like I was a corpse. I felt like I knew in that moment what it was like to be dead. I lay there for an hour and a half watching them pump my blood out and then pump it back into me. It felt like an eternity. I was so disgusted by the blood. Finally they disengaged the tube that ran from my heart to the machine and wheeled me back to the room, but the heart valve stayed, sticking like an alien out of my chest. From time to time they would come and check it for infection. As far as I knew, I would have that thing sticking out of me for the rest of my life. Like the rest of the undead in that room I would have to visit that machine twice a week.

My drug detox was heavy, and I started having sleepless nights. The pain medication they were pumping me full of made it worse. I was getting even more strung out from the liquid Morphine in my drip and on the Demerol and Valium they were giving me. It was a pharmaceutical junkie's fantasy, only I didn't want it anymore. My dreams became weird, twisted, sexy, and horrific. In one of them I was in a hellish sex dungeon laying on my back, strapped to a rack. One taut-bodied, tattooed dominatrix straddled my cock whirling her neck, her hair flinging as she oohed and ahhed in an orgasmic frenzy. The other vixen sat on my face smothering me, grinding her clit into my lips. Her pussy tasted like a combination of an airless, odorless rainbow of antibiotic medication and an onslaught of bacteria from all the gnarly abscesses I'd had before. A dead-dog discharge taste whipped lightly into a yeast infection soufflé. Right before I was about to come, the face-sitter shot me up with a half-gram of pure China White. As it hit me my pupils shrank, the come spurted, and a flood of bile pushed from my belly to my throat. Her cunt was clamped to my mouth, so the vomit seeped out the sides. She was suffocating me. I couldn't breathe. I wanted to push her back but I was tied to the rack. Vomit spewed from my nose. I couldn't breathe. She was coming and didn't see me. Then the heroin high hit me. The fat lady sang. I blacked out and fell into a dark hole.

I came to screaming, sweating, and coming. This Asian nurse came in, "Are you okay?" she asked.

"Ahhh...I just had a crazy dream," I said and kind of stared at her for a minute because I didn't really know where I was. Being in the hospital you can get so disoriented.

She said, "Oh, it's okay. I can give you something to help you go back to sleep." She gave me a glass of water and two Ativan.

I didn't want to go back to sleep. I was scared. But I didn't tell her that. It was drugs and I'm a drug addict so I took it.

In the days that followed I began having horrific nightmares. In them I was surrounded by dead and dismembered bodies. After the first of these dreams, the theme was always the same: every night I was trapped in a never-ending state of dying, unable to get out or rise up to free myself. Each night ran scarier than the next.

One night I dreamed that I was strung up to a tall tree by a rope around my neck, but I was unable to die. I was to be kept there, swinging and suffocating for eternity. I had another dream that an angel came to me. There was a brilliant white light around her and she hovered effortlessly, coming towards me. As she came closer my skin began to crawl. She came right up to my face, her nose almost touching mine. She opened her eyes. They were black, cold, and hollow. I knew it was the angel of death, but once again she passed me by. Why my body would not give up is a miracle, or a bad joke.

After three weeks the Asian doctor said my kidneys had started working again. I could pee on my own. I got physical therapy for a little while, but I would be in a wheelchair and on crutches for a few years on and off after this accident.

As I was discharged they gave me a bottle of Vicodin and I let them. I came back again and again to get refills. "We can't give you any more of this," the doctor told me as he gave the last bottle to me. There I was, no band, no money, no nothing. I was a hopeless, disabled guy. I did not want anyone around to see me like this, skinny, unable to walk, unable to feed myself. For the next two years I would go back and forth from a wheelchair to crutches, and I dwindled down to one hundred and thirty pounds.

Although I couldn't walk I was still getting to meetings, thanks to my friends who would come and pick me up. Mark Greville would come and get me in his Porsche. He would lift me into the seat and shove the wheelchair in the hatchback where it barely fit. Everyday I sat at the window, listening to the sound of buses and kids playing. I desperately wanted to make up for the way I had ruined everything so I started working on some songs. These days were beautiful in a way.

Some guys had not completely given up on me and would still come by. Sherry moved in downstairs, and I became friends with some of the neighbors who would also come visit me. But I had not really stopped using. I felt entitled to take the Vicodin. I was taking about twelve every couple of hours. When I ran out of the Vicodin the pain returned and so did the cravings. I kept it a secret, and it only took me a couple weeks to start using street drugs again. I blamed it on the pain. To get in the shower, I had to prop myself up and could not stand on my leg as it hurt like hell. Heroin was the best painkiller. When I used I was able to put my foot down. Three weeks later I was dragging myself onto the bus on crutches, sweating bullets, rushing and hobbling to cop dope. Then I would come home and just want to die. Please, God, just let it be over. I killed all the nerves in the bottom of my foot so even now I have a limp. It's still really hard for me to walk around barefoot.

Thank God Musician's Assistance Program was willing to help me again. This time I went to Liberty

D. H. Peligro

House, a treatment facility run like the Third Reich. Every single thing we did every day had to be according to a plan. The punishment for any little infraction was to write an essay on our behavior or we would be put on restriction for thirty days. We had to be downstairs with our beds made by 7:00 A.M. We all had breakfast together, then morning meditation.

Next up, chores. Everybody had to do chores on a rotation, had to take shifts cooking, cleaning the fridge, sweeping and mopping the floors. There was horticulture detail. Some people got the cushy jobs like vacuuming the living room and straightening up the office. These went to the people who had been there for a year or more, which I couldn't fathom. There were two mandatory therapy groups a day. In the evenings you had to discuss your plans for the next day to the whole group. If you didn't have a job you had to make two meetings a day. After thirty days you could leave for a weekend pass, but all your passes had to be approved twenty-four hours in advance. Weekend curfew was 11:00 P.M. If you were late you were locked out and had to sleep outside. There was a house meeting every Tuesday. If something was out of order, someone wasn't pulling their weight or just fucking off, they would get grouped.

When you got grouped you had to sit in the middle of a room surrounded by everyone. They would go around in a circle, pointing out your character defects. This was fucked because you thought these guys were your friends. Having to say such horrible truths about each other was trying, but it brought us together more than it tore us apart. Some guys would sugar coat it if they liked you and not dig too deep. But if it was a motherfucker you didn't like, you just unloaded on him until he broke down and cried.

Once a week, on Tuesdays, a facilitator would come in and give us a therapy session. The therapist was an older, gray-haired lady in motorcycle boots. *Trying to be hip*, I thought, *and hustling clients for her private practice.*

Pretty soon I was nurturing my resentments, feeling like a victim. Of course this could have justified my using again. First, I grew resentful because I had to pay out of pocket. I felt entitled, forgetting that MAP and Music Cares were paying for two months of the stay. I refused to cook because I was a vegan and 90% of the people in there were meat eaters. People stole my food. There was always a line for the bathroom, the shower, and for the refrigerator. Even in the early days when I was sick, kicking, and on crutches they wouldn't understand and let me sleep in. They didn't care that I was sick and achy, you were not allowed to sleep during the day.

I was angry and resentful all the time and hated all those nosey motherfuckers around me, prying into my life. I got into a fight with some guy and Larry, the owner of Liberty House, assigned me a five hundred-word essay.

"Five hundred words? Are you crazy?" I said.

"One thousand words," he replied.

"You trippin' man."

"Two thousand words."

"Kiss my black ass!"

"Five thousand words."

"FUCK YOU!"

"Ten thousand words."

I shut up after that.

I had to wear this fucking dunce cap and sit in a corner. A friend of mine in the house named Alex was a writer. "Hey, man, you got any of those essays, around? Can I get one? Let me get one of those essays, man, hook me up," I whispered to him like it was a Compton corner dope deal or something. So Alex gave me some of his essays. I dated them, put my name on them, wrote a bunch myself, and handed it all in.

I was so full of ego. I thought I was better than all of the other guys in there. One legged, all high and mighty. During one of the process groups I was the one sitting in the chair in the middle of the room, "D. H., you are not helping out enough, you are not taking enough people to meetings or looking out for your brothers like you are supposed to."

All I thought was how geeky the other guys were, how they would ruin my game at meetings when I was flirting with the girls. In my mind I was Casanova, socially savvy and popular. I had been around forever, and I could talk to people. But the point was that these were supposed to be my newfound brothers, and I was supposed to be looking out for them and taking care of them.

They restricted the amount of time I could leave. I had to ask permission to go to the studio. "You still haven't taken responsibility for yourself and your addiction," they said. They were right. I stayed in Liberty House long enough to feel better, but not long enough. There were people who had been there for two years and still hadn't graduated. *Bullshit!* I thought. *I am not spending the rest of my life in here. Having to ask permission to go to the studio? I am a grown ass man.*

I left on a pass one day and never came back. I went home and did the same crap all over again. I still had Dead Kennedys residuals to live on, and I pawned everything, guitars, my car, and my amp. I used alone mostly, but there were always other people to use with. When I got out, Jay came over to use with me. He was losing everything quickly. I had been so jealous of him because he was Megadeth's guitarist while I was in the DART rehab. Meanwhile, Dave was in town and on a bender. We all sat around and got loaded, me on my crutches talking about the good old days, then his wife came over and dragged him out screaming and fighting. Then she threw his ass in rehab.

A couple of weeks later I was back on the phone for help. I called Buddy Arnold from MAP. "You again? There's no hope for you! You gotta stop wasting our money and wasting our time!" Still, he managed to get me a placement at the ranch in Desert Hot Springs. "I want you here twice a week for MAP groups after you get out," he said.

Geza X drove me two and a half hours out to the ranch in Desert Hot Springs. The Ranch was no more than a bunch of little shacks. It was full of white trash girls, tweakers, and Indians from the reservation. At night the coyotes howled and during the day vinegaroons, rattlesnakes, and scorpions snapped at your feet as jack rabbits fled for their lives, sometimes getting picked off by rattlesnakes.

Vinegaroons looked like scorpions without the stingers, but it was hard to tell which was which. If a vinegaroon bit you everything you ate for a week tasted like vinegar. If a scorpion stung you and you didn't get to the hospital in time, you died.

There were two or three people to a room the girls in one shack, guys in another. Regardless, everyone was fucking everyone else.

Even though I was desperate when I called Buddy, as soon as I got in there I wouldn't surrender. My boy Dave had hurt his back lifting a boulder. They took him to the hospital and gave him some pain pills. He was a tweaker and he didn't want them, so he gave them to me. I took them all. After three weeks I called it quits and left the ranch. Then I called a taxi to take me to the Greyhound Bus terminal. Straight off the bus I was downtown and back at my place in Koreatown.

Robbie, who was watching my apartment, answered the door. "Lizard, what are you doing here?" He called up Geza X, who was furious.

"What the fuck are you doing? You know how long it took us to get you in there?" I really took for granted all those people who tried again and again to help me. I was at it again for a year or so. Then I landed in County Hospital with another huge abscess that almost killed me, this time from skin-popping Dilaudids.

Strung out, sweaty, and stinking, I had an eight by three inch spongey lump on my left thigh. The orderlies did my intake and decided that I needed immediate surgery.

When I came out of the surgery, I could hear them talking. Now this was weird. I was supposed to be unconscious, yet I could hear them saying "What's this scar, what's that one?" The doctor started poking around, and I said, "No, that's from another overdose and another abscess," only I couldn't speak or move. I saw them and I heard them but I couldn't speak a word. I guess I came out of the anesthesia partially but not totally so they started cutting on my arm which had some small lumps. I was saying, "No, no, no, no! I signed the release form for my leg. Not for my arm!" But they couldn't hear me because I couldn't talk.

I came to about thirty minutes later, and they were squeezing puss out of my thigh and leg. It was flying over their heads and landing on their masks and face-shields. Their scrubs were dripping with really stinky puss; the smell was heinous. I could tell that they were exhausted after the procedure. From my experience you had to push really hard to get all of the puss out.

After I left the recovery room and was back in the orthopedic ward, the doctor came around to my room with a team of student doctors, "This is Mr. Henley, a thirty-four year old African American. He has what's known as a shooter's abscess. We extracted approximately a liter of puss from his left thigh." The doctor showed them the wound and they ahhhed and oooed and cooed and booed then left. I felt lower than a fly on shit.

Sherry came to pick me up from County Hospital, and I went back to Tarzana. They didn't want to admit me because of the size of my wound, since I didn't want a skin graft at County Hospital. I couldn't take one more operation. I refused, and the doctors left it open. Again I had to do a wet-to-dry treatment. Tarzana said, "We are a rehab, not a hospital, and your wound will take a lot of maintenance." They still let me stay five weeks for a detox, then moved me to the Tarzana Family, which is a residential treatment.

I met a guy named Jay Bird who had just gotten out of prison and was a Nazi low rider who would later be one of the head guys at Cri Help. Robbin Crosby from Ratt was my roommate, and later some kid from Chicago named Matt from the band Mary's Window lived with me. We would sit and play guitar together for hours.

Then Robbin came out with the shocking news that he had HIV. He seemed to know all along but was keeping it a secret. When he told us in group we all cried. There were a lot of people there with the virus, as Tarzana was the best place offering the care they needed. This was an eye opening experience for me. I really understood how easy it would be for me to die. One woman had been infected after sleeping with a guy one night, and he knowingly gave her a load of infected semen. But everyone there had such a will to live, to stay sober no matter what, despite their ailments. It gave me hope and humility. If they wanted it, in their situation, then I had better want it too.

But my disease got the best of me again. I was going back and forth from rehab to the hospital for my abscess. I started groaning about the pain, and they gave me some Codeine 3s. I consequently failed the daily drug test and was asked to leave the Tarzana Family. This time I cried. I almost got it this time, but I knew right then I was going to go back to using.

Sherry had given up. "I can't help you anymore," she said. I listened to the familiar cadence of her voice, a voice that had always soothed and consoled me. I could hear the love in her breath penetrate the warmth in my heart. I knew that she had released me with love. Now, I conceded to dying. I had destroyed all of my friendships. No one wanted to be around me.

Then I got a phone call. It was Anthony Keidis. "Hey Dirty."

"Yo," I said.

"What's up?" he asked.

Now, I heard he was out on a run, and I knew he had dough. So I figured I was going sing him some sad, sad song to get some money so I could cop some dope. But what came out of my mouth was, "Help. I'm strung out. Can you help me, please?" I started to cry. I just didn't want to do this any more. "Please help," I cried.

He said, "I'll call you back." I think he called Music Cares because he called me back and said, "I'll be over to pick you up in the morning," and he took me to Las Encinas to detox.

29

The Sum of Our Surroundings

By this time all the detox units and rehabs and were full of musicians. I knew, and had worked with, some of them. This time I was in Las Encinas with Brian, a filmmaker, who turned out to be my best friend, and John Frusciante, who had really changed from his young Green Horn days when I had first met him. John went from being the straight young kid to the most rampaging junkie of us all. He used more drugs than a drugstore.

I remember Bob Forrest telling me stories of John shooting and snorting more heroin and coke than we had ever seen. He was just this little kid who went from being in Thelonious Monster to being in his all time favorite band, the Chili Peppers. He had to follow in Hillel's footsteps, one of his favorite guitar players in his favorite band, like Chris Farley after John Belushi. Since all of the artists and musicians John admired used drugs, he thought he had to, too. Fame and fortune had not been good to him. As soon as the big money came in he started using like a monster. He was snorting, at first, huge piles of it, then he went and bought maybe $10,000 at a time worth of heroin and coke and went on epic binges while he was painting and writing music. Eventually the house he lived in burned down. Instead of calling the fire department he grabbed a few things, went to the neighbor's house, and called a taxi.

He called Norwood from Fishbone for help. Norwood and his girlfriend Michelle put him up in the Mondrian Hotel. It got worse in the Mondrian Hotel with blood splattered on the walls, his classic guitars sold to pay off the bill. Then he toured with Norwood, who looked after him, and got a big check, which he spent on crack. He looked like a cadaver, doing yoga in his Fruit of the Looms, all these positions with his balls hanging out. John's addiction was just as gruesome and as much of a gore-fest as mine. The disease mangled his body as it did mine. He had to get all his top teeth removed, otherwise the fluid building up in his head was going to push into his brain. The only way to get it out was to take out all his teeth and drain it through his open gums. His arms blew up with puss and were so swollen they stuck straight out.

He had incredible cocaine psychosis and became convinced that there were police behind his eyeballs. He was screaming, "There's pigs in my eye! There's pigs in my eye!" and he tried to dig them out with a spoon. He popped his eyeball trying to get the pigs out of his eye and when they found him it was hanging by two tentacles. Flea had to take him to the hospital to put his eye back in. Afterwards, he still had an eye fixation—even years later when we were in Las Encinas. He was sure that he couldn't watch color television and would only watch black and white. So we had to put up with hours of Marx Brothers, *The Twilight Zone*, and The Three Stooges. That was is until we got an advanced copy of *Jackie Brown*—my boy Brian was in the academy, a special effects supervisor and cinematographer. "Oh, this is the new Quentin Tarantino movie! Put it in!" From then on color was okay, apparently.

After detoxing in Las Encinas, I went back to Liberty House. There were a lot of musicians there this time as MAP started sending them there. They instantly put me on restriction with no time limit. They put me in that process group and just broke me down. "Did you forget?" They asked. "You used the last time you were here. Remember when you were in a wheelchair and on crutches? And then you went downtown and got some dope. Not only that but gave it to another guy in the house, Mike, who killed himself. Goddammit."

I didn't think about what that really meant, only that Mike Roberto, that motherfucker, had snitched on me. "You're fucked up, man!" Larry, who ran Liberty House, shouted at me. "You need to get the fuck over yourself, get over your ego and your problem with authority!"

While I was in Liberty House I would see Flea from time to time. I had such conflicting feelings about being kicked out of the band, but I could also see why they did it. I still had a level of animosity toward them I had to keep under wraps.

Anthony had some time clean by then. He would always come up and give me a hug at meetings. He really took an interest in helping me stay clean and started coming to visit me when I was in Liberty House. We walked and talked, and he really helped me to see how I needed to take responsibility for my addiction. I started to make peace with what had happened. I was finally able to let go of my resentment and be friends with them again.

Eventually, I did tell Anthony that I held a resentment against him because I felt the Peppers threw me to the wolves and kicked me to the curb when I was down, then left me at my lowest point where I felt I had nothing left to live for—granted I was selfish, egotistical, insecure, and strung out like a lab rat. He held his head down and said, "I know." We looked at each other in the eye, hugged, and then let the healing begin.

I also began to heal other relationships that I had neglected or destroyed. Norwood called me up and came to see me. We resolved the rift that had come between us. He had been really angry at me because I wouldn't tell him where his ex-wife Sandra went when she ran off, and he knew that I knew. That burned him up because he felt I had broken the black man's code of honor and kept him from seeing his own child. But it was big that he was coming to see me. He wasn't a junkie but had really borne the brunt of everyone else's addictions. He had been at the center of all of us as we self-destructed. Norwood had always been like the brother figure among us. He felt it when we were hurting.

He had been close to Hillel, and our behavior at Hillel's funeral had infuriated him. His band mate Chris betrayed the band, stealing from them. Then Norwood and his girlfriend had taken care of John Frusciante through the worst of his gruesome adventure, putting him up at a hotel and employing him.

Flea and I began to hang out again. At one point when I was in rehab, every morning I would get a pass and go to his house to workout. He had bought this amazing million-dollar house up in the hills, across from a Frank Lloyd Wright house. He had this beautiful main hall, in the middle of which sat an eighteen-foot tall Yogi statue in meditation. It was a tremendous sight as its blessed body rose up into a ceiling that was as tall as the observatory. I loved visiting there.

He had this wonderful, friendly Bull Mastiff named Martian who weighed about 160 pounds. I also loved his gardeners Sally and Peter, two hippy activists, who had sculpted this beautiful landscape all around his house. When they would start in on some eco-friendly talk Flea would just roll his eyes, but I loved them. I still see them today when we go to feed the homeless out in Pasadena at Christmas and Thanksgiving for the Union Station Foundation.

The street Flea lived on was a steep upgrade from what I was living in. As part of our workout, we ran furiously up and down the hill. Flea had a new set of weights so after we ran we'd lift weights for a couple sets. Pretty soon we had a name. We called ourselves The Stud Club and had t-shirts made up with our names on them: Stud 1 and Stud 2. We were sitting around brainstorming, trying to come up with a slogan to put on the shirt. It was 1999, just about to turn 2000, so Flea came up with "Spreading the Joy of Studliness Throughout the Next Millennium." At the bottom it was signed "Nietzsche." But after about a month Flea wimped out, "I don't want to do this anymore," he said.

Just as The Stud Club was coming to an end, Bob Forrest organized a big birthday party for me, and Flea agreed to host it. So many people came. I was overwhelmed. Anthony was there, Norwood and his new girl, a sassy New Orleans ghetto sizzler, our old friend Sweet Pea, people from the PG, the Pepper's tour manager, Louie, Dougie from Teenage Millionaire, artist Phil Bower, John Denny, Richard Edson, and Flea's mom.

I was clean and sober, and I felt overwhelmed with happiness and really grateful for my life. It was hot, everyone was eating and laughing, enjoying a harmonious good vibe. I was having a great time running around. I had jokingly told everybody to bring me a present, and they did. This made me feel uncomfortable. I still didn't feel like I deserved anything good.

Some people were starting to get out of control. We had done the best to keep out the riff-raff. Flea knew most of the people there, but some people were getting in under the radar, coming in just to say they had been in Flea's house. All kinds of strangers were coming in drunk and being really disrespectful of Flea's space. Flea started to get a little bit edgy. "Dude," he said to me, with those serious blue eyes. "Dude. There's people hanging out here throwing cigarettes on my lawn and throwing trash everywhere. And they're feeding my dog. I specifically told people not to feed Marsh."

Then people started roaming around his house. He went from edgy to pissed off when he saw people were smoking, drinking beer, standing really close to a huge Jean-Michel Basquiat hanging in his central hall that was worth about $100K, and they were climbing all over the Yogi. It was a nice neighborhood and all of these people were coming in punk rock style, fucking shit up, parked all crazy up on his neighbors' lawns. These weren't the punk rock days anymore. Not like we knew it. We were supposed to be grown ups.

When I saw that this was out of hand, I started to clean up, but I got distracted. I was really overwhelmed by the attention, the gifts, people being friendly and warm with me. I felt like I was being given yet another chance with people, actually back in the land of the living. I got overexcited, as I do, and I guess started acting like a kid myself. I left quickly without really saying goodbye as someone was honking for me.

The next time we talked I apologized for the anarchy in his house. "It wasn't that, dude," he said. "It was that you didn't even say thank you." That just crushed me. I know I'm a better person than that, and I was definitely feeling thankful. Here we go again, I thought. Somebody gave me an opportunity and once again I didn't do the right thing. That old shame that I had tried to get away from by using came back with a vengeance. I was that grubby, second-class citizen running around the projects. But I felt especially bad because I really, really loved him. I still do.

The next few times we hung out things went wrong. I met him for lunch and then to go to a gallery with him and his daughter. He was driving this beautiful Porsche, and I was riding my friend Brian's Harley Davidson. I parked next to his car. We spent too long in the gallery, and both of us got tickets. "Here, you pay this one too," I said, and threw the ticket to him to pay.

He said, "I know I'm a rock star and everything, but that's fucked up. That's not right." And he was right. I could have paid that. And I should have been more responsible to park the bike properly anyway. It sounds small, but I felt like it was the hugest thing. He brought it up again the next time we met at The Viper Room.

I was starting to mess around with the guys, not doing serious music, but silly things on stage. Every Monday night at The Viper Room, Manny Chevrolet hosted Fantasy Island, where Manny would come up with these fantasies, and we would act them out. We put together crazy skits before the bands came out. That night the Circle Jerks were playing. Me, Jeffrey Lee Pierce from Gun Club, Pete Weiss, Bob Forrest, and this lively girl choreographed a skit. The story went that she got bitten on the ass by a poisonous snake. Her last wish was that she could have Stevie Wonder suck the poison out of her ass. I was Stevie Wonder. In the second part of the skit, Eldridge Cleaver wanted reparations for hundreds of years of slavery, so Bob, Pete, and Jeffery came out in white sheets and Klan hoods and I beat them with a whip while singing "Jump Down Turn Around Pick A Bail Of Cotton." As I beat them, I made them say: "Yes, Master!"

Afterwards, Flea and I were hanging, and out of the blue he brought up the ticket again. I knew it was about more than the ticket. He had been really hurt and disappointed in me and was letting me know how angry he was at my selfish behavior. It felt like our friendship could never get back on track, or at least we couldn't pick up as we were before.

But we didn't totally lose each other. When I got out of Liberty House I found a little one bedroom in Silver Lake next door to Maureen. Flea came over to see it, and we spent some quality time sitting on my little futon. We chopped it up, I played some guitar, and we reminisced about old times. The thing that hit me was he said he liked Henry Rollins, and I said, "Yeah me, too." He said, "The thing I like about him is he's so into being Henry Rollins." I thought, I should be more into being D. H. Peligro. Nothing more, nothing less.

Before I moved into that studio, the shit started hitting the fan with Jello and Alternative Tentacles. We found out that Jello had been underpaying us royalties for years. All the other bands were getting paid a higher royalty rate than Dead Kennedys. DKs accounted for most of the sales in the catalog—fifty to seventy percent of the label's total income. It was only fair we should be getting paid at the same royalty rate as whatever fucking pet bands Jello had at the time.

A lawsuit started brewing. Soon Jello was calling. It felt like he was trying to manipulate me like he always manipulated everyone for everything he wanted. Was Jello trying to befriend me? Even the odds? I thought what he really wanted was for it to be an even battle—East Bay Ray and Klaus Fluoride on one side, Jello Biafra and D. H. Peligro on the other side. He knew he had a better chance of winning if he conned me into being on his side. I was vulnerable, just out of rehab, damn near ready to do anything, but something in me knew that it was wrong. I was going to go with the band.

Besides, I was in the band, and we were the ones being underpaid. He was the one that filed for complete ownership of the record label after we supposedly started it together. He reaped the profits and grabbed all the money. Why am I living in a fucking hovel where gangs are constantly at war in front of my front door, when he has a giant house in Noe Valley? We are the guys that helped you get to where you are, and this is how you treat us? Fuck that.

The next two and a half years were a very trying time in my life. I had to go back and forth to San Francisco for the court appearances and the trial. I started going broke. Every time I went up there it tore my heart out to have to listen to all the lies. We wanted to settle it out of court, but Jello refused. He didn't want to let us see the books. He didn't want us to see that he was wrong, like a little selfish child. I could practically hear him saying, "I'm right, and that's that," while he stomped his little foot.

Now, a crisis and territorial disputes can pull a band together or tear a band apart. In the case of Klaus, Ray, and me, we grew closer. After a tumultuous two-year tug of war, the rope slipped through Biafra's fingers. Be it justice, or equality—however you slice it—the right thing was done. We won the lawsuit. All the expensive lawyers and all the King's Men couldn't put DKs back on Alternative Tentacles again. Klaus, Ray, and I decided to release a live album from shows in the Bay Area called, *Mutiny on the Bay*. After all we'd been through I really wanted to get everybody together. I suggested that we play a show to celebrate the release of the record.

I started looking for a new singer. Eventually I found Brandon Cruz, a former childhood actor who had starred in the 1970s television show, *The Courtship of Eddie's Father*. I knew him as the front man in the band Dr. Know. He was a true Dead Kennedys fan. He agreed to sing for us, and the show was great. Chuck, a booking agent from Artist's Worldwide, came up to us after the show and suggested that we do a tour. We told him we'd do a couple of gigs and see how it worked out.

So began a new era for Dead Kennedys. What a surprise it turned out to be. It felt fantastic doing what

I loved to do, playing drums and touring again. Now that we could relax after the trial, we actually started having some fun. An incredible amount of fans were in attendance, and we were playing not only for the old fans, but for a whole new generation. *Some of these kids weren't even born when the band first came out,* I thought. But these kids knew all of our songs. It was the year 2000, but the music was still relevant for the times. When we played the X Games, it was amazing to see how we influenced skateboarding, snowboarding, biking, and other extreme sports. I had young drummers coming up to me, telling me how much my drumming had inspired them. It really lifted my sense of self.

30

Jets to Brazil

With Brandon Cruz as the singer we toured across America. We mostly played for crowds that varied from four hundred to twelve hundred in the clubs. We'd eventually do festivals where the crowd ranged from 35,000 to 110,000 people. There was still controversy going on, though. Jello started talking to the press, calling us "the world's highest paid karaoke band." Jello's supporters came to some of our shows to heckle and throw stuff at us on stage, but it didn't stop us. We wrote the music and played it because we loved the music, and for the new generations that wanted to hear it and didn't get a chance to see us back in the day. Kids in small towns who listened to our recordings were so glad we came and that they got the chance to see us live. Some of the best shows we did were in Canada. The crowds were psyched.

Our worst shows came later, in Mexico City, after we had gotten a new singer, Jeff. Jello put out flyers slagging the band and this started a full-blown riot. Jeff got hit in the arm with a Jack Daniel's bottle. I got hit with a brick. It was mayhem. We co-headlined with The Misfits so all their gear, their amplifiers and instruments, were on the stage. It all got thrashed.

In Europe and South America we played lots of festivals where the crowds were huge. One of our best gigs in Europe was in Leipzig at the With Full Force Festival. We played with Slayer, Rob Halford, and Biohazard. Slayer was pissed because they got held up at the German border, and we were the only band they wanted to see at the festival. The day before, we had played at the People's Festival in Prague with Agnostic Front in the rain and mud. However, the weather didn't deter the crowd from having a good time. They fucking loved it.

On our first tour we ended up going to South America. Argentina has a huge punk rock following. The two biggest bands of all time in Buenos Aires were the Rolling Stones and the Ramones so we were well received as we played at Cemento, a rock solid concrete club. It was packed. I couldn't remember that kind of reception since we had toured in the early '80s.

Some of the smaller spots we played were really rough. This is where I learned to appreciate how good we have it in the United States. We played one really divey place in Cordova. The stairs were rickety with nails sticking up everywhere, and we had to crawl down between two walls and up a ladder to get to the stage. All of the stage equipment was outdated, rusty, and falling apart. The electrical cords were dangerously plugged into janky looking sockets. During sound check we could see a couple of them sparking and smoking. The techs didn't even blink, they just kicked out the fires and kept going. The drum kit they provided for me was a broken down rusty set of buckets with a dangerous broken dagger-looking snare stand. But this was what they had, so I had no choice but to use it and play the best show I could.

After Cordova we went to Chile and played to a gigantic crowd. We pulled up to a forty foot gate with kids screaming and beating on the side of the van bellowing, "DK! DK! DK! DK!" It was a huge arena with massive security everywhere manned by guards with huge water cannons at the ready. At first I thought that was too much like a police state, but after I saw how crazy the fans were I realized they needed those hoses. Coming onto the stage, I heard my name chanted by what sounded like a million people. "Pe-li-gro! Pe-li-gro!" They liked that my name was Spanish. It felt like they knew me. So I went to give them a handshake and they mobbed me, tearing at my dreads, tugging and pulling at me, knocking me over, and dragging me into the crowd. Way out of control. After I fought them off and got back on the other side of the barricade I thought, *Holy shit!* These fuckers are crazy. I knew the fans were full of passion, but never, never have I been mauled like that.

After that gig, we were to leave Chile and head to Brazil. We were on our way there, but somehow Brandon overslept. By the time we got all our exit papers, passports, and gear to customs, we'd missed our flight. Ray was pissed. We couldn't get a flight out unless we were in business class, and we'd have to pay out of pocket for that. So we tried to cancel the gig. We called Matthais, our Brazilian tour manager, and he said, "Hell no. If you don't get on the next flight there's going to be a riot. Leave now." So we came out of pocket, paid for business class, got on the next flight, and high tailed it to Brazil.

We skipped the hotel and went straight to the venue. Matthias was yelling and snapping his fingers, rushing us. Backstage we got dressed and ready to play. I went out to check the drum kit. I peered out to roaring applause and saw the floor covered in beer, vomit, and the sweaty condensation of a merciless crowd of bloodthirsty renegades ready for war. When they saw me they started chanting like Brazilian soccer fans, "Pel-li-gro Pel-li-gro Pel-li-gro!" My heart pounded like I'd shot up ten grams of cocaína. I ran backstage and told the guys, "It's crazy out there! Let's go on now before they tear this place apart."

We walked onstage. I started "Forward to Death." The crowd broke the barricades. The mosh pit was so insane it started pushing the stage backwards. Ray looked back at me. Klaus looked over at me. I put my head down and barreled through the set. We finished "California Über Alles" and said, "Thank you, goodnight" (boa noite). The crowd kept screaming, but we couldn't go back for an encore because the stage was falling apart.

The next stop was São Paulo, a real metropolitan city. The traffic was so thick that most of the high-rolling businessmen took helicopters to get around. Since I had a few days off, we had a press conference where tons of punk rockers came to get autographs, and we answered their questions about the history of the band and waxed philosophical over politics.

In São Paolo all of the people working in the busy city center—the stewards, ticket collectors, bus drivers—were all different colors and textures, from eggplant black, to honey gold, to the whitest white. Eye colors ranged from hazel, blue, green, grey, amber, light and dark brown. Everyone seemed to treat each other the same. There I felt like I finally fit in.

We stayed in the middle of town. All around our hotel were sex shops and gambling joints. There was a big shopping center nearby. We did press stuff there, signing autographs and shit like that.

We flew to Rio de Janeiro after São Paulo. From the window seat of my plane I saw nothing but thick, overgrown, lush green jungle, a green like I had never seen before. The jungle reached right up to the edge of the ocean, that bright green touching the turquoise blue sea. It felt like a new place, a new adventure, but it also felt familiar. Even when I was still on the plane I knew this place was some kind of spiritual home for me. As we flew lower I could see the hills surrounding the city, covered with shantytowns. People lived in cardboard boxes and makeshift shacks, jumbled all up and down

D. H. PELIGRO

the hills. Sometimes these homes were no more than a couple of boards leaning on each other, with rusty pieces of corrugated steel acting as roofs. Flying lower I saw the sweltering hot, dirty streets filled with skinny, barefoot children. I was speechless.

On the way to the Center Hotel in downtown Rio, where we were staying, Matthias drove us through the city. We passed the notorious Cidade de Deus, the favela that inspired the film *City of God*—where I would later end up. He took us down some of the roughest streets I had ever seen, filled with all kinds of hustlers, kids holding guns out in the open, dirty animals. Matthias gave us a lecture. "Life doesn't mean a whole lot down here. People die regularly of hunger or disease and murder each other all the time." We passed narrow streets of tiny shacks, next to streets filled with giant apartment buildings, like the projects back home. "Here the drug dealers run everything," Matthias continued. "They don't give a fuck about the law. The cops won't go in there because the drug lords will kill them. No cops except the corrupt ones, who bring in the drugs, protect the dealers, and split the profits," he told us. "I am from São Paolo, which is violent, but not anything like here. In Rio ciudad, be very careful. Here eight-year-old kids have UZIs and will shoot your fucking kneecaps off for your wallet. People will try to sell you stuff all the time."

By that time we had passed through the area and were walking around downtown. He told us that here it was not as violent as in the favelas, but you could still get robbed. I wasn't listening. I was buying some peanuts from a guy on the street, and he had just started trying to sell me a watch and then a lighter. "Don't! Whatever you do, don't buy anything!" Matthais said. "When you pull out your money, they see it, and you're a mark. The only color down here is green."

I was overwhelmed and sad. I felt really related to everybody, that these kids out here living so hard were my people. I know what it means to grow up poor in a rough city, but I was not prepared for this kind of poverty and suffering. Later on I would get to experience first hand a lot of joy and life and hear incredible music coming from the favela, but this first visit was a shock to my heart.

The next day we went to a place called Villa Mimosa, down at the docks. Pete Shelley from the Buzzcocks had said it was one of the greatest places on earth. "You have to see this, it's a horror show!" Villa Mimosa was a boardwalk and a historical sex stop for sailors. There were Brazilian smugglers, arms dealers, drug dealers, pimps, and bikers. And most of the women there were whores on the stroll, selling blowjobs for two reais—a fuck for two bucks. Our roadie Paulo said the only thing you were sure to walk away with was some kind of STD, as he went in to buy a fuck for two reais. But besides all of these lurid attractions, my life was about to change.

Back in Rio we did a gig at the Teatro Americano. It was chaos. The acoustics were horrendous. Communication with the Brazilian techs was non-existent so we couldn't

D. H. PELIGRO

get a sound check. There was a lot of screaming at the interpreter back and forth with the Brazilian sound crew. It was hot, sweaty, and grubby, and all my clothes were dirty, so I was playing in just my underwear. It was an insane show but the audience loved it.

At sound check a local roadie, Paolo, introduced me to a ghetto fabulous sexy morena in a mini skirt and calf high boots with heels. She was short, curvy-slender with that oh so familiar, yet smaller, action-packed bunda that many Brazilian women have. She had two spiders tattooed on her shoulders peeking out under a leather jacket that she wore despite the hundred degree heat, and a Sid Vicious portrait tattooed on her upper hip. I was instantly turned on. Backstage after sound check she asked if she could interview me. "For what?" I asked.

"Oh, just for me," she said.

Of course I said yes. Paolo saw us talking. He pulled me aside and said "Watch out for Thais, she smell too much the coke!" He warned me, but I thought nothing of it.

After the gig I was outside by our truck, wiping myself down with a towel and stretching while we were waiting to get paid. Thais came over. "You yoga?" she asked. "My father teach here." Whipping her leg up to her shoulder, she put it behind her neck and spread her arms as if she was a one legged Corcovado statue.

Right away I asked her to come back to the hotel, but she said, "No I'm not prostitute girl, not group girl." We hung outside, still waiting for the money. We were signing autographs. We were waiting with the bus because Cariocas are so sketchy about money that the promoter had gone to his house to get our fee. We were waiting for hours, and I talked with Thais the whole time. So she came back with me in the minivan to the hotel. Thais asked me if I wanted to go to her place, but I wasn't sure about that, as I didn't know my way around Rio. "I don't know, I think we should probably go to my hotel. Where do you live?"

"I live in the Beverly Hills of Rio," she assured me.

Yeah, right, I thought. "Is it your place?"

"I live with my mother and my father and—"

"No. No way" I quickly said, "I do not want to meet your mother and your father, no, no, no."

So we went back to the hotel. She mentioned that she had been sniffing coke that night. I figured that was why she would not shut up so I grabbed her, started kissing her, and then I gave her a beer. After she had calmed down, the rest of the night was amazing. I was tantalized by the force field of untouchability she wore around her like a cloak, and when she showed me some vulnerability it was unbelievable. Her skin was so soft, and the way she moved when I caressed her was like a supple-squirmy-sexy-kama-sutra-yogini-vampire.

I pulled off her leather jacket and revealed the Ganesh tattoo she had on her left arm. I thought, *Damn this is sexy.* I love girls with tattoos. As I stroked her arm I asked her, "What is this? What does your tattoo mean?"

"He's Ganesha, he bringa de good vibes, and de money, and the balanca for de life-eh."

D. H. Peligro

"Oh, cool," I said.

We spent the whole night having sex and talking. She stroked my leg. She put her palm on my scar and quickly jumped back, as if it had given her an electrical shock. "My love, I saw-ed you in the hospital! With de people standing over you in white clothes and de doctor he was shaking he head! They were so serious! You were blue and grey and these...tubes...they come out of your arm and finger...and a lot of blood."

"How did you know that?" I asked.

"I am a witch," she told me. "I see things, I have the vision. I can see were you've been and were you're going."

I didn't really believe in all that mumbo jumbo, but over the next few months I began to believe that she truly had powers. She could tell me things about myself that only I knew. If I called her on the phone, she could tell me what I was wearing, where I had just been. But she insisted that she didn't practice her powers, that she did not cast spells, although she could if she wanted to. She said she could make me do things with black magic, then she clammed up about it.

The next day I went to meet her family who lived in a modest condo. It had a pool and doorman and was in an upper middle class part of town, but by American standards the place was fairly small and it was no Beverly Hills like she told me it was. Her father, Danilo, was a leading yoga instructor and taught classes and private lessons all over Brazil. He was mixed Italian and Brazilian, and her mother was a stunning Brazilian Indian Gypsy. Her father was gone all day; sometimes he would be gone overnight. Gloria, Thais' mother, stayed at home.

I fell in love with Thais. There were so many things that were attractive about her, the way she spoke and moved. When she walked down the street she'd always draw a crowd. Her ass was like a whirling dervish. When she felt pleasure or happiness she expressed it with her whole self. I loved her loyalty and her passion. She was not one of those girls who slept around. She wouldn't fuck anybody unless she loved them. She said she didn't trust Brazilian guys. "Fucking Brazilian playboys," she called them.

I also loved her toughness. She had a fearless demeanor. She was very street savvy and could hold her own in the favelas and could speak the dialect. She was so forceful that many nights her mouth alone got us in the underground clubs in the favelas. This is how I learned that even though she and her family had moved to Baha Tajuca they had originally come from a really poor favela. Like many other Brazilian girls she had worked for the department of tourism as a tour guide. Then she had gone to school to be a pilot. She dropped out of university when she met me, saying she saw something better. I asked her not to quit. I wanted her to have a good career, and begged her to follow her ambition. But she had started giving up on things. I think the biggest reason was all the cocaína. I don't know for how many

D. H. PELIGRO

years I had tried not to be judgmental about it and let her be her own self. It was only later that I learned how much of a hustle Thais really had.

One of the most memorable times I had was when Thais introduced me to the biggest rapper in Rio—MV Bill. She knew him through the underground hip-hop scene in Rio. "There are some people who would like to meet you. I want you to meet MV Bill. He is a big hip-hop producer and performer and MC." Eddie Velto drove us. He was the go-to guy. Instead of a taxi, we would call him. He would take care of us then give us a bill at the end of the day. He was an all around guy, could get you anything you wanted: girls, drugs, anything. When we pulled up outside Cidade de Deus and saw the cop cars outside she was pissed off. She hated police, "Police Militaire!" Thais was hissing and spitting at them, "I hate these muderfuckers."

One of MV Bill's guys came down and opened the gates, let us in, and took us to his apartment. There were naked children and sick dogs running around. The poverty was parallel to what I had seen in Trenchtown, Jamaica—not a lot of hope. Everybody came out to look at me. I had a shirt with a fist holding a mic, and they seemed to know I was from the USA and I had come to visit MV Bill. I looked dressed up to them, like a gringo Americano. "They don't let the police in here," Thais said, "they will kill them. They don't let them interfere. This is their territory."

The place was dark, and the stairway up to MV Bill's apartment smelled like piss, and the tile was busted off the walls. We took the steps all the way up to his apartment. There was no elevator, and if there was one it was most definitely broken. It was a dingy apartment. Rio is humid, and Cidade de Deus dripped with the sweat of poverty that oozed down the walls, all the way up to his apartment. I can still see the rusty, gooey teardrops running down the tile walls. They seemed to put tile on most of the walls to keep it cool.

MV Bill welcomed me to Rio. He was about 5' 8", bald head, goatee, and weighed about 140 pounds. He didn't know much about punk. He asked me if I could get him any Public Enemy, Tupac, or Biggie Smalls tapes. This was 2002, but they wanted stuff from the '80s and '90s. They had limited internet access, and other places seemed to get music first, but I guess they were so isolated or behind the times in the favela. It took a while for new music to trickle down to South America. It was easier to get Shakira than it was to get Pharoahe Monch. Pirated and black market music is everywhere in Brazil. It was easier to get black market goods; they were much cheaper than the shit in the shopping malls.

In broken English he started asking me about early hip-hop—KRS One and Scott La Rock. I didn't have the heart to tell him that I was not a hip-hop musician. MV Bill and Brazilians were angry about the way they had to live, just like I was. However, they were blatant about wanting to make money, whereas in punk rock we didn't care about money as much. Quiet as it has been kept, we punk rockers needed to make money, too, but I didn't think fucking over people or exploitation was the way to get it done. I knew if I was on the right path all that shit would come, or it wouldn't matter.

31

Welcome to Jamrock

After my first trip to Brazil I went back to Los Angeles and then took a short trip to Jamaica. I had booked the Jamaica trip before I'd gone to Brazil and met Thais. I had been chasing a former Miss Jamaica, and I'd never taken a vacation on my own. This trip was to be another chapter in my education. Like in Brazil I could see how much we have in common with black folks around the world, but also how different we are.

My friends Kate and Chan invited me down to a video shoot they were doing in Los Angeles. I brought Fez along for company. They were working on a video with DMX for the song, "What These Bitches Want." On set I was surrounded by all these sexy little half-naked chicks, but I didn't dare touch any of these girls. After finishing his take, DMX walked up to me. "What's up, dawg?"

He was known for his no shows, and people said. that he is always somewhere smoking crack and fucking all the video girls. Kate asked me to babysit him, make sure he didn't leave the video set. Getting to know him, I admired how heartfelt and down to earth he was. His crew was kind of fucked up, but when you are a high profile artist, sometimes that's part of it. I still can't see why you need a bunch of do-nothing leeches hanging around all the time.

There was this super sexy, light-skinned angel gliding around the set. She saw me, looked at my tattoos. "So you either been to prison or you really like art," she said in this gorgeous Jamaican patois. I said I really like art. "Hi, I'm Shani," she said.

"Why yes, you are," I said. "I mean, hey I'm D. H., wasup?"

I couldn't believe she was talking to me. I was completely enthralled by her accent. I gave her the once over as I looked her up and down, from her pretty painted toenails, to her beautiful face and her mind-boggling body. Her whole vibe was of greatness, and I'm thinking, *I would follow this angel to the ends of the earth.* We were chatting it up and then Kate screamed, "That's lunch!"

Fez and I walked to the craft food service table. All the brothers were hitting on her so I didn't think I stood a chance as I watched her tell them to fuck off in so many words. The one thing I know about Jamaicans is they'll cut you.

I watched her cut these cats to ribbons; she was a feisty fireball. She didn't buy no shit, and she didn't take no shit. I was petrified to talk to her. She came over to our table and started talking to me, asking what I do, and I was thinking, *Be nice and answer the questions with no sarcasm or else she might slap the shit outta you.* Shani commanded my respect just like that. I was humbled and in awe.

I had booked a ticket to Jamaica to go hang out with her. After all these years of touring I didn't even know how to plan a trip for myself or have a vacation. So Sherry and my friend Caroline showed me how. I ended up staying in Kingston and then Montego Bay, then another week in Negrille, and Ocho Rios.

Shani McGram and her family lived in a gated community called The Sharrows in the Hills of Kingston. I landed in Kingston, side-stepping the hustlers and cabbies.

I was finally hailed by man in a yellow truck. "You D. H.?"

I say, "Yeah."

"RES-P-ECT Rass," he said. "Yes-I," I said being the Yankee dread that I am.

"I am David, Shani's fiancé."

I gulped. I thought I had come to get some. I was so embarrassed. As soon as he said respect I knew everything was going to be all right.

David extended his friendship, set me up in this legendary English colonists' club, the Liguanea Club, where they played squash, tennis, and some other sports. It was in full view of the Pegasus Hotel, where The Clash stayed when they recorded some of *Sandinista!* I was shocked by the segregation and the fucking poverty. I had come to have a good time, but I felt torn. Here I was going into this fancy hotel, surrounded by some of the poorest people on the planet.

David became my tour guide and showed me around Kingston. He took me to see everything except what I really wanted to see. I had three things I really wanted to do: go to Trenchtown, see Bob Marley's house in Kingston, and buy some of those rough-neck, brightly-colored net tank-tops I saw the island boys wearing.

Shani ripped me a new asshole about those shirts. "Why you want those ghetto shirts like some poor street hustler or petty criminal!" She said, "You can't wear those here!" Neither of them, David nor Shani, would take me to buy those shirts.

In the morning I met a girl named Tasha who worked as a waitress at the Liguanea Club's restaurant. She had beautiful features and a beautiful soul that shined through her perfect chocolate skin. I started flirting with her.

"What you going to do today?" she asked.

"I am going to come with you today, Tasha."

"Me don't have problem."

Those island girls are forward. I asked her to take me where they sold those shirts. She said maybe I could find them in the part of town where she needed to go for her second job. We shared a taxi and went on a quest for the net-tanks.

We went down to some part of town where they do hair and nails. I couldn't find the shirts, but I got a really good manicure. Sitting in the chair I was surrounded by all these hot young Jamaican girls doing themselves up. All of them were getting their hair straightened, undergoing these extreme torture tactics to make themselves look white or European. I saw a girl with a some kind of weave on holding her head back over the sink while the hairdresser poured a tea kettle of scalding hot water over her hair. She tried not to burn her scalp, but the girl was screaming and jerking her hips and back up off the chair as the hot water straightened her weave. That was a hell of a thing to see.

I wanted to remember Tasha as a light and fluffy chocolate waitress that I had known and loved. I didn't really want to see the reality of her life; I knew it would break my heart. So I quit flirting with her and let her get back to her second job.

Meanwhile, I went back on my quest for those net shirts. I asked a cabbie to take me to Trenchtown. He refused but told me I could find the shirts in downtown Kingston. The streets were full of confusion in downtown Kingston; some of them were blocked off by the military.

"Why are those streets blocked off?" I asked.

The cabbie told me "There's too much violence. You can't go there."

So I kept looking for the shirts. I did find a stall with the net shirts, but they were all too big—I wanted one that hugged my chest. I asked another cab driver to take me to Trenchtown. He said no. I asked two more cabbies and they both said the same thing to me.

He looked at me curiously and said "TRENCHTOWN? You want go to Trenchtown?" Then he looked at the meter. He asked me why I wanted to go to Trenchtown.

I said in my best patois accent, "Mon, me have the money here. You can take me or no?"

He grabbed a machete, made a stabbing motion, put the knife back in the side pocket. "Okay, now we can go." Hackney Cabs was his company, and I was aware of the colonial past as he drove me through streets which all had English names. I had been to City of God in Brazil, but Trenchtown was the worst poverty I had ever seen. Alongside of us were kids chasing a garbage truck. They wanted to rob it and try to find the good trash from neighborhoods like the Sharrows before it went into another neighborhood and then to a landfill.

I started to cry. Next we came up to a tin roof propped up by four sticks forming a gazebo. Sitting under it was an old man with long, sun-drenched, sun-reddened dreads. The Cab driver knew him. He said, "Rufis, wha-happ-um rass?"

He stopped to chat while the meter was running up a long bill. I didn't care; you can't buy a cultural experience like that. This was Rufis' crib and had been there forever.

In the middle of this poverty was a wall left untouched by graffiti. "Welcome to Trenchtown. Home of Bob

Marley," was written proudly across it. In the middle of the wasteland—the worst of human conditions, poverty, pain, and violence—that wall was a cultural oasis in the desert of life. And I guess that's what I needed to see in Trenchtown.

Back in Kingston, David took me to Bob Marley's house. I took the tour of the house. While the guide was explaining Rastafarianism these stupid Swedish tourists asked, "Wasn't Bob Marley a Muslim?" I wanted to smash them in the face. Their ignorance of Rastafarianism made my blood boil.

The guide showed us a living area, bedrooms, and other parts of the house as we walked to the kitchen. There, she showed us the hole in the wall where Bob was shot.

On the way to the kitchen I'd noticed that on the wall there was a picture of Bob Marley's father sitting on a horse. The guide said he was from England and everyone called him The General. I thought, *Damn. He look like a white dude.*

I stood there pointing at the picture asking questions. "Is this his father? How'd he get—wait—his father was a white dude? Wha—" Before I could finish my questions the guide got real snappy.

"Com' now! Ya'll gon' miss the rest of the tour," she said. Apparently I wasn't allowed to ask questions.

She rushed us through the rest of the house to the screening room, where you could sit and watch his videos. On the way to the video room we walked through a small yard where Bob and his friends used to play soccer. As we were leaving I just had this vibe of the house filled with the spirit of Bob Marley.

I went outside and David was talking with these Rastafarians blowing ganja. There was an old crazy guy who had played in Bob Marley's band at one time. Now he sat outside of Bob Marley's house playing a guitar with no strings and begging tourists for money. David was talking to these Rastas, and I walked up and said, "Wha-happ-um Rass?" I say, "I'm friend of David. Me name D. H.," I looked up, and it was Steve Kumani and Damian Marley. We took a picture with them.

I spent the last couple of days with Shani and her family in her genteel home, with servants bringing me cool drinks and fresh towels. Then I flew into Negril to spend a week at a Yoga center that I had spotted in a Lonely Planet guide. Every morning I would go to the market for fresh coconuts and fruit.

One day I found a young girl, dazed and wandering on the beach. She told me she was the girlfriend of an Egyptian drug dealer who had abandoned her. My friend from the Yoga center and I took her in, fed her, gave her a place to sleep. But the next day we found out that the drug dealer was looking for her. They would follow her, and us, and pay off the taxi drivers to give them information. Wherever we were these Egyptian mafia dudes would show up. I thought they were just tourists frequenting the same spot as we did, but my German friend didn't think so, and he had just dealt with similar situations in Medellín, Columbia. Now, I wasn't about to get stabbed or shot in Jamaica, so we dropped her off near the beach.

Leaving Jamaica I began to think about the suffering all around the world. In Jamaica, the only export sources of income were tourism, reggae, coffee, and rum. There was such a drastic contrast between people, truly beautiful people working really hard to get by, and then these con men, criminals, drug dealers, gang-bangers and smugglers. In the midst of it is the most amazing music. Even Jah can't figure that one out. Reggae musicians are born with a gift of pure genius, damned to live in paradise with limited options.

32

Tug of War

*A*fter I came back to Los Angeles, Thais called me non-stop. I began going back and forth from L.A. to Brazil. For the next five years I canceled all other trips and made Rio de Janeiro my second home.

Like her Father, Thais was a powerhouse of Yoga, and she had a deep spirituality. Everyday we would get up and greet the sun. Her house had a great view, and we would go out into the back and stretch our salute to the sun. She taught me yoga like I had never learned before. Her father would teach all day, and then when he came home at night he would give me private instructions. He taught Astanga, Hatha, Kundalini, and many other forms that I didn't recognize. He also taught customized yoga to help wherever you had a problem. Since I was a drummer he gave me personalized yoga stretches so that I was loose, lucid, yet powerful. He was in all the Brazilian yoga magazines. While I was there he wrote a book on yoga that included some photos he took of Thais and I demonstrating various poses.

But even with all that spirituality I saw him slap Thais in the face so hard her nose bled. They would argue all the time, and she would push and push him. And that was how it went there in Brazil. I had seen it in the streets, the woman would not think a man was really all man unless he slapped the shit out of her. It was a whole different culture that was reminiscent of my upbringing.

Now for my private yoga lessons he gave me these gems: "This is for your lungs if you smoke," he said in very broken English. "Blow the air three times out of your lower stomach in stages until all the air is out of you. Then breathe in through your nose and hold your breath. And repeat. Beat on your chest, and hold your breath three times." He taught me about my mental field, and meditation exercises in which you focus on your third eye, placing your longest fingers over it while practicing the breathing exercise. He also taught me to stand on my head.

I came alive in yoga. It helped me to take steps towards balance in my life. I am a very physical person and express myself through my body. I must let the energy out of my body or it goes crazy inside of me and it becomes self-destructive. The techniques I learned from her father were incredibly healing in this way as I began to release all of the pent-up toxic energies in my body, especially in my neck, shoulders and back. Danilo taught me a powerful exercise for my neck. I'd breathe the breath of fire, alternating my head from left to right very fast, shooting my arms out to the side and opening my hands to release the energy. I could feel the electricity shooting out from my fingertips. When I'm not playing drums this keeps me balanced and not trying to kill myself. However, Danilo also taught me that I don't have to be dependent on physical movement to disperse energy. He taught me how to sit with it, to just breathe through it and process it in meditation. Through our yoga practice, eating fresh food, and living in this beautiful paradise I began to really heal a place deep down inside me.

I loved staying with the family. All of her relatives would come over Sundays and holidays, her cousins and aunts bringing food and all talking at once. I have a special place in my heart for her grandmother, who was off the hook. Old as the hills, she would truck all around Rio, walking or taking the bus wherever she needed to go. She didn't speak a word of English, but I understood her. She would come at me, blaring in Portuguese, hug me, and cover me with kisses. The aunts and female cousins would all smother me with kisses, too. "Oh, he's so beautiful!" they would say. They lavished me with so much attention that Thais would get jealous. "I saw the way you look at my cousin! You want to fuck her!" she would yell, which was not true.

The relationship with Thais was fun, never boring, but the amount of drama was incredible, and the language barrier didn't help. I did learn a little bit of Portuguese, but I would spend most of the time just trying to figure out what she was saying. Her English was so funny I often couldn't help laughing. This made her mad. "What you do? Why you smile of my face?" she would yell. But after our fights she would get so emotional. "Oh, my love, why you do these things to me, you know I love you too much, my love. I waited for you all my life. I waited for you, this beautiful black man all my life!"

Everyday was a struggle. Everything was a fight or an argument. I would say something, and it would literally take four or five hours for the shit to roll over. It never would completely roll over; it would just roll into the next day. She would go on and on and on, worrying about things that hadn't even happened yet. She was always trying to figure me out, to tell me how I tick. Sometimes she was right and would call me out when I was acting like a jerk. "You can't do things like that. You think you are king? You think because you are in Dead Kennedys that you are king?"

The worst day was the day we had to go to the consulate for her Visa so that she could come back to the States with me. This became such a big deal, and it took us hours to get to downtown Rio, which was not that far away. I left her in the street screaming at me and jumped on a van service back to the house. I packed my shit up to go stay in a hotel. When I tried to leave, her mother Gloria grabbed my arm. "Oh Darrie, Darrie, please, don't leave Thais, she so crazy, she crazy!" she pleaded, pulling the bag out of my hand. Thais then burst in and threw herself at me. "My love, forgive me. Don't leave!" I am such a sucker that I put

D. H. PELIGRO

my bags down. We finally got to the consulate, got the visa sorted out, and Thais came back to the States, two days before I had to go on tour.

"I'm going on tour. I'll see you when I get back," I told her.

"You can't leave me all alone! You are not to leave me here! Pick me up, then abandon me!"

That's one thing you learn as a touring musician. You never take your girl on tour.

But she didn't know anybody in America, so she had to go on tour with us. It was a nightmare, but it was also funny as hell cause she had never seen America. We went through Texas, and then Colorado—she had never seen snow. She instantly lay down in a snow bank and started rolling around in it.

"Thais! Get up! Don't lay in the snow!"

"Ooh, too much wet!" she said.

She was always doing something. We would be backstage during sound check, and she would just start doing Yoga and standing on her head. The road guys would marvel. "Oh, my God, Bro! Your girl is so hot!" They were a bit jealous. They would soon see that there was another side to the coin.

We were in our hotel in Breckenridge, and she thought I was fucking some girl downstairs in the hot tub. I didn't even go to the hot tub. I had just gone down in the lobby to get something to drink. But she had created this wild fantasy somehow based on gossip she had heard about Ozzy Osbourne having sex with groupies in the hot tubs of hotels before going back to his wife.

That night, a whole other fight occurred out of her delusional jealousy. Klaus came into our hotel room because he could hear us screaming all down the hall of this swank Breckenridge hotel. He wanted to just tell us to keep it down, but Thais, with one hand on her hip and the other on his shoulder, dragged him in to mediate. Klaus was a good diplomat and she knew it. Within a half an hour, he realized she was out of her ever-loving mind. He threw his hands up and left it to us to figure things out.

Back in L.A. things were difficult with Thais. She went to hip-hop dance classes but found it hard to keep up. The classes were run by a well-known choreographer and filled with *real* dancers working toward their big break. They were in the latest hip-hop videos, films, and television. This was something she saw on American television in Brazil and thought, *Well, I can do that.* She didn't understand the discipline and dedication it took to be a professional dancer—all the pain and rejection that goes with the territory. And she took her unhappiness out on me.

Then she started having premonitory dreams that her father was very ill and that she had to return quickly to Brazil to be with him. I knew that she didn't need to be there. In fact he only needed a hernia operation. But I was glad when she flew back the next week after the tour.

Soon after that Dead Kennedys were booked to do a festival in Istanbul. We were one of the first punk bands to play in a Muslim country after 9/11. Right after our tour religious extremists blew up the British embassy. Blondie was going to play, but that fell apart because nobody wanted to go to Istanbul or anywhere in the Middle East. George W. Bush had already invaded Iraq, which made things even worse. Everyone told us not to go to Turkey because it was too dangerous, but we went anyway.

The show was fantastic. We performed for over 20,000 people. Many different bands were on the bill: The Pet Shop Boys, The Delfuegos, Simple Minds, The Cardigans, and a local Turkish punk band called Rashit.

My first relapse, after almost six years of sobriety, was on the flight to Istanbul. It was on a morphine lollipop. I started talking to a guy and his kids about music and the band. He was sucking on a lollipop, and I asked if I could have one. I thought it was one of those Nicorette things to help you not crave cigarettes during the flight.

But he said, "No, man, its for my back. I was in a car accident. It's Morphine." I had never heard of a fucking morphine lollipop.

"No, man, I'm an alcoholic I can't take that," I said.

But he stuck it in my hand, and I took it back to my seat. I really meant to go give it back to him but instead I stuck it in the magazine pouch in front of me. That flight was so long, and there it was, for hours, staring at me. Finally, I ripped it open and I started sucking on it.

It didn't feel like it got me high, but it altered my mood, and later on I felt relaxed.

Once we were in Istanbul, after we fought through a slough of media, we checked into our hotel—the Ramada Istanbul. I felt very woozy. I went to my room and laid down on my bed.

"Dammit, man, I'm fuckin' high...ughhhh...gotta keep it together," I said to myself. Later, we went out to dinner. A guide showed us around Istanbul. We were surrounded by gypsy guitar players and people trying to sell us cigarettes, cigars, and trinkets. This was supposed to be a great adventure, but by the time I got back to the hotel I felt like shit. *Wow*, I thought. *I think I just relapsed.* I was filled with a sense of brutal dread. I did not want to go back and start all over again, but I knew I had to because I was high. I was not going to lie about it. Not this time.

When I returned to L.A. I started my sobriety over at day one. That lollipop had released the phenomenon of craving. Now I told all my peers that I'd relapsed. They were like, "What happened? Man you were like the fuckin' Buddha of sobriety!" Then they asked about the chain of events that led up to it. "What were you not doing? Why didn't you call?" It freaked me out. After all, I'm a drug addict and alcoholic. What do you expect? I didn't start using heavily right away, but I was drinking and using enough to put a gap in my relationship with Thais.

I did want to get sober, and at the same time Thais and I decided to give it one more try. I continued to travel to Brazil, but Thais was getting crazier and crazier. She began praying more often to what she called her Gypsy goddess. She was pretty much a witch all the time now, although she mixed in a little Catholicism and would drag me into each Cathedral to pray. Once I came up behind her as she was worshipping her Gypsy spirit. She turned toward me, and I saw, for an instant, a disturbing change in her face and eyes. The way the light hit them—she looked demonic. It made my skin crawl. I tried to ignore it as I was focused mostly on not drinking.

One night we went to the sex motel, taking a night away from her parents. She was snarfing some coke, which was normal for her. By then I thought nothing of it, and by then I wasn't shooting up yet. After we had sex for a while Thais sat up abruptly. Her face took on a totally different shape. She always kept her hair in a power pony, but she raised her hands slowly and took her hair down. A low growl was coming from her throat.

"What's wrong, Thais?" I asked.

"I am not Thais! I am Virid! Her gypsy god!"

"Okay you need to stop playing, Thais, cause you're scaring me."

She insisted she was not Thais as she blew the coke out of her nose. Thais loved cocaine, but apparently Virid hated it. I hated it, too; it blocked my connection to her. *Oh damn*, I thought, *this bitch could kill me. I'm in a sex motel in Rio de Janeiro, ain't nobody ever gonna know. Wow, I don't quite know what to do but I am freaking right outta my skin.*

Virid said she came because Thais had ceased her vigil; she was not tending the altar, putting the water up, lighting the candles, or leaving offerings of fruit. It was true; after I came back Thais started neglecting her alter. Virid wrapped herself in my orange gym clothes because she was nude. Gypsies love red, and it was the closest color she could find to it. Virid started touching her hair, her breasts, belly, and face.

"Ooooo, I am beautiful," she said touching herself repeatedly. "I love this body. I...love...this...body," she said in a low, guttural voice of gratification.

I didn't know what to do. Then Virid grabbed my hand and started reading my palm.

"Your father is going to die, very soon. Your bassist will have trouble with his heart. And you will have a deformed child," she told me.

"Will I get a record deal?" I asked.

"Yes, the name on the record is some ball..."

I said, "Like a globe? Like a planet? Mercury Records?"

Then Virid began discovering Thais' body again. "I can't believe I am in this body!" She got up and rubbed herself all over. "This beautiful body!"

Thais had never behaved this way. This went on for hours. She was chain smoking, grabbing cans of beer, swilling them down. This was definitely not Thais, who would usually nurse her drink all night.

D. H. Peligro

Virid began rubbing on my body. My eyes widened. I was afraid. Then I thought, *Having sex with a goddess? What could be better than that?* So I took her into the shower. I washed her body while she ooood and ahhhd. Again, this was not like Thais, who very much liked to shower alone.

So after the shower I had sex with a spirit through my fiancé's body. Her pussy was totally different. It was more succulent. I was afraid to kiss her. I was afraid a forked tongue might catapult from her mouth like a juggernaut decapitating me. And I was trying to hurry up and come because her hips started jackknifing off the bed, and she was squirming. She couldn't control this body anymore. After I came, she said: "Why you stop?"

I said, "Uh...let's take another shower."

She kept going on about "this body, this body," all I could think is that I just fucked a goddess. Then we fucked again, and she fell asleep, but I was too afraid to close my eyes.

When Thais woke up she asked me, "Have I been asleep?" I told her Virid had paid a visit. "Oh, Virid! I forgot to give my offerings to the gypsy goddess!" she said, as if possession were an everyday event. "If she comes again, give her anything she wants."

That was when I realized that she had gone out of her mind. Koo-koo, ca-ca, cra-cra...run. She was no longer fun crazy, freaky crazy. She was completely brujería crazy. People would tell me it was cocaine psychosis, or she had multiple personality disorder. But I had seen plenty of that in people who did a hell of a lot more coke than she was using. What I saw happen in her was another thing entirely. I used to not believe in that supernatural mumbo-jumbo shit. But now that I've seen it first hand, I believe. Coke or no coke, I had seen with my own eyes what it looked like for a being to enter a body.

She used to say to me, "You can never leave me, I have your hair and your fingernails, you can never leave!" At the time, I didn't think it was a big deal, but to this day I still feel connected. I'm compelled to call her every so often, even though I know she's not good for me at all.

That night and the next I couldn't sleep. Thais gave me Rohypnols to get to sleep.

I said, "What is this?" after I took it like a dumb ass. She said "Houpinoals."

"HOUPINOALS? Roofies? You gave me roofies?"

I woke up the next day with the craving on me like I had just unleashed the hounds of hell. I went to the farmácia and bought some syringes. Then I told Thais to go get some coke. Two days later we wound up at the Center Hotel, still awake.

Thais gave me a handful of roofies to go to sleep. We each took a handful. Thais lay still like the dead, but again I could not fall asleep. I went downstairs and worked out like a freak.

Thais was still asleep when I needed more coke. I got up and went out on the street to search for some. I know I looked crazy. I had already dropped about twenty

D. H. Peligro

pounds, and I was sweating bullets and gnashing my teeth. I had twitches and tics in my muscles. I felt like I was suffocating. I tore my shirt off. I was stumbling, and I couldn't see straight. I ran into Henanni, a local artist, and started yelling "Cocaine! Cocaína!"

He said, "I know where we can get some," so we jumped on the bus. I was pulling huge wads of money out of my pocket but no one dared try to rob me because by now I looked crazy. I went to a different kind of favela, one I'd never been to before. This time we were walking. It was nothing like the favela in São Paulo. There were no nice trannys, no carts selling food, no guys readily selling cocaine. I was on a mission—we had to find it.

Henanni went up to some guy and jibbered to him in Portuguese. He came back and said, "No, he no gotta."

So we walked another three miles in the hot, humid, burning sun to another Brazilian cat and he didn't have any either. Now it seemed like we were walking for twenty miles but I had to have some coke so we finally got to a little house deep in the favela. This black Brazilian chick looked at me, and the look on her face said, *You're a mess.* My shirt was off. She pointed to my track marks all up and down my arms and my tattoos. She said, "He's a gringo."

I said, "What?"

She said, "Americano. I got some coke."

I bought six bindles then rushed back to the coffee shop on the corner near the house. I went in the bathroom and used the water out of the toilet. All I had was a plastic spoon. I filled the syringe up with water but the cocaine was shit so it gummed up the rig and bubbled up in the spoon. The guy in the coffee shop knew me by now so he was banging on the bathroom door, "My friend, are you ok, my friend?"

"FUCK!" I burst out of the bathroom. So once again I let Mr. Hyde out and began fiending for coke, hanging out with just Henanni from the neighborhood.

Two days later, Thais and her mother, Gloria, sided against me. Thais showed her mother the bindle of coca I gave her. I was pissed off—that snitch bitch.

"You're the one who got me on this shit now you wanna make me look like the bad guy?" I told her. "Fuck you!" So we had a huge fight. "I'm out."

She said, "Go!"

There was no Gloria there to grab my bag and say, "Stay Derrie don't go, she's crazy." So I called Eddie Velto to take me to the airport.

I got on the airplane, and I was drinking heavy, and the flight attendant was giving me shit for listening to my headphones. She said I couldn't have them, and she tried to take them. I was still pissed off from Thais snitching and bitching so I just came unglued with no principals and no structure. I would lash out at anybody, so I told her "Go fuck yourself!" at the top of my lungs.

D. H. PELIGRO

She got scared and asked for my passport number.

"I ain't givin' you shit, you cunt," was my response.

She went and told the captain.

"Wooooo, I'm shakin'...*not!*"

She saw it had no effect on me. Snoop Dogg had just done a show in Rio de Janeiro, and his security crew was on board, so the stewardess thought it would be fitting for them to come have a word with me. So these three big black niggas came up to my seat. The real big one looked like Dee Bo from the movie Friday, complete with the crazy lazy eye.

They say, "You making people scared. Why you trippin'?" One of them looked down in the seat pocket and saw an empty beer can. He says, "Man, you trippin' off some beer. Nigga, please. I just did twelve calendars at Terminal Island, I ain't scared. Look man, whatever's going on you don't want the problems we had, so chill yo' ass out. They got prisons full of niggas like you 'n me locked up fa life. You think you tough? I seen the biggest hardest niggas fall, don't take yo' freedom fa granted lil' nigga."

They sat down, and the stewardess came back and asked for my passport so I just gave it to her. She took my passport number, and I chilled my ass out. With all the talk of prison I thought about the DART rehab in St. Louis where I shared a room with J-the-Wig, Black, Coldpepper, and Vince. I had visions of getting my grippins ripped out as I had recalled the story Vince told me.

I was enraged and disappointed when I got home. Everything was falling apart again. I told myself there was no reason not to keep getting high, that I deserved some heroin after all that suffering. Despite myself I did get sober again, but not for long.

I was making some dough with DKs, so I had already invested in a new Peligro record where I paid for recordings, mixing, mastering, and pressing. So there went my dough.

I thought I could get distribution of my music and start a record label. Just before I had gone to Jamaica, this girl, London, emailed and stalked me, wanting to meet up. She saw my picture in the L.A. *Rock City News* and she told me, "I knew that you were special."

I told her I was going on a trip to Jamaica and I would meet with her when I got back. I finally met up with her years later, after I came back from Brazil and we started Dirrty Records. As it turned out she was a lovesick chick who wanted to have my baby, and after some time working with her I soon started to figure it out. I told her I didn't want to mix business with pleasure, but we did. We had the record label together, so I stayed in a bad relationship hoping that things would get better.

What I found out is that she didn't know how to run a record label. She worked for a publicity company, and all they did was make up lies; she seemed to be used to that. Her website was more a web of lies than anything. I didn't know how long she thought she could get away with it. The label had no real money, no distribution, and a phony clientele of artists, and when it all fell apart she filed for complete ownership of the company and tried to steal my record. She stole my name, Dirrty Records, and as I had relapsed and was on a serious dope run, it was easy for her to swoop in and take over. I'm pretty sure she hadn't seen a drug addict like me. To her credit she did take me to a bunch of different rehabs and would come over and bring me food. But I knew there was something wrong with her. My sixth sense told me that she was maniacal, manipulating. Besides, I was not available because I had a girlfriend already—her name was Lady Her-ron, my Mistress to which I had to pay homage everyday. Everything else was secondary.

So she left when things fell apart, and boy did they fall apart.

33

Sick Up and Fed

Soon after my split with Thais/Virid, I went to Birmingham, England, to tour Europe with the DKs. Parts of Birmingham looked sort of bombed-out; it reminded me of Serbia. There were nice parts near the college campus, where we were set to play, that had coffee shops and food vendors. As I ventured off the grounds and walked around, I had this feeling that I could easily be mugged.

I went to a strip club and hit it off with one of the dancers. She had some stripper name like Velvet, or some shit, and she wore blue contact lenses.

"That's not your eye-color, that's not your name," I said. "What is your name?"

She said, "My name is Katuchia, but you can call me Katie."

She was beautiful, sweet, and supportive. She was also Brazilian but the opposite of Thais in many ways. We hooked up, and she came and met me in Oslo at a DKs gig. Katuchia's father ran a number of radio franchises, one of which Katuchia managed. I sent her my Peligro CDs to see if they would play them on air, and pretty soon we were making plans for a Peligro tour of Brazil. She pushed and negotiated really hard for me and booked us a great, well-publicized tour with a huge open-air festival and a spot on Brazilian MTV, but I fucked it all up. About two weeks before the tour I started using heavily. G-Rock and Steve had already left the band. I was already strung out and needed two new band members to do the tour. I wanted to cancel it, but Katie was persistent in calling and confirming. I just kept saying, "Yes, yes, yes," but what I wanted to say was, *no*. I thought I could maintain, but it soon got out of control, like it always did.

Atma, Randy, and I showed up at the São Paulo airport. Katuchia was shocked when she saw me get off the plane. I was super skinny, my skin was gray and lifeless, my eyes clouded. I was a hot mess. In São Paulo we did MTV Brazil and some other interviews.

We had three days off before Porão do Rock festival. I refused to rehearse, which was stupid since I had a new bass player and drummer, and they didn't know the songs as well as I did. In the world of professionalism I should have given my all to make for the greatest show on Earth—but I was sick. Sick and strung. All I could do was whine for my medication. There was no H to be found in Brazil, so I went to the bar at the Ibis Hotel and just drank.

Before I left L.A., I'd started shooting up in my leg again, until it looked like one open sore, bleeding all over the place. In a blackout I remembered bits and pieces. I got into a taxi and went to the hospital in São Paulo. "I'm hurt. I'm fucked up," I told them. In my broken Portuguese I started begging for treatment. "I need morphine," I demanded. "I need Vicodins and I need methadone." I was asking for help, but what I really wanted was dope.

The nurses were not sympathetic. The one English-speaking nurse said, "*Nao*, we can't give you that. We can't give you anything but these bandages and some antiseptic spray," she told me. "Now get out of here so we can help someone who deserves it."

Aw fuck, man. Funny, in Brazil you could get all the coke you wanted. Our drummer found coke and a big-butted prostitute. I saw him walking by with a girl as I was sweating and drinking at the bar.

He came up to me and said, "Hey man, coke is only seven bucks a gram here. And I got this girl for only twenty reais."

I did not want coke, and I definitely couldn't fathom the thought of anyone touching me.

The following day we flew into Brasilia. Katuchia came to the hotel and had to feed me like a baby. I was so weak and dope sick. She took me to the hospital to see what they could do for my dope-sickness so she could get me through an interview and then onstage for the Porão do Rock Festival.

The doctors took me into a room partitioned off with a curtain and brought out a transparent plastic box of liquid. "Ow, ow," I said as they started poking

D. H. PELIGRO

me trying to find a vein. They finally found one in my hand, raised the box onto an IV drip pole, and the nurse cracked the box.

I said, "Ahhhh..." as I immediately started to feel relief. I didn't feel high, but the pressure in my brain and my back and legs started to relieve a bit. When you're strung out you don't really realize how dependent you are on every little grain of opiate. Usually this would be enough to get me off of the couch so I could score and get *real* high. Since we were in Brazil this was all I was going to get; after three days of shitting and puking and sweating it felt like heaven.

"What is that?"

Katie said, "Morfina."

I said, "What did you tell the doctors to get them to give me morphine like that?"

She said, "I told them he had to do the Porão do Rock Festival—and that he's an American junkie."

I met Katuchia's father that night. He told her, "Stay away from that guy. He's a piece of shit," in Portuguese. As I was about to go onstage I was getting pumped up and didn't really give a shit what anyone thought of me.

I did my best to cancel the tour because I was really too sick and out of my mind to perform. But it was bigger than me, and they wouldn't let me cancel. *I'm here now*, I thought. *So let's do the best we can.*

People were screaming. I thought, *Fuck, man. I finally got a crowd of 35,000 for my own band.* But I just knew, deep inside of me that I could have put on a much better show. I could have given a lot more.

After the shows, Katuchia packed my bags to put me on a plane to L.A. She had to clean up the mess I had left in the hotel room—the towels soaked with blood, bloody gauze, and rubber gloves everywhere. She collected all my money, which was wadded up in various pockets, and held on to it for me.

Back in L.A., my bass player and drummer left the band because I was tore up, and they were tired of watching me die. Confused and not sure how to work this out, I sat in a deep depression. I made myself unavailable; I shut off my phone so no one could reach me. The next day Brian Jennings, a special effects director I had been in rehab with, came over to my house to tell me that my father had died. Apparently my sister Dianne had called him.

Russell Sr. had a triple bypass a few years earlier. The doctors told him he needed to stop drinking and smoking—of course he didn't—and he ate really bad food. He had gone in for a routine check up, and they had to do an emergency operation. It was a routine procedure, but he died on the operating table. Damn. That crazy witch had been right. Three major relationships crashed right there. The band, Thais, and my father's death. They all hit me at once.

I took those deaths as an excuse to use. I started hitting more bottoms and more bottoms. Pretty soon I was getting enough balloons of her-ron to last two or three days. I would get the biggest amount I could at a time, which was around an eighth of an ounce. Normally it went for about $120, but you could get it for $80 depending on who you talked to. It was shitty dope, but if you did enough of it, you got high.

I met another dealer that would sell me these asteroid sized chunks. Each chunk was about fourteen grams. At that point I was doing fourteen grams every two or three days. I was just fixing, fixing, fixing. I was getting more and more abscesses, so many that sometimes I couldn't walk. On top of that I was drinking. I was constantly trying to get Klonopin or Valium just so I could feel high. By that point I took the dope just to make me feel normal so I wouldn't feel sick.

My lawyer, David Given, called me up and asked how I was doing. I meant to say, "I'm good, man." What I said was: "I'm on the H-Bomb."

"What's that?" he asked.

I slurred in a half-nod, "The H-Bomb, man...Hiroshima, Horse, Boy, Dogfood, Gorilla biscuits...her-ron."

"What? I'm coming down from San Francisco and personally taking you to rehab." And that's just what he did. So, once again it was back to rehab for the twenty-fifth or twenty-sixth time.

David called Music Cares, which I was already familiar with; they knew me very well. He talked to Harold, and they came up with a plan to take me to an upscale joint out on the Malibu coast. That was a whole new kind of rehab. Brand spanking fresh. I had never been in rehab with rich kids before. And they were really rich. It was $30,000 a month and their parents were happy to pay for it. They were all spoiled, and I was real angry. I wanted to kill one of those little motherfuckers. I was so resentful and full of self-hatred. This time, I had to pay for my bed. Of course I didn't pay the full amount, as I had the Musician's Assistance Program's rate (MAP, which later merged into Music Cares, also part of the Grammy Foundation), but I still had to pay $7,000 to $8,000. Even with a discounted rate, I thought, *fuck I'm gonna be broke*. I wasn't really thinking about how much life is worth.

Music Cares had just about had enough of me. Harold said my cap was up, and they told me that they could no longer pay for my rehab anymore. With Bush in office there was not as much state funding either. Before, when I got strung out, I could just cry poverty and get into rehab instantly. But there were no more county beds or General Relief beds like there used to be. There was none of that shit that I used to take for granted. I had to start paying for it myself.

"If you really fucking want it then you should be willing to fucking pay for it," one of the counselors said. "Just like you had to pay for your dope."

I thought, *Fuck you, ya prick. Are you going to help me or not?* When you need some help you don't want to hear all that tough love bullshit.

I stayed out in Malibu for all of October 2004. This new kind of rehab was a huge drug dispensary.

D. H. PELIGRO

Pharmaceutical companies were designing new miracle drugs for everything, and scripts were handed out like candy. They were giving some of the clients Valium and Klonopin. The first drug they gave me was Subutex, which they can only give to you if you have been really strung out, but you have to be kicking before they give it to you because it sends you into immediate withdrawals. They waited until I was pretty sick, sweating bullets and puking, before Dave the tech finally gave me a dose of Subutex. Then I felt fine. It truly was a miracle drug.

I had never been to a place like this with an in-house chef, daily yoga, classes, therapists, healers, doctors on call, and our own private rooms. In the bathroom the tile floors were heated. The beds had 5,000 thread-count sheets, and soft new age music wafted through the rooms on demand. Clients could stay up as late as they wanted and sleep in until 9:30 A.M., which was really rare for rehab. Some of them didn't get up at all.

We had private therapists visiting our rooms, which I had never experienced. We also had weekly bodywork, including acupuncture. About a month earlier I was loaded, fell off my bicycle, and damaged the nerves in my right arm. My wrist was bent inward, and my hand was closed like a claw. It wouldn't open on it's own. Kaiser had given me a contraption that held my hand open with little wires attached to a brace. The acupuncturist concentrated on the area where the nerve injury was, placing needles along meridian points in my arm. Then he burned some sort of smoldering coals and placed them close enough to my skin that I could feel the warmth without getting burned. He waved them up and down the underside of my arm.

One morning a hot yoga-bootie-ballet chick came into my room and said, "Hi, I'm Nia." I thought she was a masseuse as I'd seen everyone else getting massages. That's what I thought I asked for, a massage.

"Cool," I said, "I'll get ready for my massage."

"Oh, I'm not a masseuse."

"OK...so what are you here for?"

"I'm here to do some body and energy work to help you."

I lay down on the table. The first thing she did was hold her hands over my head and chest, running them up and down as if she was feeling my energy. A flash of terror and pain shot across her face. "Oh you poor thing," she said with her eyes closed, moving her hands down my legs. "All that's happened to you...you're still holding on to a lot of pain."

She moved her hands to my abdomen. "Why are you blocking Jesus Christ?" she asked, her eyes still closed.

I felt stripped of all defenses, all ability to lie. "I think it's because that's my mother's God, my father's God," I said. *How could that God be any good if he let us live that way? I saw the face of my mother, eyes full of anger, ready to whip me bloody. Then my father, drunk and full of rage, coming at me with his double barrel shot gun...* "Well, ya see in our neighborhood everybody would beat their kids, get drunk, shoot one another, and then go to church on Sunday and get saved and redeemed. I don't think that's very spiritual."

D. H. PELIGRO

She said, "People are people. People can be spiritual, but unfortunately we have this human condition and are chock full of defects—but Jesus was not." She went on to tell me some of the great things he had done.

"You're so full of hate. Let it go." She talked to me softly for what felt like hours. She talked about how Jesus was a humble man, a noble man, who gave more of himself to other people than he would take. Somehow I could hear her in a way I had not been able to hear anyone before. She told me that all spiritual efforts around the world were really about the same thing, love. That my hate was not the truth, just a lie my pain and my disease was telling me. "Stop fighting everyone and everything," she told me.

After she left I lay there, my heart hurting, with pain in my abdomen like I'd been kicked in the gut. I'd had spiritual awakenings before: doing yoga in Brazil, and the ceremony at the Indian sweat lodge. It was the last thing I was looking for in rehab, but this healer unlocked something in me that I hadn't experienced before, some truth in me that had been struggling to keep me alive all these years.

I allowed her to plant a spiritual seed. I could see that the paths of Jesus, Buddah, Allah, and Jah all led to a greater power. I was opening up to it then, after all my old thought patterns had gotten me as far they could; I'd kept relapsing over and over. On that day I became a lot more open to new and old spiritual ideas. I stopped fighting against many spiritual concepts that I had rejected because I didn't completely understand, or care to understand, them. I was finally willing to be available to whatever kept me from a slow death and would bring me into the wide world of enlightenment. Soon I started getting up before anybody else and exercising. It was a really beautiful place so I did my salute to the sun before a panoramic view of the ocean with the mountains right behind me.

Things were being uncovered in me, but I still had reservations, because I still loved to get high. They had prescribed me Seroquel, and I was taking it every night; how I got up at 6:00 A.M. every day is a mystery. At one point they asked me if I was sleeping okay. I lied and said no, so they would give me more. Without any question they upped my dose from seventy-five to a hundred and fifty milligrams. *I love Malibu*, I thought. This is great. They also had prescribed Cymbalta for me because they thought I was manic. I would wander around all day screaming lyrics and being obnoxious. I didn't know I was going to get charged for those pills until my lawyer told me I was paying for it out of my royalties. Paying for things made me feel a lot differently about it all. I was pissed OFF!

After my stay at Malibu they said I should go into sober living so I went to New Perceptions. Once there I was told, "You can't be in sober living if you're still on meds, you have to stay in the treatment phase." From the Malibu facility I was on Subutex, Depakote, Cymbalta, and Seroquel. Why had they put me on so many drugs?

D. H. PELIGRO

I don't know. Maybe it had something to do with the drug companies, or maybe it was a stabilization thing at Malibu. But if I wasn't on so many meds I could just go straight into sober living. That was my plan and that's what I was told at Malibu.

I was pissed off. All my newfound spirituality was gone. I had just done thirty days in treatment, I was not about to do thirty more. I bitched and moaned, acted a fool in group, and left after about four days. I came back to my apartment on Heliotrope Street with a bag full of psych meds, sleeping pills, and no program. Stoned again, the cycle started right away.

Brian Jennings would come by from time to time to check up on me. "You've lost a lot of weight," he told me. My memory started going; I didn't know what I was doing. "Hey, man, when did you get back to town?" I'd ask him.

"Man, you ask me that every time I see you—and I saw you yesterday. Jesus. I haven't been out of town. I haven't gone anywhere. What the fuck is wrong with you?" He knew what was up.

My publicist, Cynthia, would also come by and bring me food and water.

Sick and unhappy I went to St. Louis to try and dry out. Yet again it was around Christmas time when I arrived. As usual everyone was enjoying the Christmas spirit and having fun except me. This was the first time I had been with my family since our father died. My family is so patient with me, tolerating my mess. I was loaded the entire time I was there, but I did get to play music with my Uncle Sam.

The revelation I had felt with Nia at Malibu had not left me entirely. A small window of curiosity remained open. Since I was already in St. Louis I was thinking, *Are these my roots? Are these my people? Are these my cousins? They don't even look like me.* I started asking my mother about our childhood. It was during this trip that my mother told me that Russell was not Dianne's and my real father. She said our biological father was a sometime guitar player in Uncle Sam's band named James Yokely, which is probably why I felt I had the music in me. He and my Uncle Sam had to be part of my musical gene pool. Now it all made sense. Perhaps it was only after Russell died that she felt she could tell us about my bio-dad. That was a life-changing blow. Suddenly what I had suspected had been confirmed. All along I had suspected there was a reason why Russell had treated us differently, why I had always felt like a misprint, as if I'd been photoshopped into the family album by mistake.

When I got back home to L.A. I was strung like a cello. I had found the dope spot in old St. Louis. I used and used until I sang the blues. So of course coming back to Los Angeles, I had to get off the H-Train to nowhere. Back on the rehab merry-go-round we go. I went back to Cri Help for the fourth or fifth time. I was really, really sick. Once I got out of detox they took me to residential. I had been such a regular over the years that many people recognized me. No one was surprised, and no one took particular notice of me. *This guy is gonna be in and out of here like he always is,* they thought. Then I got a personal visit from Shireen from Music Cares, which was strange. You usually don't get a personal visit from one of the heads of Music Cares. I told her I could stay twenty-eight or thirty days, then I had to go.

She looked me in the eye and pointed her finger in my face. "LOOK. This is not a revolving door, D. H., and you're gonna die." Of course I had heard these words before, but they struck at my heart this time.

"What's four months out of your life to save your life?" Fuck, four months seemed like a lifetime the way time seemed to stand still in rehab. I took that as the voice of God. I felt really vulnerable and started to cry.

I stayed there for sixty days. I was still two different people inside: the one who did not care and wanted to die and the other fighting to stay alive. The first month I was so sick with night sweats, anxiety, achy bones, and a racing head, so sleep was nearly impossible. This guy Patrick started giving me some of his Seroquel at night so I wouldn't leave. I thought, *OK. This'll be cool...I think I can make it as long as I get some sleep.* Then Patrick got kicked out for fucking, talking, and passing notes with these girls, which was not allowed—and they busted him with the Seroquel in his drawer. He had been so enthusiastic about getting clean. "I'm gonna be here for six months!" he announced. *Why the fuck would you want to stay that long?* I thought. But slowly I was able to change my mind, to decide to stay for myself.

Some nights I couldn't sleep. Occasionally I'd get three or four hours, which was just fine. I also started stepping up and participating. I had usually been so hostile with the other guys, but now I realized how many of them were good people who really cared. I began to appreciate that they came from all walks of life and they were all there for the same purpose I was. I started doing things contrary to what I thought.

A lot of the shit they would have me do I thought was straight up beneath me. There were about a hundred and fifty guys in there. The same four guys would volunteer to do the extra work: Darren, Patrick, Popeye, and Rudy. So I just did what they did. I started volunteering to clean the bathroom, take out the trash, sweep the floors, help out in the kitchen. Before long they made me kitchen aide, and I had a crew of people working for me. I was careful to keep busy, keep my time structured. During the day I worked in the kitchen. I had to get up at 4:30 A.M. to prepare for breakfast, then I went to groups, came back at 10:00 A.M., prepared for lunch and then dinner. When we went to meetings I focused in on the meeting and did what I needed to do. I didn't want to be back out there in the drama and bullshit outside on the patio where people would talk shit like they were on a fucking prison yard.

I knew I had to hang out with positive people. I had been in enough rehabs, twenty-eight at that point. There was always drama. I knew myself, and I knew that if I started hanging around with that prison crowd

D. H. PELIGRO

chances were I was going to go to prison—if I stayed alive—which I knew was highly likely at this point. I might have a chance.

Three months later I got out of Cri Help and did the X Games with Dead Kennedys in downtown Los Angeles where Bob Timmons came down to see us. That made me happy because Bob and Anthony were my first introductions into sobriety. Bob was actually one of the first sober coaches I ever knew—I think he coined the term. Bob also worked with Mötley Crüe, Aerosmith, Doug Fieger, and Bob and Mark Mothersbaugh. My liaisons into sobriety were Bob, Dallas Taylor, Denny Seiwell, Nick Gilly, Steven Levy, Mark Groubert, Harold Owens, Tony Sales, Carey and Doug Caruso, Wag, Pete Downing, Jeff McFarland and later on Tommy Davidson. These guys hooked me into man-style sobriety.

Tommy was a different kind of brother. He held onto this shit like it was the last morsel of food on the planet Earth. I'd call him up for a simple, "Hey man, how you doin' I just wanna check in."

He'd say, "Grab tha book, nigga." Then he'd give me a lecture on the twelve and twelve. "Turn to page twenty-two. Now go to the bottom."

I would try to tell him that I was in rehab and only had ten minutes of phone time, but I couldn't get a word in edgewise. Meanwhile, an hour and a half later he was still talking. He would just go on and on, but what I did hear him say was something about going after sobriety with fervor. You know, like if you were drowning in the ocean hanging onto your life preserver with all the fervor you could muster. I don't like people to lecture me, but I heard that loud and clear. He colored it in a way that I could clearly understand—no sugar coating, but a rainbow spectrum of stark reality. He used funny stories and wove stuff from television shows, Bruce Lee analogies, *Star Wars*, and *The Exorcist* in his description of how to work this whole sobriety thing. It was funny, diligent, enlightening, and frightening all at the same time. Funny how when you stop thinking of shit to say, you can actually listen.

Doug Fieger was the spiritual guru out of all of us freaks. He always had something deep and meaningful to say in ways I couldn't fathom. He was always very kind and gentle, like he loved me. I mean like he really cared. While I was in my very last rehab in Georgia, rehab number twenty-nine, Harold told me Doug had died. Doug had been battling brain cancer for a couple of years. Harold said, "I know you should do it for yourself, but do it for Doug."

It tore me up inside. Bob had died the year before and I went to his funeral loaded. Now I'd missed the end of Doug's life. Now I just miss him, period. He always went out of his way to show that he cared. I remember once he put both of his hands on my shoulders and looked me dead in the eye, straight down to my soul. He gave me a gentle shake and said, "Just stay." But I couldn't be there for him because I was loaded. I thought about that day after day after day for six weeks in that Georgia rehab. It was a guilty motivation that sprung me into reality.

DKs hadn't been touring for a few years. I don't think the guys knew I was in and out of rehabs, so I didn't tell them. Some gigs came along, I was sober, and it was just business as usual. We did Wakefest in Toronto and a string of gigs, some European gigs where l met a lovely little Dutch gal named Hyacintha. She had a thick little bottom, thick calves, and long brown hair. She was strong and endearing. She had a cute little nose, made you want to just bite it. She was a feisty, brazen vixen, full of fire and very sparky. We talked and talked and pretty soon I found myself going back and forth to Amsterdam, all the while telling myself I would not start another long distance relationship, but then there we were again. I don't know what I was thinking.

I asked to meet her father. I knew that Holland was the first country to import slaves from Africa and to colonize Suriname. So being the genius that I am, I decided make this the dinner conversation. I got there and I met her father, a very tall, striking Dutchman named Casper. All I could think of was whitey-cracker-casper-the-friendly-ghost. But he was cool. He invited me in with open arms; they were so welcoming. He showed me the lovely Dutch house with narrow hallways and teeny tiny stairwells—which was odd as he was so tall.

Hyacintha's father took me downstairs and showed me his wine cellar and a European map of where he traveled to get his wine, which was mostly in France. Casper was very particular about his wine and the temperature of it, how it was stored and all. He would take some sips of some expensive liquor and offer me a snort. I said, "Oh no, I can't, but thank you."

He had this large wine collection, and, me being a recovering alcoholic, I was thinking, *Why don't you just fuckin' drink it? What the fuck are you saving it for? What's the point in storing and collecting wine?* I guess that's the difference between me and people who can just have a glass or two of wine. Shit, I would be getting drunk. Fuck how pretty it is or where it came from as long as it would get me drunk.

So we went back upstairs to have dinner. It was quite the spread, five courses; it just kept coming. Everybody was having wine, and I started to ask about the history of Holland. They told me how Amsterdam and Rotterdam had the biggest docks in the world, and Holland would trade spice from around the world, mostly from India. I said, "Oh really?"

"Yes, there is a long history of pirates ships, trading ships, explorer ships, the lot."

I said, "The food, it always tastes so fresh since you import so much. How is that possible?"

"Well, lets just say we've got it down to a science."

So I lowered the boom and said, "So Holland was the first country to import slaves?"

He simply said, "Yes, this is true. We were no angels, in fact we fought off the British, we fought off the Nazis, and then some."

D. H. PELIGRO

I really respected that he didn't dodge the issue. I liked this guy.

Then he said, "Come now, have some wine."

I said, "No thank you."

He was getting a little loose and tipsy and asked again, "Why don't you drink?

Finally I said, "Because it leads me to heroin." It got real quiet, like uncomfortably quiet.

"Hummmm, okay then," he said and never bothered me about drinking wine again.

Being in a long distance relationship, we could only get together every three to six months. My brother Russell was getting married and had a wedding in St. Louis, so Hyacintha got to meet my family.

As my family was from the Bible Belt they couldn't believe her sailor's tongue; every other word was *shit, fuck*, those *mudda-fuckers, piss-off*, and *you cunt*. That was how she talked on Sundays, and her last name was Convent. I mean it's usually all good when the adults are hanging, but when the kids and elders are around there's an unspoken PG rating that's in effect. However, Hyacintha had no filters—she was full throttle. She thought it, she said it. There's a certain charm to that for me, but the family was shocked.

For the next five years I went back and forth to Amsterdam, talking on the phone and running up a long distance phone bill. Unsatisfied and lonely one Easter Sunday, after two years clean and sober, I thought it would be a good idea to go downtown and cop some dope. It started with a bag like it always does despite all my abscesses and trips to the county hospital and hospitals in L.A. and Brazil.

I showed up in Holland skinny and strung like a Stratocaster again. We had booked some gigs in Brussels, Belgium, and Haarlem, Holland. Hyacintha showed up only to see my hand again in a stabilization device. I could barely play drums.

"Damn, you look like shit!" she said, with her filterless tongue. Everybody in DKs knew it, but they didn't dare say anything. They were just talking shit behind my back. It should have been a tip that I kept saying we should stop at different coffee shops so I could buy weed. Plus I was drinking all night in between running up to my room and fixing dope, pinching from the golf ball sized chunk of her-ron that I smuggled into Brussels. Yeah, she was right, I did look like shit—and I felt even worse. So I began another journey of more rehabs in Holland, and then back to Cri Help.

At Cri Help the counselor said, "What are you gonna do different? You've been here five times, and frankly we have no hope or faith that you're gonna make it." I just hung my head in shame and left. At that point I didn't have any faith in myself so I was crushed yet again. Quite frankly, I didn't know what I was going to do differently. When I was already lower than fly-shit on a windowsill it was easy to say fuck it. So for the next two years I just stayed on the drink and the dope. People would call, and I wouldn't answer the phone or just lie and say I

D. H. PELIGRO

would meet them at a meeting. The lies, the lies. I got so tired of lying, and one day Harold called from Music Cares. He said, "Hey man, we miss you at the Monday night meeting." I said, "Man, I'm fucked up. Help me, please!" I had asked so many times before, and he had told me again and again that the cap had run out. So I figured I would be left to die a slow painful death. Then he showed a bit of mercy. He said, "Do you want to go to Cri Help?"

In my arrogance I said, "Naw. I've been there five times," then with all my manipulation—being a dope fiend, you always want to get the best deal you can get, for free—I said, "Can you send me to Aruba? Ya know the Eric Clapton rehab in the Caribbean?"

He said, "HELL no."

You can't snow an old dope fiend like Harold.

"Tell you what I can do," he said, "do you have frequent flier miles?"

I said, "Yes."

"OK. I have a friend in Georgia that has a rehab. I need you fly down there on Feb 20th, can you do that?"

"Yes sir."

The rehab was called Willing Way. It was owned by the Mooney family—which sounded like a cult to me. You know, c'mon, being from San Francisco and all the "Mooney" sounded like some Christian death brainwashing church. I was like, *Fucking Harold. What have you got me into now? I told that motherfucker I wanted to go to Aruba...he got me all in the South and shit. Willing Way my ass. I'm not willing to be brainwashed by some Christian fools.*

He was able to get me in because, a year before, Harold had kidney failure. A lot of the guys from our group had been tested to see if they had a kidney match for Harold. None did. But one of the relatives of the Mooney family and a friend of Harold's, Jimmy, had a kidney that matched. When I think about it, that's a hell of a kind thing to do. To be sliced open and give one of your kidneys to someone else, the fact that Jimmy would do that restored my faith in mankind. So Harold had called in his favor for me.

On February 20th I flew into Atlanta. At the airport there was a big Dr. Martin Luther King, Jr. memorial. It was a civil rights piece that showed all the trials and tribulations people went through so I could be free. It had photographs, one of his suits, and the "I Have a Dream" speech. It was tough for me to take it in, even though I was a little high and dazed. But it seemed to cut through the drugs right to my core. How many people died so that I could have this freedom? How many slaves stood on auction blocks so that I could have this freedom? How many people were whipped, beaten, bled, tortured and lynched? How many people were forced to pick cotton and eat scraps so that I could be free...to shoot dope? God. What a fucking loser. What a fucking loser. I gotta make this right.

I thought about that on the next plane to Savannah. I got there, and I was to meet some old dude named

Les. He was holding a sign at the airport with my name on it. I didn't think that much about having to meet Les. I was thinking more about how tore up I was; how bloated from alcohol; how my kidneys and liver were taking a beating every day; and how yet again I was given another chance. My soul was crying out to be part of society again. But my belly was distended, my ankles were swollen, my face was so blown up it looked like I just fought twelve rounds with Mike Tyson and lost. I was sore and beat up, heroin and alcohol were oozing out my pores—and I had on a sweatsuit that I hadn't washed. I figured since I was chunky, I'd just take my fat clothes to rehab.

So Les drove an hour to Statesboro, Georgia. He was a short, mouthy, thin, white-haired white man sporting a little paunch. He was spry, chipper, and happy to show me photos of his motorcycle and his gun on his iPhone. And he loved his classic southern rock, cranking up Molly Hatchet on the radio. He also had a peachy Georgia accent that sounded a little scary when he talked about guns. *Oh shit. I'm going in*, I thought.

So once again I went to intake. They took all my worldly possessions: one cell phone, check; one set of keys, check; three lighters, check; wallet, credit cards, smokes, $150 cash, check. After they took all my stuff, this brother Mike took me in the bathroom to search me. I had a stash of Suboxone in my underpants just in case the meds weren't right. He didn't find it since it was taped to my underwear, right next to my Johnson.

When they took my stuff they put my toiletries in a box, and when I wanted to shower or shave or brush my teeth I had to go to the nurses' station and ask for my toiletries. The nurses' station was a glass-enclosed, caged, round house nerve center for all the detox patients, where we would circle around like angry ants lurking for meds. All our detox rooms surrounded the glasshouse nerve center, as well. To the left of the entrance, there was a kitchen where we had groups and breakfast, lunch, and dinner, and a shit load of snacks. It was very much like a hospital: fluorescent lights, white walls, office carpeting, you know, hospital style. All the nurses wore scrubs or white coats, and the doctors would roll through their morning rounds in white coats and stethoscopes.

The thing about this rehab that bugged me was that they frowned on swearing. Once again I tried to follow the rules. Every time I would get ready to act a fool, I would remember Harold telling me, "Don't fuck up down there." I likened it to a scene in *Casino* where Robert DeNiro comes to Joe Pesci's restaurant to get his wife, who Joey's been fucking. Joey puts his finger in DeNiro's face and says, "Don't fuck up in here." So I kept my cool.

It was hard to keep my mania in check with yet another crazy cast of characters. First there was Bob. He was an older gent who spoke like a 1950s radio announcer. He seemed to be very smart. He was in a wheelchair. I think the alcohol had damaged his nerves so he couldn't walk. He was a chubby talking head of a guy who always had an opinion on politics. He later told me he was a lawyer and that he supported the death penalty. The staff was slowly weaning him from his wheelchair and teaching him to walk again. Eventually he was back on his feet, at least part of the time. But he shuffled along, going back and forth from his wheelchair to a cane, real shaky.

One morning he drank an awful lot of coffee. We were at the breakfast table and Bob got this stunned, shocked look of urgency, dropped his coffee cup, and tried to shuffle away as fast as he could. He got about three steps, and I heard that brrrta-ta-tat-tat-tat, and I said, "Whats that smell? Oh damn, Bob shat his pants."

Then there was Clint. He was about 5'9" with a light brown Sideshow Bob sugar-bowl haircut parted in the middle. He told me he was from Dodge County.

I said, "Huh?"

"I had to get out of Dodge," he said.

"Where is that?"

"It's the deep deep south, where they still make moonshine."

I said, "Oh! Where the KKK cracker rednecks come from?"

He said, "That's kinda racist *Dee Haytch*."

"Oh I'm sorry man, I just wanted to see if you were payin' attention."

"Ummm...Yeah, right."

When he read in group it sounded like the dueling banjos of *Deliverance*. His accent was so thick I couldn't pay attention to what was going on. He sat across from me at the lunch table one day. He was very serious and had this puzzled look on his face and asked me why I was so happy. I gave him some slick citified answer and was like, "Man, you just don't know the half." He explained to me that, "Man I jus wonna git sober. I gotta git right with the Lord." Then I thought of him as more of a child of the Gods instead of a southern-fried fool with a fucked up haircut and a dueling banjo accent.

One of the techs, Robert, Googled my name and YouTubed some of my videos. He told me I was a somebody, which made me a bit nervous. He seemed weird and self-righteous, but he liked music, and we liked some of the same music. He was cool, but I'd felt this vibe before. He told me he liked one of my Peligro songs, "Negativity," and my version of "King of the Road." He also went on to talk shit about Barack Obama and how the Mexicans are taking over Georgia. Our conversation took a Jim Crow kind of twist. I was listening mostly because I was still kicking her-ron and I wasn't trying to do a lot of talking. The only reason I was listening at all was because I could not sleep. I was a little tired of rolling around in my bed. So he went on to tell me that if you hung around Statesboro long enough, some of the KKKs would show you some pictures of lynchings.

"Oh, joy," I said.

He went on to tell me that black people wanted to be slaves; they were submissive.

D. H. PELIGRO

I said, "You'd be submissive too if you had a gun at you, or your mother's head, and your brother's head on a stick. Yeah, I guess we asked for those beatings and asked to pick cotton because being free in Africa was getting a bit boring. And I guess you're the chairman of the *bored!*" I was fuming mad, but Harold's voice came to me, "Don't fuck up in here!"

So I told the staff. They did nothing. I just had to stay away from this guy. All I want to do is get sober, and this time was the real test. Detox alone was murder enough to make you shit your pants, like Bob, and I nearly did a couple of times. The nurses would give you baskets of pills without telling you what they were for. If you had some real anxiety, they would give you the silver bullet, which was a chrome syringe filled with God knows what.

Being the drug addict that I was I kind of liked it. Nurse Heather would come in the room. "Now pull down your pants," she'd say. "Oh my, look what you've done to your bottom." I had been skin poppin' in my arse for years and had all the scars to prove it. Again it hit me. I had been killing myself for a long time, and the party was now over. I would go to the meetings and groups. I'd volunteer to read aloud, afraid of making mistakes. If there's one thing about me: if I make a mistake it's big, and when I do something good it's big.

It all started getting easier with repetition. I would say good morning to people I didn't like and started to not take things so personally. After three weeks I started to get some sleep. First an hour or two, then four hours, and then on through the night. Sleep makes a big difference in attitude towards annoying dummies.

As I started to get close to being discharged, my family came to visit. This was the only time other than DART that they had come. They could never afford the trip to Los Angeles, but Georgia was closer, and the counselors insisted that they be a part of my recovery.

We had some family groups and counseling where they said how they were worried. Dianne, my sister, said that when she didn't hear from me she would always think that she was going get that call from the police. My mother said when she talked to me on the phone she could always tell when I was high. She started to cry, as did my sister Dianne, as they told other sordid stories of what of a mess I was.

I didn't think they had a clue. I don't know if I really cared, but it sure was the full flavor of stark reality when they sobbed and told me in so many ways what their take on my addiction had done to them. I thought about all the abuse I'd suffered as a kid and realized that it didn't serve me to be a victim of the past. It's good to draw on for experience, but as a template for life it just doesn't work.

I remembered how Mary in St. Louis had told me that I pretty much belonged to the world, that I had an obligation to fans and people worldwide. Well shit, I never thought of it like that until I was actually sober enough to sit down and listen to what my Mom and

D. H. PELIGRO

my sister had to say in those groups. It broke my heart knowing that I was affecting people other than me.

Dianne said, "I think you should move back to St. Louis."

I told Dianne I wanted to go to school for acting, and she said, "Damn. Well, I didn't know that." She was sort of supportive, but she thought that acting might be another nest of snakes I'd have to slither out of.

So I was at the jumping off point. I could do what everyone else wanted me to do, or I could do what was right for me.

Charles, this grumpy older guy with thinning white hair and a pouty lower lip, who was running group, which was always boring, dropped this gem on me. He said, "The reason you have a mirror in your room is to take a long look at yourself and find out who you really are."

As much as I disliked him, I took his suggestion because all of my ideas kept bringing me back to this same place. So I went back to my room and stared at myself in the mirror, deep into my soul until I felt like I was hallucinating. My eyes burned as if I had never used them before. I stared long and hard every day, for weeks, sometimes falling asleep and having vivid dreams of a long, slow, painful death. Corny as it seems, part of me died looking at my reflection in that mirror. Maybe it was a part of me that needed to die. Shooting all of that dope had served a purpose: to beat me up, break me down, and slow me down long enough to where I could listen to my soul. I started to flash back to points in my life. I realized that I'd always avoided looking inside of myself. I was always so concerned with being the life of the party that I hadn't really sat, looked, and listened to my inner self.

When I did at first I felt as though my sprit was malnourished, as if I had been asleep for years. I'd had a vortex of dope and alcohol robbing me of life, and all that I had to give to life. For weeks I just sat, stared in the mirror, and listened. I heard lots of different voices saying all types of shit. *WHAT am I doing? Where have I been? Beware of bloodthirsty renegade punk rock Republicans...Never give up. It's not to late to start anew–the savage mutilation of the human race is set on course–live for today.* I thought I was going insane. I just could not stop thinking. People would speak to me and I would just stare at them. My heart would pound, and I would overthink every situation while I tried to stop my mind long enough to process what they were saying, then my brain would slow down enough to where I could breathe.

I started to meditate. It made it easier to slow down. Once my brain slowed down I realized I had reached a turning point. The point of forgiveness. Letting go of the childhood beatings, the abuse, the anger, and even most of the racism. If I want to grow, I have to let go. This soul exploration was part of an unlearning process.

It was pretty clear that it was all right here for me to unlock. With this newfound roadmap, I had the key to discover the mysteries of inner peace. All the Buddha practice, all the Rastafarian teachings, yoga, meditation, all the old ladies in the big hats at the Baptist church, all the sunsets in California, the bums, the fake tits, the ocean breeze, the desert heat, the love for others, the birds, butterflies, dog shit, the cotton field plantations, slave hymns, and now more than ever the love of self. It's all spiritual. The Gods are all that or nothing at all.

I felt a little stupid, but better late than never. I'm damn sure glad I didn't miss the boat like so many people I knew, who were now dead. From that day forward my spiritual awakening allowed me to see when I was giving thanks for my food, shelter, clothes, talents, my history, and the legacy of D. H. Peligro. In that time my spirit reawakened; all the relapsing, all the hospitals, all the jails, rehabs brought me to that moment.

From then on, to the best of my ability, I promised I wouldn't take things for granted or people's attitudes as personally. No more ten-year naps under the Laurel tree. I nurture my talents, my acting, writing, guitar, bass, drum, and vocal skills. Wherever I felt like I was lacking I tried to do better. I didn't kill myself or beat myself up if I wasn't a perfect ten.

I started to read daily meditations, thanks to Doug Fieger, and daily affirmations for African Americans: *Black Pearls, The Courage to Change, Answers in the Heart, Just for Today—* about six daily reflections books—only after I asked for the knowledge of God's will for us and the power to carry it out.

I discovered this light inside me that would burn at its brightest when I wasn't using drugs or drinking.

Where I was a social misfit before, I was now able to hang out and get involved, or not. I learned to be okay with just *being*.

My life got better. I started to do some gigs with DKs again and got some new guys for Peligro. I developed an exercise routine that would keep me healthy and on a spiritual path. Now it's a regular part of my life. If you change something, you have to change everything.

Now I wake up in the morning and go to the YMCA, but not before starting my day by thanking Buddha for the focus and meditation. I thank God for being sober today. I thank Jah for the experience, strength, hope, courage, faith, humility, responsibility, patience, unity, love, and respect. I work hard, and it's a lot easier without a monkey on my back.